COMMUNITY SAFETY

Critical perspectives on policy

Edited by Peter Squires

First published in Great Britain in July 2006 by

The Policy Press
University of Bristol
Fourth Floor
Beacon House
Queen's Road
Bristol BS8 1QU
UK

Tel +44 (0)117 331 4054
Fax +44 (0)117 331 4093
e-mail tpp-info@bristol.ac.uk
www.policypress.org.uk

© Peter Squires 2006

British Library Cataloguing in Publication Data
A catalogue record for this book is available from the British Library.

Library of Congress Cataloging-in-Publication Data
A catalog record for this book has been requested.

ISBN-10 1 86134 729 4 paperback
ISBN-13 978 1 86134 729 9 paperback
ISBN-10 1 86134 730 8 hardcover
ISBN-13 978 1 86134 730 5 hardcover

Cover design by Qube Design Associates, Bristol.
Front cover: photograph by Peter Squires.
Printed and bound in Great Britain by Hobbs the Printers, Southampton.

Contents

List of tables and figures

Tables

Figures

List of abbreviations

ABC   Acceptable Behaviour Contract
ACPO   Association of Chief Police Officers
ASB   antisocial behaviour
ASBO   Anti-Social Behaviour Order
BCS   British Crime Survey
BCU   Basic Command Unit
CDA   1998 Crime and Disorder Act
CDRP   Crime and Disorder Reduction Partnership
CFF   Crime Fighting Fund
CPS   Crown Prosecution Service
DAT   Drug Action Team
GCHS   Gay Community Health Service
HMIC   Her Majesty's Inspectorate of Constabulary
LAA   Local Area Agreement
LGA   Local Government Association
LGBT   Lesbian, Gay, Bisexual and Transgender
NAO   National Audit Office
NIM   National Intelligence Model
NPM   New Public Management
NTA   National Treatment Agency
NTE   night-time economy
PI   performance indicator
SCI   Street Crime Initiative

List of contributors

Peter Squires is Professor of Criminology and Public Policy at the University of Brighton.

Adrian Barton is Senior Lecturer in Criminal Justice Policy at the University of Plymouth.

Mark Button is Principal Lecturer in Criminal Justice Studies at the University of Portsmouth.

Marian FitzGerald is Visiting Professor in the Kent Crime and Justice Centre at the University of Kent.

Matt Follett is Lecturer in Criminology at the University of Leicester.

Carlie Goldsmith is a postgraduate researcher at the University of Brighton.

Chris Hale is Professor of Criminology in the Kent Crime and Justice Centre at the University of Kent.

Lynn Hancock is Lecturer in Criminology and Sociology at the University of Liverpool.

Barry Loveday is Reader in Criminal Justice Administration at the University of Portsmouth.

Derek McGhee is Reader in Sociology at the University of Southampton.

Lynda Measor is Reader in Applied Social Science at the University of Brighton.

Dawn Stephen is Senior Lecturer in Criminology at the University of Brighton.

Steve Tombs is Professor of Sociology at Liverpool John Moores University.

Sandra Walklate is the Eleanor Rathbone Chair of Sociology at the University of Liverpool.

Dave Whyte is Lecturer in Criminology at the University of Stirling.

Paula Wilcox is Senior Lecturer in Criminology and Sociology at the University of Brighton.

ONE

Introduction: asking questions of community safety

Peter Squires

As the various chapters in this book make clear, the emergence of a substantive concern with what became known as 'community safety' policy marked a significant shift in forms of local and national governance. This shift had far-reaching implications for local authorities, for crime and disorder management, for the politics of community, for social policy and for the variety of agencies (the police, local authorities, probation, Drug Action Teams, witness support services and so on) that, following the 1998 Crime and Disorder Act, came to form the Crime and Disorder Reduction Partnerships (CDRPs) charged with the responsibility of delivering local crime and disorder reduction strategy.

For some, the new ways of working embodied in the community safety agenda entailed a certain 'breaking of the mould' of traditional forms of local government. For others, the new policy development and evaluation arrangements were instrumental in ushering in the forms of 'New Public Management' endorsed by the New Labour administration (Rhodes, 1997; Stoker, 1999). Some commentators saw community safety policy as a new field of action in which more progressive social policy objectives, informed by 'left realist' social crime prevention thinking (Gilling and Barton, 1997), might be inserted into Britain's overwhelmingly 'situational' (and neo-classicist) approaches to crime prevention (Hughes et al, 2002). Others, by contrast, perceived a threat summed up in the phrase 'the criminalisation of social policy' (Muncie, 2000; Crawford, 2002). By this was meant a concern that social policy priorities might become distorted around crime prevention objectives and that, whatever the intrinsic merits of given social policies (housing, education, youth services, for example), policies would gain preferment according to their ability to advance the cause of crime reduction, irrespective of their other merits.

Finally, other commentators detected, in the new policy development arrangements, forms of priority setting, risk analysis and modes of intervention, legitimation, audit and evaluation, the arrival of a new phase in late modern governance, namely 'governance through crime' (Simon, 1997; Stenson and Edwards, 2003). In short, many important debates and controversies are caught up in the attempt to understand, interpret and come to terms with the discourse and practice of community safety policy making. It has proven to be a vital phase in the development of social policy as an applied and academic discipline and a critical stage in the evolution of the politics of crime and disorder in the UK (Garland, 2001).

That said, it is not the intention of this book to provide definitive responses to the essentially academic issues and interpretations outlined above, although they do serve as a backcloth to the themes addressed in the various chapters. Rather, the aims of the book are more directly critical and questioning. Thus the purpose here is to interrogate various aspects of the discourse, policy and practice of the community safety paradigm in order to ask some straightforwardly sceptical questions, questions familiar to a social and public policy readership, concerning what has been achieved in the name of community safety and, perhaps just as importantly, for whom?

While each of the various chapters will present to some extent its own particular interpretation of the origins of this policy area, it seems reasonable to begin by outlining something of the context, and conditions of emergence, of the community safety idea.

The beginnings

At a time when some commentators were detecting a worrying drift towards a more neo-classical, punitive and situational drift in law and order policies (Brake and Hale, 1992) and, as we have noted above, an emerging 'criminalisation' of social policy, community safety policy appeared to offer a more optimistic and progressive alternative. It has been seen as a direct descendant of the 'left realist' shift in academic criminology (Lea and Young, 1988; Matthews and Young, 1992), giving new emphasis to patterns of victimisation (Mawby and Walklate, 1994) in relatively deprived communities, whereby crime was understood as yet another burden compounding the poverty and social exclusion endured by some UK citizens (Hope, 2001).

Yet community safety sought to extend beyond mere 'crime prevention' (see Gilling, 1997; Hughes, 1998; Squires, 1998), receiving a major fillip with the 1991 Report of the Home Office Standing Conference on Crime Prevention ('the Morgan Report') (Home Office, 1991). In the face of government opposition, the Morgan Report, drawing on good practice and innovative multi-agency working in many local authority areas where the Labour Party held power (see Chapter Six in this volume), went on to spell out a central, positive and progressive role for local government community safety planning. Community safety was to be about rights, opportunities, enhancing 'quality of life' and citizenship values, always recognising that crime and victimisation were the direct result of disadvantage, discrimination, social divisions and blocked opportunities. The rest, as they say, is history. New Labour picked up the community safety baton and, in the 1998 Crime and Disorder Act, required local authorities and the police to collaborate as partners in new statutory CDRPs.

Outline questions

In the process, what has happened to the original ideals and aspirations of community safety? A number of questions have begun to emerge regarding the development, the working and the achievements of community safety (Loveday, 1994), and it is around these questions that the idea for this book originated. So, for example:

- There has been the suggestion that, in fact, community safety policy making has been rather eclipsed by 'crime and disorder management' (Pitts, 2001; Hughes, 2002) and that localised community strategies are unlikely to be sufficient to address national (even globalising) criminogenic contexts (Squires, 1999; Taylor, 1999; Crawford, 2002; Pitts, 2003).
- There have been complaints that community safety has become a 'stalking horse' for intolerance, legitimating the perennial complaints of an older, settled constituency (speaking now as consumers of community safety resources) against young people in particular (Brown, 1998; Squires, 1998; Measor and Squires, 2000) and various 'others' whose lifestyles and behaviours do not conform (Hancock and Matthews, 2001), culminating, perhaps, in the new antisocial behaviour enforcement strategy (Squires, 2006), and legitimating racist or xenophobic attitudes regarding, for example, asylum seekers (FitzGerald, 2001).
- There have been claims that the goals of community safety have been subverted by a new corporatist local policy making, prioritising economic regeneration over community values, quality of life and safety (Crawford, 1994), while area-based initiatives such as New Deal, in which community safety development teams are often based, have come to prioritise a rather selective form of disciplined inclusion at the heart of their working (Stephen and Squires, 2003).
- There have also been questions asked about conceptions of 'community safety' that were open and inclusive or rather more exclusive. For example, the Local Government Management Board survey of local authority community safety initiatives in 1996 found that the most common community safety investment involved CCTV projects (LGMB, 1996). Virtually all such CCTV schemes were in town centres, where a commercial interest in 'safer shopping' (an orderly and crime-free retail and business environment) appeared a more obvious objective than community safety itself. Subsequent research has pointed to the fact that, for almost 10 years, public CCTV camera schemes accounted for approximately 75% of the entire Home Office crime prevention budget (Goold, 2004), which is testimony, perhaps, to the aspirations invested in this particular technology. However, this hardly suggests a particularly 'balanced' approach to community safety development, nor one in which every community safety 'interest' carried equal weight (Squires and Measor, 1996b; Coleman, 2004). Subsequently, commentators have argued that the particular value of the successive rounds of 'CCTV challenge competitions', in which the Home Office promised to match local funding raised by local partnerships comprising

local authorities, the police, the community and local business and retail sectors, lay precisely in the way the promise of central government funds acted as a catalyst to get local partnerships working together (on a voluntary basis) before the Labour government's 1998 Crime and Disorder Act made it mandatory (Squires and Measor, 1996a; Goold, 2004).

- Finally, and arising most directly from the last point, questions also have to be asked regarding whether all sections of the population have been equal beneficiaries of community safety. Evidence already exists suggesting that they have not (Hope, 2000; FitzGerald, 2001; McGhee, 2003; Coleman, 2004). Community safety, like citizenship, implied an indivisible, or holistic and inclusive ideal, something to be worked towards, so the idea that some might be benefiting more than others, or even at the expense of others, for example where criminal activities might be displaced onto more vulnerable victims, implied a major weakness. It had always been an implicit goal of the community safety movement that new priorities for crime prevention resourcing should be allowed to emerge. Community safety was intended to unearth the hidden and underreported patterns of victimisation, such as domestic violence, racial harassment and the victimisation of vulnerable groups. Inevitably, therefore, this made 'community safety' policy making inherently political and contested. In fact, however, a national evaluation of consultation by CDRPs (Newburn and Jones, 2002) suggested that relatively few new priorities had emerged. This might prompt a suggestion that 'community safety' consultation might simply represent a process of legitimation whereby existing local interests continued to demand and to receive a larger share of crime prevention resources. Community safety might thereby be seen as part of the problem, rather than as a solution.

The social divisions of safety

These last questions, above all, relate directly to some rather fundamental questions asked of social and public policy more generally by Richard Titmuss, in particular, Titmuss's reflections on what he referred to as the 'social division of welfare' (Titmuss, 1958). Likewise (from 1964), his related observations that 'welfare could serve different masters [and] a multitude of sins may be committed in its appealing name' pose some interesting questions for community safety policy (Titmuss, 1964, p 28).

When this book was first contemplated, therefore, the relatively straightforward initial questions envisaged and presented for potential contributors to consider concerned, first, the extent to which there might be said to be 'winners' and 'losers' from the community safety policy development process. We have already noted that the development of a community safety perspective was also about change, and that the very processes of community safety consultation, crime and disorder auditing and strategy development were intended to redistribute 'crime prevention resources' and wider opportunities and life chances to relatively deprived and vulnerable groups. In this way, as we have seen, community safety policy making will inevitably become politicised (as Matt Follett discusses in Chapter Six in this volume).

An important question, therefore, concerns the extent to which community safety policy development processes actually do achieve a redistribution of resources and opportunities towards those groups enduring disproportionate levels of crime, disorder and victimisation or whether more powerful or more vociferous groups continue to demand, and to receive, more than their fair share. So, can we talk about winners and losers in community safety terms, and what are the consequences of politicising this area of local governance? Are there groups, communities or sections of the population who have yet to benefit appreciably from this new arena of policy development – communities for whom the community safety project can only be seen as seriously incomplete? With these questions in mind, contributors to the book were sought with a view to discussing the experiences of a number of potential 'consumers' of community safety policy, groups for whom existing criminal justice servicing or priority setting had proven problematic or that were, for a variety of reasons, either particularly vulnerable to forms of criminal victimisation or experiencing difficulties in accessing services or obtaining appropriate support (for example, from the police) to meet their needs.

Thus, a range of groups and communities that a significant body of existing criminological research indicated were encountering inadequate levels of support and service from criminal justice agencies suggested themselves. Thus, Paula Wilcox considers the extent to which community safety policies entail particularly gendered conceptions of 'safety' and whether these adequately reflect the interests of victims of domestic violence, while Sandra Walklate discusses the ways in which community safety has embraced and in some ways redefined the needs, concerns and interests of victims. Derek McGhee likewise discusses the relationships, more effectively fostered under the banner of community safety partnership working, between lesbian, gay, bisexual and transgender communities and the police, relationships that have not always been characterised by mutual trust and confidence.

Marian FitzGerald and Chris Hale discuss the community safety experiences of minority ethnic communities, particularly in the light of broader crime, disorder and security threats, not to mention police practices such as stop and search, which may fundamentally contradict the aims of community safety. Lynda Measor, Carlie Goldsmith and Dawn Stephen discuss the community safety issues relating to young people – respectively, young women, marginalised young people with recent youth custody experiences, and lastly young people subject to 'antisocial behaviour' enforcement processes. All three contributors make the point that it is hard to see young people, especially these particular groups of young people, as noticeable beneficiaries of community safety policy processes. Rather, youth still appears something of an Achilles heel for community safety policy (Measor and Squires, 2000, p 257). Finally, Lynn Hancock explores the relationships between policies for social inclusion and policies for community safety, suggesting that these may not be easily compatible.

A second set of issues reflected in the commissioning of contributions for the book concerned not the consumers of community safety but the providers. Returning to Titmuss's observation regarding welfare 'serving different masters', the question arose as to the extent to which community safety might reflect certain powerful 'provider' interests. To this end, Barry Loveday's chapter discusses the police contribution to community safety policy development, while Matt Follett explores the increasing politicisation of community safety policy processes as a result of local authorities (and, by definition, local political groups) starting to assert their own concerns and priorities. Adrian Barton, by contrast, explores the extent to which management and audit processes within community safety partnerships are impinging on the work of outreach drug agencies and thereby potentially restricting their effectiveness. Mark Button explores the relatively overlooked contribution made by private sector security agencies to community safety strategies and questions the issues (perhaps the 'mixed blessings') to which this may give rise. Finally, Dave Whyte and Steve Tombs discuss the equally overlooked question of corporate crime within community safety policy making, arguing the case for taking the harmful consequences of corporate malpractice more seriously in the course of community safety policy development.

Although the original structure of the book sought to reflect these 'consumer' and 'provider' themes, things did not quite turn out this way. This is not to say that these kinds of interests are insignificant, just that the complex and interlocking issues raised by and across the various chapters suggested a different set of organising principles. In the end, the following grouping of the chapters was settled on:

- community safety as an incomplete project;
- community safety as a contested project;
- community safety as a flawed project;
- community safety overrun by enforcement.

In a brief concluding chapter, a more developed explanation and defence of this structure and these issues is outlined, although, perhaps it goes without saying, the above themes are certainly not confined to the set of particular chapters included within each sub-section.

References

Brake, M. and Hale, C. (1992) *Public Order and Private Lives: The Politics of Law and Order*, London: Routledge.

Brown, S. (1998) *Understanding Youth and Crime*, Buckingham: Open University Press.

Coleman, R. (2004) *Reclaiming the Streets: Surveillance, Social Control and the City*, Cullompton: Willan Publishing.

Crawford, A. (1994) 'The partnership approach to community crime prevention: corporatism at the local level', *Social & Legal Studies*, vol 3, no 4, pp 497-519.

Crawford, A. (2002) 'The growth of crime prevention in France as contrasted with the English experience: some thoughts on the politics of insecurity', in G. Hughes, E. McLoughlin and J. Muncie (eds) *Crime Prevention and Community Safety*, London: Sage Publications, pp 214-39.

FitzGerald, M. (2001) 'Ethnic minorities and community safety', in R. Matthews and J. Pitts (eds) *Crime, Disorder and Community Safety*, London: Routledge, pp 145-66.

Garland, D. (2001) *The Culture of Control*, Oxford: Oxford University Press.

Gilling, D. (1997) *Crime Prevention: Theory, Policy and Politics*, London, UCL Press.

Gilling, D. and Barton, A. (1997) 'Crime prevention and community safety: a new home for social policy', *Critical Social Policy*, vol 17, no 1, pp 63-83.

Goold, B.J. (2004) *CCTV and Policing: Public Area Surveillance and Police Practices in Britain*, Oxford: Clarendon Studies in Criminology.

Hancock, L. and Matthews, R. (2001) 'Crime, community safety and toleration', in R. Matthews and J. Pitts (eds) *Crime, Disorder and Community Safety*, London: Routledge, pp 98-119.

Home Office (1991) *Safer Communities: The Local Delivery of Crime Prevention through the Partnership Approach*, Report of the Standing Conference on Crime Prevention ('the Morgan Report'), London: Home Office.

Hope, T. (2000) 'Inequality and the clubbing of private security', in T. Hope and R. Sparks (eds) *Crime, Risk and Insecurity*, London: Routledge, pp 83-106.

Hope, T. (2001) 'Crime victimisation and inequality in risk society', in R. Matthews and J. Pitts (eds) *Crime, Disorder and Community Safety*, London: Routledge, pp 193-218.

Hughes, G. (1998) *Understanding Crime Prevention*, Buckingham: Open University Press.

Hughes, G. (2002) 'The shifting sands of crime prevention and community safety', in G. Hughes, E. McLoughlin and J. Muncie (eds) *Crime Prevention and Community Safety: New Directions*, London: Sage Publications, pp 1-10.

Hughes, G. and Edwards, A. (2002) *Crime Control and Community*, Cullompton: Willan Publishing.

Hughes, G., McLoughlin, E. and Muncie, J. (2002) 'Teetering on the edge: the futures of crime control and community safety', in G. Hughes, E. McLoughlin and J. Muncie (eds) *Crime Prevention and Community Safety*, London: Sage Publications, pp 318-40.

Lea, J. and Young, J. (1988) *What is to be done about Law and Order?*, Harmondsworth: Penguin.

LGMB (Local Government Management Board) (1996) (with Association of District Councils, Association of Metropolitan Authorities and Association of County Councils) *Survey of Community Safety Activities in Local Government in England and Wales*, London: LGMB.

Loveday, B. (1994) 'Government strategies for community crime prevention programmes in England and Wales: a study in failure?', *International Journal of the Sociology of Law*, vol 22, part 3, pp 181-202.

Matthews, R. and Young, J. (eds) (1992) *Rethinking Criminology: The Realist Debate*, London: Sage Publications.

Mawby, R. and Walklate, S. (1994) *Critical Victimology*, London: Sage Publications.

McGhee, D. (2003) 'Hidden targets, hidden crimes: community safety and sexual minority communities', *Crime Prevention and Community Safety: An International Journal*, vol 5, no 4, pp 27-40.

Measor, L. and Squires, P. (2000) *Young People and Community Safety*, Avebury: Ashgate.

Muncie, J. (2000) 'Decriminalising criminology', in G. Lewis, S. Gerwitz and J. Clarke (eds) *Rethinking Social Policy*, London: Sage Publication/Open University.

Newburn, T. and Jones, T. (2002) *Consultation by Crime and Disorder Partnerships*, Police Research Series, Paper 148, London: Home Office.

Pitts, J. (2001) 'The new correctionalism: young people, youth justice and New Labour', in R. Matthews and J. Pitts (eds) *Crime, Disorder and Community Safety*, London: Routledge, pp 167-92.

Pitts, J. (2003) *The New Politics of Youth Crime: Discipline or Solidarity*, Lyme Regis: Russell House Publishing.

Rhodes, R. (1997) *Understanding Governance*, Buckingham: Open University Press.

Simon, J. (1997) 'Governing through crime', in L. Friedman and G. Fisher (eds) *The Crime Conundrum*, Boulder, CO: Westview Press, pp 171-89.

Squires, P. (1998) 'Cops and customers: consumerism and the demand for policing services. Is the customer always right?', *Policing and Society*, vol 8, pp 169-88.

Squires, P. (1999) 'Criminology and the community safety paradigm: safety, power and success and the limits of the local', in M. Brogden (ed) *British Criminology Conferences: Selected Proceedings*, Volume 2 (www.britsoccrim.org/bccsp/vol02/12SQUIR.HTM).

Squires, P. (2006) 'New Labour and Anti-Social Behaviour', *Critical Social Policy*, vol 26, no 1, pp 144-68.

Squires, P. and Measor, L. (1996a) *Closed Circuit TV Surveillance and Crime Prevention in Brighton*, Health & Social Policy Research Centre Report, Brighton: University of Brighton.

Squires, P. and Measor, L. (1996b) '"Here's looking at you kids": gender, youth and CCTV. Accountability in crime prevention', Paper presented to the Democracy and Justice Conference, Brunel University, April.

Stenson, K. and Edwards, A. (2003) 'Crime control and local governance: the struggle for sovereignty in advanced liberal politics', *Contemporary Politics*, vol 9, no 2, pp 203-17.

Stephen, D. and Squires, P. (2003) *Community Safety, Enforcement and Acceptable Behaviour Contracts*, Brighton: Health and Social Policy Research Centre, University of Brighton.

Stoker, G. (ed) (1999) *The New Management of British Local Governance*, London: Macmillan.

Taylor, I. (1999) *Crime in Context: A Critical Criminology of Market Societies*, Cambridge, Polity Press.

Titmuss, R. (1958) 'The social division of welfare', in R. Titmuss (ed) *Essays on the Welfare State*, London: Unwin University Library, (first published in 1955), pp 34-55.

Titmuss, R. (1964) 'The limits of the welfare state', *New Left Review*, no 27, pp 28-37.

Section one
Community safety:
an incomplete project?

TWO

'You just know you're being watched everywhere': young people, custodial experiences and community safety

Carlie Goldsmith

Introduction

This chapter is based on a small-scale qualitative research project carried out in 2005 with young people who had spent time in Young Offenders Institutions. The research had three aims:

- to investigate the participants' psychosocial well-being prior to imprisonment, during their time in custody and after their release;
- to assess how safe they felt while in custody and subsequently;
- to explore how they felt that imprisonment had impacted on their aspirations for the future.

In April 2005, the total prison population in Britain was 73,228 and of that number 10,581 were aged under 21 (www.howardleague.org.uk). Britain has the largest number of young people in prison in Western Europe, a figure that has been rising steadily since the 1990s despite continuing questions surrounding the effectiveness of imprisonment in reducing recidivism. Reconviction rates for young offenders are high. In 1999, 71% of young people released from custody were reconvicted within two years (Solomon, 2004).

Many of the young people who go to prison have been excluded from school, have spent time in care, have mental health issues, are unemployed at the time of their arrest or have drug or alcohol problems (Campbell and Harrington, 2000).

All of the research participants live in an area traditionally associated with economic deprivation and problems of crime and disorder. For the past seven years, the area has been subject to regeneration attempts by a New Deal for Communities initiative that has placed community safety and, in particular, tackling antisocial behaviour high on its list of priorities. The area, although predominantly a residential housing neighbourhood, had seen CCTV crime prevention cameras installed in 1998.

Methodology

The primary data were collected using a series of semi-structured interviews and one self-completed transcript. All the research participants were between 17 and 21 at the time of their incarceration (Home Office, 2003). Snowball sampling was used as a means to contact potential research participants. Ethical considerations were a key issue in the research. All the participants had experienced a significant amount of upheaval in their lives and only one had completed full-time education. As such, all of the interviewees could be described as vulnerable. Involving vulnerable groups in research is an issue that has been explored thoroughly in the area of health (INVOLVE, 2002; Corrigan, 2003) and vulnerable groups have been described as 'those who do not have access to full citizenship rights because of a variety of personal, social and economic factors' (INVOLVE, 2002, p 3). Accordingly, a key priority of this research was not to treat participants in ways that might compound any feelings of vulnerability or marginalisation.

Late modernity

It was important that the research was grounded in the debate associated with the transformation of social and economic life that some argue has occurred since the mid-1970s: the transition from a modern to a late modern society (Giddens, 1990; Beck, 1992). This transition has serious implications for young people in general and those living on the margins of society in particular (Furlong and Cartmel, 1997; MacDonald, 1997; Mizen, 2004; Barry, 2005). These changes are identifiable in both individual experiences and in wider society's shifting attitudes towards young people, crime and punishment (Goldson, 2000a; Garland, 2001; Pitts, 2001; Smith, 2003).

The concept of 'ontological security' (Giddens, 1991) has been employed to explore how the confidence that human beings have in the continuity of their self-identity and the constancy of their social and material surroundings may have been eroded by the developments of late modernity. Trust and reliability in others may have been eroded. However, some groups, such as marginalised young people, are sometimes said to exist in conditions of 'high' ontological insecurity insofar as their early lives and domestic and material circumstances may not have supplied them with sufficient resources of reassurance and resilience or trust and security (Chan and Rigakos, 2002).

Building on such questions concerning how individuals experience the world, Beck (1992) identifies one of the defining features of late modernity as the development of a 'risk society'. This implies that the overall advantages of living in a modern capitalist form of society may be outweighed by the risks that this entails. A sense of risk is increasingly important in both public and private spheres, transforming a world associated with religious belief systems and notions of fate into one concerned with risk management and control (Green et al, 2000).

Understandings of life in late modernity are said to revolve around an 'epistemological' fallacy that although social structures such as class continue to shape life chances, these structures have become increasingly obscure as the collectivist tradition has weakened and individualist values intensify. In turn, the social world is seen as unpredictable and filled with risks that can only be negotiated on an individual level (Furlong and Cartmel, 1997). Risk, unlike wealth, which accumulates at the top, tends to accumulate at the bottom of society and, for young people, subjective feelings of risk have become a much more significant feature of their lives, having implications for their experiences and lifestyles (Beck, 1992). The traditional pattern of home, school and work has altered radically, leaving marginalised young people, who often experience a fractured education and economic deprivation, in a state of reduced opportunity and social immobility (Furlong and Cartmel, 1997; Young, 1999).

Bauman (2004) takes this interpretation one stage further by suggesting that marginalised young people who have no skills, no economic use or consumer power are, in effect, 'redundant':

> To be 'redundant' means to be supernumerary, unneeded, or of no use … the others do not need you, they could do as well and better, without you…. 'Redundancy' shares its semantic pace with 'rejects', 'wastrels', 'garbage', 'refuse' – with 'waste'. (p 12)

The consequences of this enforced redundancy for marginalised young people are stark; they are increasingly dislocated from a society that places the individual and the market at its heart:

> The protective functions of the state are being tapered to embrace a small minority of the unemployable and invalid, though even that minority tends to be reclassified from the issue of social care into the issue of law and order: an incapacity to participate in the market game tends to be increasingly criminalized. (Bauman, 2004, p 51)

In a wider societal context, these shifts in individual experience have significantly altered the public's response to crime and punishment. A fundamental shift has occurred whereby high crime rates are now seen as a social fact and experiences of crime are now seen as ordinary collective experiences (Garland, 2000). This has led to governments implementing policies of punitive segregation, lengthy sentences in 'no frills' prisons that are supported by the public, for whom this process of condemnation and punishment serves as an expressive release of tension and unity in the face of crime and insecurity (Garland, 2001; Roberts and Hough, 2002):

> The public's priorities seem clear, incarcerate first, then rehabilitate if possible. (McCorkle, 1993, p 76)

The new penology (Feeley and Simon, 1992) is not about punishing or rehabilitating individuals but about identifying and managing apparently unruly groups. An example of this might be the work of parole officers whose primary role is no longer the reintegration of offenders into the community but rather comprises the cost-effective way of long-term management of the dangerous. This is problematic insofar as effective reintegration might help individuals move on from a past that included offending.

When specifically relating these shifts to young people and crime, there appears to be a widespread public perception that more crime is committed by young people and that the crimes they are committing are now more serious. This leads to an erosion of the principle that juvenile offenders should be treated more leniently than adults (Roberts and Hough, 2002). This can be reflected in the increasing number and length of custodial sentences given to young people.

Psychosocial issues

There is considerable evidence that young offenders suffer increased psychosocial difficulties, including mental health problems, increased levels of problematic substance use, general health problems, poor educational attainment and higher instances of risky sexual behaviour or pregnancy (Ulzen and Hamilton, 1998; Nicol et al, 2000; Singleton, 2000; SEU, 2002; Vermeiren, 2003; Carswell et al, 2004; Farrant, 2004).

Research conducted with young offenders on remand concluded that two thirds of those surveyed had a drug or alcohol problem prior to prison (Gilvarry, 2000). Research commissioned by the Youth Justice Board (2003) found that 70% of young offenders have been previously excluded from school, suffer high rates of sleep and health problems and find accessing drugs easy. However, research has also highlighted that many young offenders use drink and drugs as a tool to enable them to block out certain aspects of their lives that cause them problems, such as very damaging early life experiences (Smith and Thornberry, 1995; SEU, 2002).

There are many explanations for such problems, including the idea that seeks to explain risky, disorderly or aggressive behaviour as a desire for immediate gratification or as 'low self-control'. Young people with low self-control are identified as being more likely to participate in problematic activity, including drug taking and risky sexual behaviour. This is linked very strongly with poor socialisation, often caused by growing up in chaotic family environments, for example, where high levels of deprivation and poor family ties exist (Gottfredson and Hirschi, 1990; Sellers, 1999; Pratt and Cullen, 2000; Junger et al, 2001). However, not all children raised in such environments go on to develop multiple psychosocial problems (Akers, 1991; Barlow, 1991).

Another, more interesting, explanation is that focusing on 'social capital' (Coleman, 1990; Halpern, 2004). This directs our attention not only to individual variables, such as personality, but also to how quality, content and structure of social relationships can affect the transmission of resources – 'capital' – across generations and shape opportunities and life 'careers'. Research has identified that family social capital can reduce rates of problematic behaviour (Sampson and Laub, 1993; Hagan and McCarthy, 1997; Wright et al, 2001). The significance of the idea of social capital is that it focuses attention on wider explanations of problematic behaviour:

> Institutional sources – including work, family, school, neighbourhood and community – that contribute to the explanation of crime and delinquency force us to move on from static explanations of crime and encourage attention to the ways in which social capital accumulates. (Hagan and McCarthy, 1997, p 235)

This provides a more satisfactory explanation as it identifies that the responsibility for problematic behaviour in young people has multiple sources and that it is insufficient to place blame upon defective family relationships alone.

Once a young person has been given a custodial sentence, it is unlikely that any of their risky behaviour patterns will be challenged. In fact, being in prison often compounds existing problems and introduces new ones. The issue of self-harm and suicide is a good example of this. Of the 172 suicides in penal institutions between 1999 and 2001, 31 involved people aged under 21 (Hales et al, 2003). Research has shown that young offenders are particularly at risk of harming themselves and that self-harmers are more likely to be identified by their descriptions of their experiences in prison than they are by any previous psychiatric history (Liebling and Krarup, 1994). Imprisonment has been identified as a specific vulnerability factor for self-harm and it increases the risk of being exposed to the suicidal behaviour of others (Hales et al, 2003). Studies in the US have found that exposure to suicidal behaviour increases rates of post-traumatic stress disorder, depression, conduct disorder and substance misuse in those who witness these events (Brent et al, 1996).

Drug use can also be prompted by (or intensified by) experiences of custody. The availability of drugs in prison is a challenging issue, and 'boredom' and lack of meaningful alternative activities are often among the reasons given for using drugs (Smith, 2000). There is also evidence that some young offenders (and adult prisoners) see an escalation in the use and type of their drug of choice. This choice is influenced by two factors: first, the types of drugs available in the prison environment, and second, how long a particular drug remains traceable in the body (King and McDermott, 1995).

Young offenders are often held long distances from home, making it difficult to maintain whatever family relationships they may have established. At the beginning of July 2004, 35% were being held more than 50 miles away from their homes, 23% between 50 and 100 miles away and 12% more than 100 miles away. Frequent moves around the prison estate while in custody have also been identified as causing further disruption and distress (Solomon, 2004).

Safety in prison

Young offenders are particularly at risk from harm inside Young Offenders Institutions. According to statistics, they are the least safe penal institutions in which to be incarcerated because of the high number of incidents of bullying, assault, robbery, threats of violence, exclusion and verbal abuse (Howard League for Penal Reform, 1995; Tattum and Herdman, 1995; O'Donnell and Edgar, 1998; Ireland, 2002; Chang et al, 2003; Kimmett et al, 2003; HM Inspectorate of Prisons, 2004). A national research project conducted between 1994 and 1999 involving more than 1,000 prisoners found that levels of victimisation and bullying are particularly high in Young Offenders Institutions, with 30% of the sample of young offenders reporting being assaulted and 44% being threatened with violence in the previous month. Based on these findings the authors of the research estimated that a Young Offenders Institution with a population of 500 would experience on average 150 assaults per month (Kimmett et al, 2003). These findings are supported by recent research funded by HM Inspectorate of Prisons (2004), which found that over a third of all young offenders felt unsafe while in custody.

Addressing the issue of fear for young people in penal settings, it is important to note that while there are a variety of explanations about the causes of fear of crime, it is nevertheless important to acknowledge that what may be happening to many young people in prison is itself criminal victimisation. Fear of crime is caused by one or a combination of the following factors: direct experience of criminal victimisation, direct experience of incivilities (behaviour that is not necessarily criminal but can be socially disruptive and personally upsetting), and witnessing the victimisation of others (Kimmett et al, 2003). A great deal of the literature on fear of crime is devoted to how crime affects communities (Bennett, 1990; Holloway and Jefferson, 1999; Stanko, 2000). It points to community deterioration, lack of amenities and high levels of social exclusion as the main determinants of fear. There is literature that addresses fear of crime within specific penal settings (Killias, 1990). This identifies exposure to non-negligible risk, loss of control over the environment and anticipation of serious consequences as the three main components of fear in prisons.

A post-structuralist approach, in contrast, highlights how individuals' responses to crime are not generated so much by calculations of probability as by a series of intuitions grounded in their experiences of their everyday lives (Sparks, 1992). Young offenders, like all prisoners, bring into custody values and routines they know in wider society and, unfortunately for many young offenders, violence is widely accepted within their communities (Hood and Joyce, 1999). Thus, violence and intimidation may have become so significant a part of some young people's ordinary lives that they no longer regard it as something exceptional, or as something that can be effectively addressed by the 'authorities' either within the prison environment or beyond it. Vulnerable young people who are regularly victimised in their own communities therefore bring their fears and vulnerabilities into the prison setting.

Yet if Young Offenders Institutions are very unsafe places to be, why do so many young offenders report feeling relatively safe in prison? Research has suggested that even when a young offender has been subjected to different types of victimisation, they may still report that they considered prison to be safe (McCorkle, 1993). The 'safety paradox' (Bottoms, 1999) addresses this particular phenomenon and refers to a prisoner's lived experience, the ability to adapt to a new environment, the development of strategies for self-protection, the stability of a predictable routine, staffing arrangements and, finally, the legitimacy of using violence as a form of self-regulation as explanations for this phenomenon. However unusual this may seem, it is not unique to the prison setting. In wider society, it is generally the elderly and women who express the highest levels of fear of crime, whereas young men are disproportionately the actual victims of crime (Ainsworth, 2000; Hope and Sparks, 2000).

Aspirations

During the 1950s and 1960s, with the existence of a healthy labour market, young people's occupational aspirations were explained using developmental models. Young people were seen as developing a 'vocational self' and 'choosing' occupations that fitted with their self-conception (Ginzberg et al, 1951; Super, 1968). Later developments highlighted how aspirations are constrained by socioeconomic structures (Ginzberg, 1972) and commentators argued that young people from working-class backgrounds were often unrealistic in their aspirations for the future and should, in fact, tailor their skills to suit local labour markets (Roberts, 1975).

Young people's life-course development, in late modernity, is no longer seen as so straightforward and the previously established transition from school to work has been replaced by prolonged, insecure and fragmented periods of training, unemployment and employment (Ainley and Bailey, 1997; Evans and Furlong, 1998). For marginalised young people, this journey has become even more insecure and problems of poor educational attainment and low skills compound their insecurity (Bentley and Gurumurthy, 1999). The rate of unemployment in the UK is currently one of the lowest on record and yet there are more that one million 16- to 24-year-olds not in employment or training and each year more than 5% of 15-year-olds leave school with no recognised qualifications (ONS, 2005). As highlighted previously, 70% of young offenders have been excluded from school and many have problems with basic literacy (Home Office, 2003). The problem of a lack of qualifications among this group is being exacerbated by a growing shift in the labour market towards skilled positions requiring academic qualifications or technical competences (Layard et al, 2002).

When research has been conducted with young offenders, having access to meaningful employment is identified as the main way to prevent recidivism

(Lyon et al, 2000). However, on average, 71% of young offenders are reconvicted of a further offence just 18 months after their release from a custodial sentence (Solomon, 2004). If meaningful employment can affect change in the minds of young people, it is important to examine what it is about going to prison that has the potential to undermine the possibility of meaningful employment on release.

Imprisonment has a huge impact on employment opportunities, motivation and expectations about what life can offer (SEU, 2002). Young offenders believe that with a criminal record there is a much-reduced probability of work even being offered (Lyon et al, 2000; Machin et al, 2005), an assumption that appears to have some foundation. A survey of 69 businesses in London found that only 46% of them would offer a job to a young person with a criminal record, even if they knew the young person had the right skills for the job (NACRO, 1999).

As the high numbers of young people receiving custodial sentences persist, so the opportunities in prison for appropriate education, work and recreation diminish, as custodial regimes prioritise containment rather than education, rehabilitation or development. Education and skills targets set by the Youth Justice Board are not being met and there are wide disparities in provision across the prison estate (NAO, 2004).

It seems therefore that Young Offenders Institutions do not protect the public from further crime by addressing psychosocial or education and skills deficiencies. It may be that they compound existing problems for young people and the overcrowding and poor physical environment of many institutions should be addressed. The research explores a further aspect of this as identified by Bottoms (1995, p 52):

> Offenders sentenced to custody had relatively more personal problems one year after the end of their sentence ... custody leads to more social problems for the offender after release, which results in higher levels of criminality in the long term.

This is supported by more recent research in the US (Johnson et al, 2004) that concluded that system involvement, and in particular incarceration, was positively related to later criminal activity and social problems.

We now turn to the research findings in order to discover the extent to which young people's custodial experiences affect their well-being and aspirations.

Findings

Psychosocial well-being

With the exception of one of the young women interviewed, all of the participants in this research reported multiple psychosocial problems prior to their imprisonment. Substance misuse was the most commonly reported issue but this was often preceded and compounded by poor (or non-existent) relationships with parents, school exclusion, periods of depression and unstable housing situations:

> Before prison I was taking a lot of drugs, not smack or anything like that but I'd go out do some Es, maybe a few lines of coke, speed, shit like that. My life was a mess, I'd been kicked out of school, my parents weren't having anything to do with me ... it was like they had given up on me and nobody cared.

The consumption of drugs and alcohol was identified as making a significant contribution to the likelihood of being involved in criminal behaviour:

> Every time I've been arrested is when I've been drinking. That's when all the fights kick off.

> ... the vallies [vallium] always did, if you went out and took vallies you would do anything, fight anyone for the slightest thing. Someone only had to brush against you when you were walking down the road and you'd want to fight them, you had no fear.

Many of the young people had experienced a significant disruptive and damaging event in their lives. These ranged from sexual or physical abuse, through witnessing domestic violence, to the death of a parent or partner. The drug or alcohol problems of parents were also a key issue. It was a combination of these problems that was often identified as a catalyst for subsequent events:

> My mum died when I was 13, we were on our own before that because my dad is a smackhead. He couldn't fucking take care of me, he was too busy robbing to get his drugs ... I ended up in a children's home and that was it, I was always running away, getting into trouble basically being angry with everyone, that was in my life. That's when I started bunking, taking drugs and robbing.

None of the young people could recall having received any formal support or help to come to terms with these life events, and feelings of abandonment, loss and anger were commonly expressed:

> Believe me, no one gave a toss. Not my teachers or social services, they just didn't care and left us alone. After my dad died I think my mum had a difficult time. Me and my brother just started to go out and go to raves and stuff. There were never really any rules like what time we had to be in. I think she was just dealing with what happened to my dad.

Prior to their imprisonment (and despite all their difficulties) over half of the participants were optimistic about the possibility of getting a job and eventually leading a 'normal' life. Education was seen as the key to making this happen and a desire to get back into education and gain vital skills was identified as the most important way of getting their lives 'back on track':

> I really wanted to be a plumber, I even applied to [name of college] but it was really hard to get a place.... I wanted to be able to look at something and go 'I did that'.

A disrupted education and lack of qualifications were seen as the main barriers to moving forward. For one participant, this was a result of deeply questionable action by the police:

> I made it right the way through to my GCSEs and took half of my exams but right before I had to take the rest of them I got arrested and kept in the cells for three days, so I missed the rest of my exams.... I told them I had my exams to take but they didn't let me out to take them.

For others, particularly those who had suffered quite acute financial hardship while growing up, issues of identity and self-worth complicated their aspirations:

> I did want to go to college but I wanted to be a bad boy. It's all about what you've got and what you haven't got ... everything comes down to money, you want money to be able to do things, to be a certain way. I started dealing to get cash so that I could go out, buy clothes, spend money on the people around me. You just can't do that in a normal job.

Prison – safety, screws and scraps

> ... you're less protected in prison than you are on the outside by miles. You would think steel doors and all the screws would protect you but you've got no chance, if something is going to happen to you something will happen to you.

What is important to recognise at this point is that although all the participants came from the same area, they had between them experiences of a wide variety of institutions housing young offenders. The experiences and the feelings the participants articulated cannot therefore be explained by the regime in one, or maybe two, institutions.

For the younger participants, prison was a much more precarious experience.

Bullying and assaults were frequently reported, as were feelings of isolation and loneliness:

> It was like no one was looking out for me, and the older kids used to take the piss ... they were always threatening me and taking my burn [tobacco] ... they used to shout out the windows and everyone could hear 'I'm gonna fuck you up'.... I never wanted to come out of my cell.

The vulnerability of the younger inmates was often supported in interviews conducted with the older participants:

> I think some of the younger lads were really scared but you can't show it ... [when asked why] ... oh, leave it out. You'd fucking fry, any sign of weakness and that's it.

> ... all the youngsters ... all the new boys. You see the older ones try it on straight away and depending on how they react depends on how their time in prison is going to be. If you walk in there and you're jack the lad, trying to give it all that, then you're gonna make enemies straight away and if you go in there and let people walk all over you and take the piss your life's going to be made a misery.

Specific spaces within the prison were also highlighted as being areas of potential danger; showers and movement between cells to activities were perceived as being the most dangerous:

> I didn't shower the whole time I was there, it was really dangerous ... there was always fights and attacks ... I used to get called a tramp but I didn't care.

Prison staff were not seen as providing any protection and were accused of antagonising the inmates and often adding to the tension:

> They [prison officers] would open the flap and tell you to 'shut the fuck up and if you do it again we'll put you on report', they were wind-up merchants at [name of prison] ... obviously because they've got a load of young boys in there they know are fiery and have got bad tempers they really used to wind you up and be cocky, bang your doors as they walked past and say stupid things.

> In [name of prison] they treated you like shit, they put you down, everything's just 'bang up, bang up', everything is just lock up, if you're not doing anything just lock 'em up. I mean we used to be

locked up during the day and you could hear the screws playing pool on your pool table, sitting in your TV room drinking cups of tea.

Prison officers were also identified as supporting the prison culture and using their powers to divide and rule:

> Its all about control … a screw would take something off you, like things you're not allowed and the next day you'd see someone else with it and they used to give me things just for the night, like magazines and shit like that, they've taken them out of other people's cells.

Older participants were more likely to say that they felt safe during their time in prison. However, they often witnessed extreme acts of violence:

> Another kiddie when I was in [names prison] was in the showers, everyone was showering and four coloured kiddies come in, they had a jagged lid off a can of tuna and slashed him all down the face, there was blood squirting everywhere, that was sick.

These attacks, however heinous, were seen in the eyes of inmates to serve a purpose and often went unpunished:

> Because this kiddie he was a boxer … he was a big hard lump and obviously a pack of them had got together because they thought he was a bit of a handful … when things like that happen in prison two or three days later either the person or the people get shipped out, they knew they could do it and there was gonna be no repercussions.

There were indications that a large number of the participants suffered psychologically in prison and were constantly confronted with the psychological problems of other prisoners. The most vocalised indicators of this pressure were bad dreams, feeling agitated, not being able to sleep and depression:

> I used to have a mad dream that the prison got set on fire, and everyone's all banged up in their cells, they couldn't run around and let everyone out. I don't think prison's safe, if there was a big fire or a riot and you're just one person I can guarantee you that the screws ain't unlocking anybody's door.

> There was this other prisoner who hated being on lock up, he would scream all day saying that the walls were coming in on him … [when asked what happened] … the screws took him off the wing and put him in solitary.

'Lock up' or being locked in cells for up to 23 hours a day for long periods of time was common, particularly for the male participants. This practice added to the tension of the prison environment, made it difficult for prisoners to use the telephones and therefore hard to maintain relationships with those on the outside:

> You can't just pick up the phone. That was the hardest, you'd read something in a letter and think 'I really could do with ringing them up' and you can't, there's nothing you can do. That's what I used to get really frustrated about, I'd wind myself up because you're banged up for that long it's all going on in your head.

One female participant with a small child on the outside articulated feelings of deep distress when speaking about maintaining contact with her son:

> I never wanted him to see me in that place, it was dirty and disgusting.... I couldn't speak to him on the phone, he just used to say 'where are you mummy?'. It just broke me up inside.

However, contrary to much academic research, the young men also found separation from their children extremely difficult mentally and emotionally:

> I can guarantee you that there are a lot of prisoners in there that every single day cry their eyes out over their kids' photos. They might be innocent, they might not, they might have done something stupid to try and help their families financially but they are paying the price and they are missing out.

Both female interviewees were incredibly candid about the level of psychological distress they encountered during their time in prison. This often began as soon as they arrived and seemed to be the result of serious drug addiction among the inmates:

> We were told to wait in this reception area and all these girls were sweating, crying and puking all over the floor, they were all clucking. I was the only one who was sort of normal. All the staff were just stepping over these girls who were obviously really sick. I felt like I was in a dream and kept thinking I was going to wake up.

Two thirds of the participants reported there being a suicide or an attempted suicide during their time in custody. This was reported to have an incredibly negative effect on the atmosphere of the prison in general:

> You all know it's happened, everyone on the landing was talking about it ... it makes you feel like shit and everyone feels down.

The young women, who were keen to express the seriousness and regularity of incidents taking place, were more likely than the men to report incidents of self-harm:

> I've never seen women's arms like it, the cuts were up their faces, all over their legs, they were walking round with open wounds. I had a friend who didn't have any razors so she smashed a metal flask and stuck the glass in her arm and cut her artery ... she had mental problems.

The young male participants were much less likely to report this kind of behaviour, although many alluded to its existence.

Many of the young people tried to participate in basic skills provision or other activities offered by their institution. There were significant barriers to this, including a shortage of staff to supervise activities taking place, and lack of appropriate teaching staff and space. Young male offenders identified a lack of meaningful educational opportunities and felt that what was provided was often designed simply to distract and occupy inmates rather than being part of a concerted effort to arm them with skills they could use after release:

> I retook the ones [GCSEs] I missed when I was in prison but they haven't sent me the results yet, I've been trying to get them since I got out but I don't think they really care. It's not really about giving you something for the future, it's just about keeping you occupied so that there's no trouble.

The female participants observed that for them the emphasis was on helping with the menial tasks involved in running the institution rather than increasing skills:

> I mostly did the cleaning, I used to mop the corridors on the wings every day and help out keeping the garden tidy.

Although this meant that they spent less time in lock up, it is questionable whether such activities should take precedence over education.

A small minority of the interviewees felt that going into custody was an intervention that prevented them from progressing to more serious crime. However, some felt that this was more a question of individual choice than something arising from the prison experience:

> Like I've said, prison is shit and it does nothing for no one but it was still the best thing that could have happened to me because of the time that it happened and the sentence that I got, it knocked the wind out of my sails and I straightened myself out. If things had got a bit worse and I had got a bit older I might have done something more serious and ended up doing a big chunk of my life, so really it's

not because of the screws or the prison system it was because of myself it was a good thing to happen.

The remaining participants all felt that the experience had had serious implications for them personally and meant they were far less likely to build a 'normal' life.

On 'the out'

After serving their sentences, all of the participants returned to the area they lived in before they went to prison. Most of them were tagged and all but one were placed under the supervision of the local Youth Offending Team. Four of the participants also had unexpired Anti-Social Behaviour Orders (ASBOs) against them. What was striking about the participants with ASBOs was the common acknowledgment of the damage they perceived this community sanction had done to them. One participant in particular, who had not been in trouble since his release from prison six months previously, was very aware of their stigmatising effect:

> I think me having been in prison might've changed the way some people looked at me but I think the ASBO has been more damaging in terms of my future. My picture was in [the local paper], that was when I was 15. I'm 18 now and I still get people coming up to me in the street saying, 'I know what you've done', I can't get away from it.

Having been served with an ASBO was perceived as increasing the pressure on those young people. They particularly complained about the level of surveillance they felt they were subjected to:

> I go out my house, the cameras watching. I go round the corner; it's the fucking police waiting for me to breach my curfew. I've got a tag on my leg. I have to see my YOT [Youth Offending Team] worker and they want to know where I've been and what I've been up to. You just know you're being watched, in prison, on the street, everywhere.

The idea of 'being watched' was a common theme for the research participants both prior to, during and after prison. Nearly all of the young people interviewed were very clear that their movements and activities were being monitored by the authorities and other residents in the area where they lived. Many also questioned the value of Youth Offending Teams and the opportunities that they were able to provide for young offenders:

> Well, if you don't mind a bit of gardening you're all right but if you want to get on with your life they can't help. I wanted to go back to

school but no one would take me and there was nothing my YOT worker could do.

Those participants who were old enough to go into full-time employment reported a significant number of barriers that they felt were preventing them from working:

> Well, according to them [a potential employer] I'm just a criminal. I'm not me any more, and all of the older kiddies who've been inside will tell you … that don't change.

The psychological effects of prison were particularly debilitating, with some participants reporting that the bad dreams, depression and agitation they suffered inside had continued after release:

> Before I went to prison I might have been a bit fucked up but now I think it's worse … I feel really down a lot of the time and keep having bad dreams about what I saw. I've definitely lost a lot of confidence.

One participant was so worried about having to go back to prison that he rarely goes out and seldom engages with anything. His mother is particularly concerned about what has happened to her son:

> What you don't understand is that for me there is always a chance that something will happen, I'll be walking along the street, something will kick off and that's it, I'm back inside. I know I couldn't deal with that … my mum is really worried but there's nothing she can do, she just doesn't understand.

Conclusion

The experience of prison had a significant impact on the lives of all the participants in the research. For a few, it had the result of stopping their offending behaviour from escalating. However, for the majority, the experience compounded their existing problems and added the new challenge of moving on in their lives with a criminal record and a prison sentence behind them.

Many of the young people who participated in this research have had difficult lives. This does not remove all responsibility from them for their actions, and during the interview process many of them expressed the view that some sort of punishment was justifiable for the part they contributed to the crime that had been committed. However, it is also apparent that society chooses to intervene at the point when they break 'the law' and not at the point of most need, like at the loss of a parent. This does send a message, however subliminal, to some young people about how little value we place on their emotional and mental health and yet how important they subsequently become when they enter the criminal justice system.

Perhaps the core conclusion emerging from this work concerns precisely the limitations of an approach to community safety in which the wider problems outlined in this chapter remain unresolved. The circumstances undermining the ability of young people to attain meaningful and rewarding opportunities are exacerbated precisely by the interventions that seek to punish them for their failures. In the process, their needs go unaddressed; we overlook how their experiences of vulnerability and victimisation are often intimately connected to their patterns of offending, but we treat them as offenders first, and young people and victims (if at all) second (Goldson, 2000b). We are preoccupied, above all, with the risks they are presumed to represent, rather than the risks posed to them and the disadvantages they are forced to endure. The argument of this chapter is that this represents a particularly retarded and inadequate conception of community safety.

References

Ainley, P. and Bailey, W. (1997) *The Business of Learning*, London: Cassell.

Ainsworth, P.E. (2000) *Psychology and Crime: Myths and Reality*, Harlow: Longman.

Akers, R.L. (1991) 'Self-control as a general theory of crime', *Journal of Quantitative Criminology*, vol 7, pp 201-11.

Barlow, H.D. (1991) 'Explaining crimes and analogous acts, or the unrestrained will grab pleasure where they can', *Journal of Criminal Law and Criminology*, vol 82, no 1, pp 229-42.

Bauman, Z. (2004) *Wasted Lives: Modernity and its Outcasts*, Cambridge: Polity Press.

Barry, M. (ed) (2005) *Youth Policy and Social Exclusion*, London: Routledge.

Beck, U. (1992) *Risk Society: Towards a New Modernity*, London: Sage Publications.

Bennett, T. (1990) *Tackling Fear of Crime*, Home Office Research Bulletin 28, London: Home Office.

Bentley, T. and Gurumurthy, R. (1999) *Destination Unknown: Engaging with the Problems of Marginalised Youth*, London: Demos.

Bottoms, A.E. (1995) *Intensive Community Supervision for Young Offenders: Outcomes, Processes and Costs*, Cambridge: Institute of Criminology.

Bottoms, A.E. (1999) 'Interpersonal violence and social order in prisons', in M. Tonry and J. Petersilia (eds) *Crime and Justice: A Review of the Research*, Chicago, IL: University of Chicago Press.

Brent, D.A., Moritz, G., Bridge, J., Perper, J. and Canobbio, R. (1996) 'Long-term impact of exposure to suicide: a three year controlled follow up', *Journal of the American Academy of Child and Adolescent Psychiatry*, vol 35, no 5, pp 646-53.

Campbell, S. and Harrington, V. (2000) 'Youth crime: findings from the 1998/1999 youth lifestyles survey', www.homeoffice.gov.uk/rds/pdfs/hors209.pdf (accessed 2 January 2005).

Carswell, K., Maughan, B., Davis, H., Davenport, F. and Goddard, N. (2004) 'The psychosocial needs of young offenders and adolescents from an inner city area', *Journal of Adolescence*, vol 27, no 4, pp 415-28.

Chan, W. and Rigakos, G.S. (2002) 'Risk, crime and gender', *British Journal of Criminology*, vol 42, no 4, pp 743-61.

Chang, J.J., Chen, J. and Brownson, R. (2003) 'The role of repeat victimization in adolescent delinquent behaviours and recidivism', *Journal of Adolescent Health*, no 32, pp 272-80.

Coleman, J.S. (1990) *Foundation of Social Theory*, Cambridge, MA: Harvard University Press.

Corrigan, O. (2003) 'Empty ethics: the problem with informed consent', *Sociology of Health and Illness*, vol 25, no 3, pp 768-92,

Evans, K. and Furlong, A. (1998) 'Metaphors of youth transitions: niches, pathways, trajectories or navigations', in J. Bynner, L. Chesholm and A. Furlong (eds) *Youth, Citizenship and Social Change*, Aldershot: Ashgate.

Farrant, F. (2004) 'A Sobering Thought: Young Men in Prison: Research Briefing 1', *Out for Good*, London: Howard League for Penal Reform.

Feeley, M. and Simon, J. (1992) 'The new penology: notes on the emerging strategy of corrections and its implementation', *Criminology*, vol 30, no 4, pp 452-74.

Furlong, A. and Cartmel, F. (1997) *Young People and Social Change*, Buckingham: Open University Press.

Garland, D. (2000) 'The culture of high crime societies: some preconditions of recent law and order policies', *British Journal of Criminology*, vol 40, no 3, pp 347-75.

Garland, D. (2001) *The Culture of Control: Crime and Social Order in Contemporary Society*, Oxford: Oxford University Press.

Giddens, A. (1991) *Modernity and self-identity: Self and society in the late modern age*, Cambridge: Polity Press.

Gilvarry, E. (2000) 'Substance abuse in young people', *Journal of Child Psychiatry*, no 41, pp 55-80.

Ginzberg, E. (1972) 'Towards a theory of occupational choice: a re-statement', *Vocational Guidance Quarterly*, no 14, pp 25-34.

Ginzberg, E., Ginzberg, S., Axelrad, S. and Herma, J. (1951) *Occupational Choice*, New York, NY: Columbia University Press.

Goldson, B. (ed) (2000a) *The New Youth Justice*, Lyme Regis: Russell House Publishing.

Goldson, B. (2000b) 'Children in need or young offenders? Hardening ideology, organisational changes and new challenges for social work with children in trouble', *Child and Family Social Work*, vol 5, no 3, pp 255-65.

Gottfredson, M.R. and Hirschi, T. (1990) *A General Theory of Crime*, Stanford: Stanford University Press.

Green, E., Mitchell, W. and Bunton, R. (2000) 'Contextualizing risk and danger: an analysis of young people's perceptions of risk', *Journal of Youth Studies*, vol 3, no 2, pp 109-26.

Hagan, J. and McCarthy, B. (1997) *Mean Streets: Youth Crime and Homelessness*, New York, NY: Cambridge University Press.

Hales, H., Davison, S., Misch, P. and Taylor, P.J. (2003) 'Young male prisoners in a Young Offenders Institution: their contact with suicidal behaviour by others', *Journal of Adolescence*, vol 26, no 6, pp 667-85.

Halpern, D. (2004) *Social Capital*, Cambridge: Polity Press.

HM Inspectorate of Prisons (2004) *Juveniles in Custody*, London: HM Inspectorate of Prisons.

Holloway, W. and Jefferson, T. (1999) 'The risk society in an age of anxiety: situating fear of crime', *British Journal of Sociology*, vol 50, no 3, pp 507-23.

Home Office (2003) *Prison Statistics England and Wales 2002*, London: Home Office.

Hood, R. and Joyce, K. (1999) 'Three generations: oral testimonies on crime and social change in London's East End', *British Journal of Criminology*, vol 39, no 1, pp 136-57.

Hope, T. and Sparks, R. (2000) *Crime, Risk and Insecurity: Law and Order in Everyday Life and Political Discourse*, London: Routledge.

Howard League for Penal Reform (1995) *Banged Up, Beaten Up, Cutting Up: Report of the Howard League Commission of Enquiry into Violence in Penal Institutions for Teenagers Under 18*, London: Howard League for Penal Reform.

INVOLVE (2002) 'Involving marginalised and vulnerable people in research: a consultation document', www.invo.org.uk/pdfs/Involving%20Marginalised %20and%20VullGroups%20in%20Researchver2.pdf (accessed 15 February 2005).

Ireland, J. (2002) 'Official records of bullying incidents among young offenders: what can they tell us and how useful are they?', *Journal of Adolescence*, vol 25, issue 6, pp 669-79.

Johnson, L., Sands, R. and Conder, D. (2004) 'Criminal justice system involvement and continuity of youth crime: a longitudinal analysis', *Youth and Society*, vol 36, no 1, pp 3-29.

Junger, M., West, R. and Timman, R. (2001) 'Crime and risky behaviour in traffic: an example of cross-situational consistency', *Journal of Research in Crime and Delinquency*, vol 38, no 4, pp 439-59.

Killias, M. (1990) 'Vulnerability: towards a better understanding of a key variable in the genesis of fear of crime', *Violence and Victims*, vol 5, no 2, pp 97-108.

Kimmett, E., O'Donnell, I. and Martin, C. (2003) *Prison Violence: The Dynamics of Conflict, Fear and Power*, Cullompton: Willan Publishing.

King, R.D. and McDermott, K. (1995) *The State of our Prisons*, Oxford: Clarendon Press.

Layard, R., McIntosh, S. and Vignoles, A. (2002) *Britain's Record on Skills*, CEE Discussion Paper 23, London: Centre for Economics of Education, London School of Economics and Political Science.

Liebling, A. and Krarup, I. (1994) 'Suicide attempts in male prison', *Research Bulletin*, no 36, pp 38-43.

Lyon, J., Dennison, C. and Wilson, A. (2000) *Tell Them so They Listen: Focus Group Research for Young People in Custody*, Home Office Research Study 201, London: Home Office.

MacDonald, R. (ed) (1997) *Youth, the 'Underclass' and Social Exclusion*, London: Routledge.

Machin, S., McNally, S. and Rajagopalan, S. (2005) *Tackling the Poverty of Opportunity: Developing 'RSB Enterprise Works' for The Prince's Trust*. London: The Prince's Trust.

McCorkle, R.C. (1993) 'Living on the edge: fear in a maximum security prison', *Journal of Offender Rehabilitation*, vol 20, no 1-2, pp 73-91.

Mizen, P. (2004) *The Changing State of Youth*, Basingstoke: Palgrave Macmillan.

NACRO (National Association for the Care and Resettlement of Offenders) (1999) *Going Straight to Work*, London: NACRO.

NAO (National Audit Office) (2004) *Youth Offending: The Delivery of Community and Custodial Sentences*, HC 190 Session 2003-2004, London: NAO.

Nicol, R., Stretch, D., Whitney, I., Jones, K., Garfield, P., Turner, K. and Stanion, B. (2000) 'Mental health needs and services for severely troubled young people including young offenders in the NHS region', *Journal of Adolescence*, vol 23, no 3, pp 243-61.

O'Donnell, I. and Edgar, K. (1998) 'Routine victimization in prisons', *The Howard Journal of Criminal Justice*, vol 37, no 3, pp 266-79.

ONS (Office for National Statistics) (2005) 'Labour Market Trends January 2005', www.statistics.gov.uk/downloads/theme_labour/LMT_Jan_2005.pdf (accessed 1 March 2005).

Pitts, J. (2001) *The New Politics of Youth Crime: Discipline or Solidarity*, Lyme Regis: Russell House Publishing.

Pratt, T. and Cullen, F. (2000) 'The empirical status of Gottfredson and Hirschi's general theory of crime: a meta-analysis', *Criminology*, vol 38, pp 931-64.

Roberts, J.V. and Hough, M. (eds) (2002) *Changing Attitudes to Punishment*, Cullompton: Willan Publishing.

Roberts, K. (1975) 'The developmental theory of occupational choice: a critique and an alternative', in G. Esland, G. Salaman and M. Speakman (eds) *People and Work*, Edinburgh: Holmes McDougall.

Sampson. R.J. and Laub, J.H. (1993) *Crime in the Making: Pathways and Turning Points through Life*, Boston, MA: Harvard University Press.

Sellers, C. (1999) 'Self-control and inmate violence: an examination of the scope and specification of the general theory of crime', *Criminology*, vol 37, no 3, pp 375-404.

SEU (Social Exclusion Unit) (2002) *Reducing Re-Offending by Ex-Prisoners*, London: Office of the Deputy Prime Minister.

Singleton, E. (2000) *Psychiatric Morbidity among Young Offenders in England and Wales*, London: Office for National Statistics.

Smith, C. and Thornberry, T.P. (1995) 'The relationship between childhood maltreatment and adolescent involvement in delinquency', *Criminology*, vol 33, no 3, pp 451-77.

Smith, C. (2000) 'Healthy prisons: a contradiction in terms?', *The Howard Journal*, vol 39, no 4, pp 142-59.

Smith, R. (2003) *Youth Justice: Ideas, Policy, Practice*, Southampton: Wilkin.

Solomon, E. (2004) *A Lost Generation: The Experiences of Young People in Prison*, London: Prison Reform Trust.

Sparks, R. (1992) *Television and the Drama of Crime: Moral Tales and the Place of Crime in Public Life*, Buckingham: Open University Press.

Sparks, R., Bottoms, A.E. and Hay, W. (1996) *Prisons and the Problem of Order*, Oxford: Clarendon Press.

Stanko, E.A. (2000) 'Victims R Us: the life history of "fear of crime" and the politicisation of violence', in T. Hope and R. Sparks (eds) *Crime, Risk and Insecurity*, London: Routledge.

Super, D. (1968) 'A theory of vocational development', in B. Hopson and J. Hayes (eds) *The Theory and Practice of Vocational Guidance*, Oxford: Pergamon Press.

Tattum, D. and Herdman, G. (1995) *Bullying: A Whole Prison Response*, Cardiff: Institute of Higher Education.

Ulzen, T.P.M. and Hamilton, H. (1998) 'The nature and characteristics of psychiatric comorbity in incarcerated adolescents', *Canadian Journal of Psychiatry*, vol 43, no 1, pp 1133-43.

Vermeiren, R. (2003) 'Psychopathology and delinquency in adolescents: a descriptive and developmental perspective', *Clinical Psychology Review*, vol 23, no 3, pp 277-318.

Wright, J.P., Cullen, F.T. and Miller, J. (2001) 'Family social capital and delinquent involvement', *Journal of Criminal Justice*, vol 29, pp 1-9.

Young, J. (1999) *The Exclusive Society*, London: Sage Publications.

Youth Justice Board (2003) *Speaking Out*, London: Youth Justice Board.

THREE

Community safety and lesbian, gay, bisexual and transgender communities

Derek McGhee

Introduction

This chapter focuses on the social and political climate in which hate crimes, whether racially motivated or as a result of homophobia, are increasingly being taken seriously by local authorities and police forces in England and Wales. The chapter explores the special place hate crimes occupy in the 1998 Crime and Disorder Act 'community safety' ethos, with particular attention being paid to how police forces, especially Hampshire Constabulary, have been attempting to win the trust of lesbian, gay, bisexual and transgender (LGBT) communities in Southampton.

In the course of the chapter, it will be argued that police forces in England and Wales are at the forefront of the project of increasing the 'civic participation' and 'active citizenship' of the members of LGBT communities in England and Wales. Homophobia is the umbrella term used to describe the prejudice expressed by societies, institutions and individuals who hate (and fear) homosexuals[1]. This classification of prejudice is also used to describe the hatred and fear of lesbians, bisexuals and members of the transgender community (although the term transphobia is increasingly being used to describe fear and hatred of members of transgender communities)[2]. The recent history of the policing of LGBT communities has been one similar to that of other minority groups in that the general perception of these communities was that they were 'over-policed and under-protected'[3]. This perception was in turn associated with two interdependent factors: the existence of institutionalised homophobia in police forces, and, as a result of this, the lack of trust LGBT communities had in the police. It will be argued in this chapter that there is currently a sea change in the policing of the LGBT community in England and Wales in the post-1998 Crime and Disorder Act context. This alleged 'culture' change is examined later in the chapter in a case study that focuses on the policing of LGBT communities in Southampton. What these developments suggest is that in Southampton, and elsewhere in England and Wales, policing is no longer concerned with driving sexual minority communities (such as gay men) underground. Rather, new policing styles and practices are emerging in relation to the LGBT community where the primary objective is to open up and improve the channels of communication between these communities and the police.

Community safety

It was with the passing of the 1998 Crime and Disorder Act that partnership and consultation under the banner of 'community safety' was to be widely institutionalised in police forces in England and Wales. The precursor to this legislation was the Home Office's report of the Standing Conference on Crime Prevention (also known as 'the Morgan Report') published in 1991 (Home Office, 1991; see Hughes, 1996, 1998, 2000, 2002; Crawford, 1997, 1998a, 1998b, 2001). It was suggested in the Morgan Report that the term 'crime prevention' should be replaced with 'community safety', which is a wider interpretation that could encourage greater participation from all sections of the community in the fight against crime (Home Office, 1991, p 3). The Morgan Report suggested that the local authority was the '... natural focus for coordinating, in collaboration with the police, the broad range of activities directed at improving community safety ...' (Home Office, 1991, p 4).

According to Newburn, the 1998 Crime and Disorder Act sought to 'reinsert' the community into policing (2002, p 109). The three key elements of this reinsertion process can be described as an emphasis on 'the local'; a tendency to deliver a 'broad-based' approach to social problems beyond simple crime and disorder strategies; and the idea that 'community safety' is to be achieved through 'partnerships' (Newburn, 2002, p 108). It is important to note that there was a compulsory element to all this 'local' activity in that the 1998 Crime and Disorder Act introduced these initiatives in the form of requirements and duties that were to be placed on local authorities and police forces for consulting with and encouraging a multi-agency, problem-solving approach to local crime problems in conjunction with local agencies, organisations and the representatives of local communities. This 'required community consultation process' in the implementation of community safety strategies and community representation in local partnerships has been described by Crawford as an attempt to implement a 'holistic, problem-oriented approach' to crime rather than a single-agency (notably police) 'solution' to crime (Crawford, 2001, pp 57, 59)[4]. It is within this ethos of consultation and participation that, I shall argue, a rather less familiar relationship between the police and the LGBT community is beginning to emerge.

Hate crime and community safety

It will be argued below that hate crime and intolerance are at the forefront of the expanding remit of community safety beyond an exclusive focus on crime and disorder to include wider definitions of social exclusion and social harm. The expansion of the remit of community safety beyond acts defined exclusively as the usual 'criminal acts' (burglary, robbery, criminal damage and so on) is already an established theme in contemporary criminology. For example, Wiles and Pease have suggested that '… community safety is the phrase to be preferred only if safety refers to the likely absence of harms (particularly serious harms) from all sources, not just from human acts defined as crimes' (Wiles and Pease, 2000, p 21). In a similar vein, Gordon Hughes has suggested that perhaps there are alternative paradigms of community safety, beyond mainstream 'crime and disorder hype', where community safety could be understood '… as a multi-agency and community-based strategy guided by the principle of harm reduction, where the notion of harm extends beyond the actions proscribed by criminal law' (Hughes, 2000, p 57).

However, what will be argued below is that at the same time as the conceptual parameters of community safety are being problematised by criminologists in terms of the absence of some of the non- or quasi-criminalised (or relatively neglected) forms and sources of social harm listed above, one could say that the emergence of the expression of intolerance especially in the form of intolerance of difference is another aspect of this contemporary conceptual renegotiation process. In fact, one could go as far to say that Third Way politics is fairly explicit in its attempt to ever expand key government concepts. For example, according to Giddens, '… exclusion is not about gradations of inequality, but about mechanisms that act to detach groups of people from the social mainstream …' (Giddens, 1998, p 104). Similarly, '… inclusion refers in its broadest sense to citizenship, to the civil and political rights and obligations that all members of a society should have, not just formally, but as a reality of their lives …' (Giddens, 1998, pp 102-3). Along these lines there is evidence that the interpretation and focus of the government's 'social exclusion' discourses are radically expanding in the face of cultural disharmony and hatred and polarisation between communities in present-day Britain (see McGhee, 2003, 2005). This 'expanded' concern over the mechanisms that can detach individuals and groups from the social mainstream, does, as we shall see below, have a bearing on the LGBT community. However, much of the emphasis of this 'concern' in recent years has been associated with racism (or more accurately 'racisms') (see Chapter Five in this volume). What minority ethnic groups share with minority groups defined by sexuality and gender is a vulnerability to hatred and a history of oppressive policing[5].

The Association of Chief Police Officers (ACPO) was one of the first organisations in the UK to focus wholeheartedly on the problems facing minority groups in society that are targeted by hatred. Significantly, the ACPO's *Guide to Identifying and Combating Hate Crime* published in 2000 included homophobic incidents alongside racist hate crime as the two most high-profile hate crime problems facing the UK. Both of these forms of hate crime, according to the ACPO, are associated with high-profile media events, for example, the Stephen Lawrence Inquiry and the nail bombing of the Admiral Duncan (gay) pub in Soho in London in 1999 (ACPO, 2000, p 17).

Hate crime in the ACPO guide is taken to mean any crime where the perpetrator's prejudice against an identifiable group of people is a factor in determining who is victimised (ACPO, 2000, p 10). The centrality of victimisation in relation to racist and homophobic hate crime is evident in the ACPO definitions. For example, a racist incident is defined as: 'any incident which is perceived to be racist by the victim or any other person' and homophobic incidents are similarly defined as 'any incident which is perceived to be homophobic by the victim or any other person. In effect, any incident intended to have an impact on those perceived to be lesbian, gay men, bisexual or transgender' (ACPO, 2000, p 13). According to the ACPO, hate crimes are special crimes that require special police attention because:

> Hate crimes can have a devastating effect on the quality of life of its victims and those who fear becoming victims. That is why we must give it priority. Hate crime victims feel the added trauma of knowing that the perpetrator's motivation is an impersonal, group hatred, relating to some feature such as skin colour, physical disability, or visible features relating to core personal values such as religion or being lesbian, gay, bisexual or transgendered. A crime that might normally have a minor impact becomes, with the hate element, a very intimate and hurtful attack that can undermine the victim's quality of life ... hate crime is a powerful poison to society ... it breeds suspicion, mistrust, alienation and fear. It promotes isolation and exclusion and sets up barriers to communication. (ACPO, 2000, pp 20, 21)

According to Moran, the ACPO definitions of racist and homophobic hate crimes are significant as they focus on the 'special circumstances' and the 'unique effects' of these 'value-added' crimes, which, although impersonal, are experienced as being very personal and thus are the source of greater harm (Moran, 2000, p 12). For example, homophobic hate crimes have been described as having a particularly spatial impact on victims and victim communities in that these incidents have been described as a mechanism for 'policing the closet', or the boundaries of 'privacy' that work to keep lesbians and gays marginalised in the fringes of society. Thus, homophobic violence can be viewed as 'a punishment for stepping outside culturally accepted norms and a warning to all gay and lesbian people to stay in 'their place', the invisibility and self hatred of the closet' (Herek and Berrill, 1992, p 3). According to McManus and Rivers, in the context of crime and disorder, homophobia can be subtle or overt, and can take many forms (2001, p 3), for example:

- verbal abuse and harassment;
- physical assault and emotional violence;
- property damage;
- other crimes (for example, extortion).

For McManus and Rivers, the victims of homophobia and homophobic incidents can experience a number of long-term mental health problems as a result of the victimisation or discrimination they face. For example, it has been suggested that the victims of homophobia in adolescence are more prone to self-harm and suicide[6] than their heterosexual counterparts; exposure to violence and harassment increases the prevalence of depression, anxiety and relationship problems among lesbians, gay men and bisexual men and women[7]. There is also the suggestion that the victims of homophobic incidents may also suffer from post-traumatic stress disorder (McManus and Rivers, 2001, p 3). However, the ACPO stresses that it is not just individuals who are affected by hate crimes, but also the families and friends of the victim (their wider 'community'). According to the ACPO, it is 'society' that is the ultimate victim of hate crime. In answer to the question, 'Why is it important to identify an incident as a hate incident?', the ACPO stresses the following:

- it does not just affect the victim;
- it can impact on entire communities;
- there can be hundreds of 'victims';
- society as a whole is a victim;
- there is a very high risk of repeat victimisation. (ACPO, 2000, p 76)

Thus, hate crimes, whether racist or homophobic, are perceived by organisations such as the ACPO as a serious threat to individuals, neighbourhoods and communities. The policy solutions to hate crime, other than introducing higher tariff offences, such as, for example, racially aggravated offences in the 1998 Crime and Disorder Act[8], are also associated with attempting to encourage the communities affected by hate crime to work with police in order to fight it. The 1998 Crime and Disorder Act requires that both the police and local authorities in partnerships with other agencies should become involved in both mapping and thereafter reducing crime in local areas (Blackbourn and Loveday, 2004, p 15). This translates into the requirement that Crime Reduction Partnerships should actively seek out and record offences identified as 'hidden crime' (Blackbourn and Loveday, 2004, p 15). The following is a five-step plan devised by McManus and Rivers for the development of a generic police–LGBT community anti-hate crime strategy:

- prepare the ground for partnerships;
- prepare a common policy statement;
- consult and involve lesbian, gay and bisexual communities;
- audit homophobic crime;
- develop and implement a strategy for dealing with homophobic crime. (McManus and Rivers, 2001, p 4)

It will be suggested below that much of the focus of police–LGBT anti-hate crime partnerships focus on the third and fourth steps of this five-step plan, that is, on the consultation with certain individuals who 'represent' the LGBT community; and on the auditing of homophobic hate crime. But what is being audited in homophobic victimisation surveys? According to Moran and Skeggs, homophobic victimisation surveys represent violence in two main ways: as hidden violence and as unreported violence (2004, p 16). Moran and Skeggs suggest that victimisation surveys are mechanisms for recognising 'what is not recognised' in official criminal statistics (2004, p 16). Moreover, the conducting of a homophobic victimisation survey is often perceived as a reflexive act associated with institutions within the criminal justice system that have failed to take these instances of violence seriously, to begin the process of doing so. This absence of data on homophobic victimisation is evident, according to Moran and Skeggs, in the absence of police reports of these instances of violence and is related to the lack of police investigation into these instances of violence; at the same time there is a dearth of prosecutions and convictions of the perpetrators (2004, p 16). However, homophobic victimisation surveys do not exclusively focus on homophobic violence and the experience of homophobic victimisation in local LGBT communities. Homophobic violence and victimisation is only one side of the problem to be audited, that is:

> Research shows that lesbian, gay, bisexual and transgender populations are at a greater risk of being victims of crime. They are also disadvantaged when they experience crime and find it more difficult to access the range of services available to many other victims of crime. (McManus and Rivers, 2001, p 2)

The examination of service provision, or more accurately the barriers preventing victimised communities from accessing the range of services that should be open to them, is therefore another important aspect of homophobic victimisation surveys or audits of homophobic crime. At the same time, the presence of an institutionalised prejudice in service provider organisations is also one of the prerequisites for the ACPO classification of hate crime. Lack of trust in service providers results in a further layer of value-added 'harm' that can impact on individuals and whole communities because hate crime offenders 'can often keep the same victim or group of victims locked in isolation and fear by keeping the physical extent of each attack at a level where it is unlikely to be reported' (ACPO, 2000, p 21). Part of the problem in relation to getting police–LGBT anti-hate crime partnerships established, according to McManus and Rivers, is the perception among members of LGBT communities that the police as an organisation is homophobic. McManus and Rivers have produced a definition of institutional homophobia modified from the definition of institutional racism found in the Stephen Lawrence Inquiry report:

The collective failure of an organisation to provide an appropriate and professional service to people because of their actual or perceived sexual orientation. It can be seen or detected in processes, attitudes and behaviour that amount to discrimination, through unwitting prejudice, ignorance, thoughtlessness and homophobic stereotyping, all of which disadvantages LGBT people. (McManus and Rivers, 2001, p 3)

The ACPO suggests that the effects of the perception of police institutional prejudice towards LGBT communities result in victims of homophobic violence assuming:

- that the incident/crime will not be taken seriously by the police;
- that there may be a homophobic reaction from an officer;
- that others may find out about your sexuality as a result of reporting;
- that information about your sexuality may be recorded/stored; and
- that you will have to disclose/talk about your sexuality to an officer. (ACPO, 2000, p 81)

The Crown Prosecution Service (CPS), in its guidance on homophobic crime, suggests that there is little that can be done at the initial stage of a police–LGBT anti-hate crime initiative other than attempting to overcome some of the perceptions (listed by the ACPO above) about police in LGBT communities through building bridges and increasing community confidence in the various criminal justice agencies:

Many homophobic incidents go unreported because the victim makes an immediate decision not to involve the police. There is little that we can do to prevent this from happening, although by building links with the LGBT communities and by using those links to help the communities have confidence in us, more victims from the LGBT communities may be willing to come forward and report crimes to the police. (CPS, 2000, p 10)

Building trust and increasing confidence are at the very heart of police–LGBT crime reduction partnership. However, it is important at this stage to explore some of the assumptions behind this strategy of 'increasing' trust. According to Misztal (referring to the trusting relationship between subjects and governments), it is assumed that people who trust that political power is appropriately exercised have good grounds for compliance. At the same time, if they feel that their government will deal with their demands fairly and equally, they are more likely to press those demands on government (Misztal, 1996, p 245). Therefore, for Misztal, there is a connection between trust and the expectation of being treated fairly and equally by a public institution that is in turn related to political participation. The social necessity of trust is therefore a two-way process that sustains social relationships; trust is thus well placed as a potential basis for social solidarity, cooperation and consensus in late modern societies associated with the erosion or decline of many institutions (family, work, discipline, the welfare state and national sovereignty) and the rise of others, such as culturally specific (ethnic, sexual orientation and territorial) identities (Misztal, 1996, p 4). However, trust, like those other centre-left (and centre-right) staples – community, civil society and citizenship – is an ambiguous concept. Trust, as Misztal elaborates, is employed as the new basis of democratic civil society in rather circular ways:

> First trust – as one of the important sources of cooperation – is seen as a socially desirable aim. Secondly, it is argued that, in order to achieve it, we must proceed in a trustworthy way. It is this double and ambiguous meaning that makes the concept of trust difficult to examine yet simultaneously attractive to use. (Misztal, 1996, p 8)

Trust, according to Misztal, is therefore a process; trust is to be achieved, increased, developed, earned. However, confidence should be distinguished from trust (which Misztal describes as a matter of individual determination and involves choosing between alternatives). Confidence is the end point of building trust, in that confidence is a more 'habitual expectation' (Misztal, 1996, p 16).

Many of the problems and issues surrounding the policing of the LGBT community raised above, including issues of trust and overcoming the perception of institutionalised prejudice, as well as the combination of victimisation surveys with audits of service provision, will be explored in the case study on police–LGBT initiatives in Southampton. One could say that the police–LGBT liaison culture that is unfolding all over England and Wales is an attempt to turn the habitual mistrust between police and LGBT communities into trust in an attempt to eventually facilitate 'habitual confidence' in LGBT communities in the form of the expectation that they will be treated fairly. Building trust is also central to Hampshire Constabulary's work with LGBT communities in Southampton in recent years. This relationship came to a head in July of 2001 with the launch of the Hidden Targets Report (Mallett, 2001)[9]. The purpose of this launch (which included a structured programme of presentations from various representatives from Southampton, for example, the Gay Community Health Service (GCHS), Hampshire Constabulary Community Support Team, Southampton Gay Community Network and the city council's Crime and Disorder Steering Group at Southampton's Civic Centre) was to promote a wider understanding of: the extent of homophobic incidents in the city; the existing initiatives that have been set up to deal with the problem; and the ways the various agencies might work more closely together[10].

In response to the Hidden Targets Report, the Hidden Targets Multi-agency Group (Southampton) was established in October 2001. The membership of this group includes representatives from 17 statutory and voluntary organisations and agencies across Southampton and wider Hampshire. It could be suggested that LGBT trust (never mind habitual confidence) in police is still far off in relation to the LGBT community in Southampton and in Hampshire. This conclusion is supported by the following passage from the 2001 Hidden Targets Report:

> This research shows that lesbians and gay men are subject to homophobic incidents. Over half the sample[11] had experienced one or more incidents and over a third have experienced an incident in the last year. Only a quarter of these incidents were reported to the police. The data shows that it is not just 'minor' incidents that are not reported. Respondents often did not report incidents such as rape and blackmail. This study identifies a number of possible reasons for the under-reporting of homophobic incidents. These reasons include a distrust or fear of the police; concerns around disclosure of sexuality; belief that the incident will not be taken seriously; or feeling that the incident is not serious enough to warrant reporting. (Mallett, 2001, p 71).

What this indicates is that the problems associated with the reporting of homophobic incidents to the police are multi-causal yet are all strongly associated with trust. The vast majority of the multi-agency group initiatives and many of the recommendations taken up by the assembled stakeholders at the launch of the Hidden Targets Report in Southampton in the summer of 2001 involve trust and esteem building where the promise of inclusion, participation, protection and justice are all bound up with the project of encouraging homophobic incident 'reporting behaviour'. This is an attack on the enduring deep-seated perception, widespread in LGBT communities, of police institutional homophobia. The ACPO recognises that institutional prejudice, whether racist or homophobic, can become an obstacle to its goal of creating an equitable police force that 'must be – and be seen to be – entirely fair to every individual and to all sections of the community' (ACPO, 2000, p 18). The way forward from LGBT communities' lack of trust in police, according to Hampshire Constabulary, is through the creation of a more informed and sympathetic police force by encouraging police officers to volunteer for Lesbian and Gay Liaison Officer service, with its specialist training in conjunction with local LGBT organisations and agencies; providing special outreach surgeries in local LGBT venues; and expanding and improving access to anonymous 'homophobic incident' reporting facilities. Hampshire Constabulary in Southampton, as will be revealed below, has been relatively successful on all three of these fronts.

The following statement is taken from the conclusion of the Hidden Targets Progress Report of 2002 in relation to the work that has been carried out in the first year of the existence of the Southampton multi-agency group:

> The Hidden Targets Multi-agency Group is working towards building greater confidence in the reporting process and the court service. This is being achieved by both training for staff working in these services and making them more accessible to the LGBT community through outreach and publicity ... the work completed in the past year has enabled services to respond more effectively to people experiencing homophobic and transphobic harassment. The next step for the Hidden Targets Multi-agency Group will be to ensure services are well publicised and promoted, and that the LGBT community are aware of the improvements. (Mallett, 2002, p 18)

These are all very welcome developments. However, one could suggest that too much priority has been given in the Hidden Targets project to improving the efficiency (and awareness) of the agencies and organisations that come into contact with the LGBT community (even though this is undeniably important work). This is a problem associated with all community safety multi-agency approaches, not just those targeting LGBT communities. Ballintyne and Fraser suggest that 'public services and multi-agency partnerships do not have a strong track record in consulting and engaging local communities' (Ballintyne and Fraser, 2000, p 164). The emphasis in the Hidden Targets Progress Report (Mallett, 2002) seems to be less on participation, engagement and consultation with the wider LGBT community than on the improvement of the agencies and organisations that might service the LGBT community and on publicising these improvements and their increased efficiency in providing services to the LGBT community.

At the same time, there is a need to acknowledge another problem associated with the role that 'agencies' such as the Gay Community Health Service (GCHS) play in the context of police–LGBT community consultation, that is, the issue of representation, which is well rehearsed in studies of participatory and deliberative democracy (see Schedler and Glastra, 2001). The central problematic that arises here is who is representing which communities in these consultation processes, with whose authority, and to what ends? In Southampton there seems to be a dearth of lesbian and transgendered 'community representatives' in multi-agency forums. In this city the LGBT 'community' is overwhelmingly represented by a small number of extremely well-organised gay men from local health promotion agencies and HIV services, for example, the GCHS. In more metropolitan settings, such as certain London boroughs, it is increasingly the case that 'political professionals' in the form of 'freelance consultants' on community discrimination issues dominate Metropolitan Police–LGBT advisory groups. There is a risk that when the police consult, for example, 'hard to reach' minority communities (Jones and Newburn, 2001) in conjunction with local authorities, they might be simply consulting with the usual suspects, the same faces, the same self-selecting (or habitually selected) 'community representatives' or established service providers, and not the wider members of these communities. Perhaps this is one of the major failings of crime and disorder 'consultation' initiatives, in that multi-agency groups recruit pre-existing agencies, and therefore, in many instances, pre-existing community 'representatives'. Perhaps these consultation and multi-agency groups do not reflect enough on the representativeness of 'the representatives' of these organisations to speak for LGBT communities. The Home Office seemed to be aware of these problems when it suggested in its guidance on the 1998 Crime and Disorder Act's statutory 'consultation requirements' with reference to LGBT communities that:

> Seeking the involvement of the gay and lesbian community must be an active process not a passive one. This community is not always visible[12], and may for historical reasons not find it easy to engage in a dialogue with some of the groups involved in these potential partnerships[13]; it will *not* be enough just to write to the local pressure group inviting it to send a representative to a meeting and then thinking that your obligation to this sector of the community is discharged. You must develop creative and flexible ways to break down any barriers which may exist locally, and to encourage full and active engagement in the work by local gay and lesbian people. (Home Office, 1998)

In many ways, Hampshire Constabulary (with other partners in the multi-agency group) has been successful in attempting to break down some of the 'local' barriers to its engagement with Southampton's LGBT communities through various initiatives. For example, Hampshire Constabulary is a partner in the Hampshire Anonymous Reporting Scheme, and the Community Support Team also holds regular 'police surgeries' in local LGBT venues. These are more recent developments, although it should be noted that Hampshire Constabulary's work with Southampton's LGBT communities pre-dates the 1998 Crime and Disorder Act. In fact, Hampshire Constabulary has been actively working with the GCHS since 1994.

This partnership emerged in response to the high rate of suicide in the early 1990s in men who were awaiting prosecution for gross indecency offences; and a survey undertaken in 1994 that indicated that, among gay and bisexual men in Southampton, the police were the lowest rated service (Mallett, 2001, p 5). In many ways, the pre-1998 Crime and Disorder Act consultation activities and initiatives such as the Hidden Targets Multi-agency Group have their origin in these findings[14]. Hampshire Constabulary has also had an established (and growing) number of Lesbian and Gay Liaison Officers since 1996. These volunteer officers have been trained by the Constabulary's Community Support Team in collaboration with the GCHS. In many ways, the LGBT communities in Southampton can no longer claim that they are over-policed and under-protected in the context of the initiatives and policies that have been introduced in the city since the mid-1990s, but this does not mean that there is nothing left to do. Perhaps the challenge that faces all police–LGBT consultation initiatives, not just those in Southampton, but across all England and Wales, is not only the thorny problem of representativeness of those individuals (or agencies) consulted, but also the relatively low priority given to the reduction of homophobic incidents relative to initiatives dedicated to building trust and improving communication between the police, partner agencies and the LGBT community (although, obviously, these are not unrelated factors). It is undoubtedly the case that within the context and climate of these 'community safety' and multi-agency interventions we do see the welcome creation of what Matthews and Pitts (2001) describe as new alliances and new lines of responsibility between police and the communities they serve.

However, it is important to note that in this context the roles of key regulatory agencies, such as the police, are changing significantly. This has important implications in that 'the police have been "let off the hook" and can now legitimately claim that neither crime control nor community safety is their sole responsibility' (Matthews and Pitts, 2001, p 5). This is an emergent policing culture that requires the police to participate in an increasingly wide range of interventions. This shifts the balance of 'policing' away from crime control towards interventions that are described by Matthews and Pitts as being increasingly related to public order maintenance and akin to 'social work' functions (Matthews and Pitts, 2001, p 5). Reducing homophobic incidents and employing the full weight of the law, in appropriate evidence situations, against those who perpetrate homophobic and transphobic incidents against LGBT individuals must now also be prioritised as police–LGBT crime reduction partnerships move beyond the initial stages of these initiatives that have understandably focused on trust building and opening the channels of communication.

Notes

[1] The word 'homophobia' (first coined in North America in the 1960s) was first used in an academic setting in K.T. Smith's article 'Homophobia: a tentative personality profile' (Smith, 1971). In 1972, Weinberg defined homophobia in his book *Society and the Healthy Homosexual* as 'the dread of being in close quarters with homosexuals' (Weinberg, 1972, p 4). In an article in 1975, Freedman later added to that definition a description of homophobia as 'an extreme rage and fear reaction to homosexuals' (Freedman, 1975, p 19); for an overview, see Fone (2000).

[2] According to Whittle (2000), 'transgender' is an umbrella term used to define a political and social community that is inclusive of transsexual people, transgender people, cross-dressers (transvestite) and other groups of 'gender-variant' people.

[3] The differences between gay men and lesbians are well rehearsed in relation to this 'community', especially in terms of gender (Weeks, 1996, p 73). However, there are other differences within this wider LGBT community, including location (European, American, third world, urban, rural, and so on), class, race and disability, to name but a few. All this being said, it might understandably be argued that there are certain key

elements of the LGBT community that make it a unique 'community', for example, stigma, prejudice, legal inequality, a history of oppression and so on (Weeks, 1996, p 73).

[4] These are the rather more 'progressive elements' of the 1998 Crime and Disorder Act. However, what this Act is best known for is its authoritarian provisions that cater for Prime Minister Tony Blair's much-quoted ambition of being 'tough on crime, tough on the causes of crime', especially in relation to youth crime.

According to Fairclough, 'tough' is a New Labour keyword that moves the government to the centre in an attempt to court 'middle-class middle England' (Fairclough, 2000, pp 106-7). The consensus-building element around the youth crime provisions in the 1998 Crime and Disorder Act was that such measures were presented as being for young people's own good. They were in the order of early preventive interventions, tackling antisocial rather than necessarily 'criminal' activities. Muncie suggests that the authoritarian toughness of the provisions were, as a result, legitimised in the name of welfare (Muncie, 1999, p 157).

[5] This is not to suggest that racism and homophobia do not intersect. For information with regard to the intersection of racist and homophobic violence, see GALOP's black services needs assessment report, *The Low Down*, in which the racist and homophobic violence experienced by African, Asian and Caribbean lesbian, gay and bisexual people in London was examined (GALOP, 2001).

[6] See Canadian research conducted by Bagley and Tremblay (1997).

[7] See US and British research conducted by Hershberger and D'Augelli (1997) and Rivers (2000), respectively.

[8] The 1998 Crime and Disorder Act included racially aggravated incidents as a crime, but did not include a similar provision that defined incidents motivated by homophobia as crime. As a result, according to Baxendale, homophobia is confirmed as the prejudice that may dare to speak its name (Baxendale, 2001). That said, Baxendale notes that despite not being written into law, homophobic, and indeed transphobic, incidents are being taken seriously by many police forces in England and Wales, and the police, unlike the Home Office, '… have no problem in understanding the thematic link between racism and homophobia, and improving their practices with both' (Baxendale, 2001).

[9] This report was a victim survey and an agency audit. Agencies surveyed in this report were Breakout Youth Project, Victim Support Service, Solent Lesbian and Gay Switchboard, Southampton City Council Housing Department, Winchester Rape and Sexual Abuse Counselling, The Rainbow Project, No Limits Youth Information and Advice Centre, Options Drug and Alcohol Counselling Service, Southampton Women's Aid, Southampton Rape Crisis and Sexual Counselling Service, and Society of Dismas.

[10] Community policing and community consultation in Southampton has been carried out within the context of significant changes, especially in relation to the creation of a centralised police division in the city. For example, in 1998, Portswood and Southampton Central police stations joined forces, and in April 2001, Shirley and Bitterne were added to form a new city-wide police division. This larger police division now matches the local authority area covered by Southampton City Council. This reorganisation will have an impact on the future local authority and police statutory partnerships and community policing programmes, especially in the light of the appointment, in February 2002, of a new Community Policing Chief Inspector.

[11] In summary, a total of 279 people took part in the study. The average age of the sample was 29 years, and the age range was 16-63. The sample consisted of more men than women (69% men, 28% women) and 3% identified as transgender. The sample was predominantly white (93.6%) (Mallett, 2001, pp 19-20).

[12] For example, Jones and Newburn suggest that even in areas where police have developed extensive consultative links with the 'out' lesbian and gay community, this will not necessarily help in fostering positive links with those gay men and women who are not 'out' (Jones and Newburn, 2001, p 10).

[13] The CPS describes this as an 'entirely understandable reluctance' on the part of members of LGBT communities due to '... the way in which members of the LGBT communities have historically been treated by individuals within the criminal justice agencies' (CPS, 2000, p 7).

[14] In 1997, Hampshire Constabulary and the GCHS (then the Gay Men's Health Project) were awarded regional and national Health Alliance awards in the category of mental health as a result of their joint efforts to reduce suicide rates in relation to men awaiting prosecution for gross indecency offences. This reduction in suicide rates to zero since 1994 is the result of the development of policy of cautioning first-time gross indecency offenders along with an automatic referral to the GCHS.

References

ACPO (Association of Chief Police Officers) (2000) *Guide to Identifying and Combating Hate Crime* (www.acpo.police.uk).

Bagley, P. and Tremblay, A. (1997) 'Suicidal behaviours in homosexual and bisexual males', *Crisis*, vol 18, no 1, pp 24-34.

Ballintyne, S. and Fraser, P. (2000) 'It's good to talk, but it's not good enough', in S. Ballintyne, K. Pease and V. McLaren (eds) *Secure Foundations: Key Issues in Crime Prevention, Crime Reduction and Community Safety*, London: Institute of Public Policy Research, pp 164-88.

Baxendale, G. (2001) 'Soft on hate crime, soft on the causes of hate crime', *Gay Times*, October, p 60.

Blackbourn, D. and Loveday, B. (2004) 'Community safety and homophobic crime', *Community Safety Journal*, vol 3, no 2, pp 15-22.

CPS (Crime Prosecution Service) (2002) *Guidance on Prosecuting Cases of Homophobic Crime*, London: produced by the Equality and Diversity Unit and the Policy Directorate.

Crawford, A. (1997) *The Local Governance of Crime: Appeals to Community and Partnerships*, Oxford: Clarendon Press.

Crawford, A. (1998a) 'Delivering multi-agency partnerships in community safety', in A. Marlow and J. Pitts (eds) *Planning Safer Communities*, Lyme Regis: Russell House Publishing, pp 213-22.

Crawford, A. (1998b) *Crime Prevention and Community Safety: Politics, Policies and Practices*, London/New York, NY: Longman.

Crawford, A. (2001) 'Joined-up but fragmented: contradiction, ambiguity and ambivalence at the heart of New Labour's "Third Way"', in R. Matthews and J. Pitts (eds) *Crime, Disorder and Community Safety*, London/New York, NY: Routledge, pp 54-80.

Fairclough, N. (2000) *New Labour, New Language?*, London/New York, NY: Routledge.

Fone, B. (2000) *Homophobia: A History*, New York, NY: Metropolitan Books.

Freedman, M. (1975) 'Homophobia: the psychology of a social disease', *Body Politic*, no 24, pp 8-19.

GALOP (2001) *The Low Down: Black Lesbians, Gay Men and Bisexual People Talk About Their Experiences and Needs*, London: GALOP.

Giddens, A. (1998) *The Third Way: The Renewal of Social Democracy*, Cambridge: Polity Press.

Herek, G.M. and Berrill, K.T. (1992) 'Introduction', in G.M. Herek and K.T. Berrill (eds) *Hate Crimes: Confronting Violence Against Lesbians and Gay Men*, Newbury Park/London/New Delhi: Sage Publications, pp 1-10.

Hershberger, D. and D'Augelli, R. (1997) 'Predictors of suicide attempts among gay, lesbian and bisexual youth', *Journal of Adolescent Research*, vol 12, no 4, pp 477-97.

Home Office (1991) *Safer Communities: The Local Delivery of Crime Prevention through the Partnership Approach*, London: Home Office.

Home Office (1998) *Guidance on Statutory Crime and Disorder Partnerships: Crime and Disorder Act 1998*, London: HMSO.

Hughes, G. (1996) 'Communitarianism and law and order', *Critical Social Policy*, vol 16, no 4, pp 17-41.

Hughes, G. (1998) *Understanding Crime Prevention: Social Control, Risk and Late Modernity*, Buckingham: Open University Press.

Hughes, G. (2000) 'In the shadow of crime and disorder: the contested politics of community safety in Britain', *Crime Prevention and Community Safety: An International Journal*, vol 2, no 4, pp 47-60.

Hughes, G. (2002) 'Plotting the rise of community safety: critical reflections on research, theory and politics', in G. Hughes and A. Edwards (eds) *Crime Control and Community:The New Politics of Public Safety*, Cullompton:Willan Publishing, pp 20-45.

Jones, T. and Newburn, T. (2001) *Widening Access: Improving Police Relationships With Hard to Reach Groups*, Police Research Series, Paper 138, London: Home Office.

McGhee, D. (2003) 'Moving to "our" common ground – a critical examination of community cohesion discourse in twenty-first century Britain', *Sociological Review*, vol 51, no 3, pp 383-411.

McGhee, D. (2005) *Intolerant Britain: Hate, Citizenship and Difference*, Berkshire: Open University Press and McGraw-Hill.

McManus, J. and Rivers, D. (2001) 'Without prejudice: a guide for community safety partnerships on responding to the needs of lesbians, gays and bisexuals', NACRO (www.nacro.org.uk).

Mallett, L. (2001) *Hidden Targets: Lesbian Women and Gay Men's Experiences of Homophobic Crime and Harassment in Southampton*, Southampton: Southampton City Council.

Mallett, L. (2002) *Hidden Targets: Lesbian Women and Gay Men's Experiences of Homophobic Crime and Harassment in Southampton – Progress Report*, Southampton: Southampton City Council.

Matthews, R. and Pitts, J. (eds) (2001) *Crime, Disorder and Community Safety*, London/New York, NY: Routledge.

Misztal, B. (1996) *Trust in Modern Societies:The Search for the Bases of Social Order*, Cambridge: Polity Press.

Moran, L.J. (1996) *The Homosexual(ity) of Law*, London/New York, NY: Routledge.

Moran, L.J. (2000) 'Victim surveys and beyond: researching violence against lesbians, gay men, bisexuals and transgender people', *SCOLAG Journal*, September, pp 10-12.

Moran, L. and Skeggs, B. (2004) *Sexuality and the Politics of Violence and Safety*, London/New York, NY: Routledge.

Muncie, J. (1999) 'Institutionalized intolerance: youth justice and the 1998 Crime and Disorder Act', *Critical Social Policy*, vol 19, no 2, pp 147-76.

Newburn, T. (2002) 'Community safety and policing: some implications of the Crime and Disorder Act 1998', in G. Hughes, E. McLaughlin and J. Muncie (eds) *Crime Prevention and Community Safety: New Directions*, London: Sage Publications, pp 102-22.

Rivers, I. (2000) 'Going against the grain: supporting lesbian, gay and bisexual clients as they "come out"', *British Journal of Guidance and Counselling*, vol 28, no 4, pp 503-13.

Schedler, P. and Glastra, F. (2001) 'Communicating policy in late modern society: on the boundaries of interactive policymaking', *Policy & Politics*, vol 29, no 3, pp 337-49.

Smith, K.T. (1971) 'Homophobia: a tentative personality profile', *Psychological Reports*, vol 29, no 1, pp 1091-4.

Weeks, J. (1996) 'The idea of a sexual community', *Soundings*, vol 2, Spring, pp 71-84.

Weinberg, G. (1972) *Society and the Healthy Homosexual*, New York, NY: St. Martin's Press.

Whittle, S. (2000) *The Transgender Debate: The Crisis Surrounding Gender Identities*, Reading: South Street Press.

Wiles, P. and Pease, K. (2000) 'Crime prevention and community safety: Tweedledum and Tweedledee?', in S. Ballintyne, K. Pease and V. McLaren (eds) *Secure Foundations: Key Issues in Crime Prevention, Crime Reduction and Community Safety*, London: Institute of Public Policy Research, pp 21-9.

FOUR

Community safety, the family and domestic violence

Paula Wilcox

For centuries, non-intervention in the private life of the family was the state's justification for abdicating responsibility for the safety of women and children in the home. With 'community safety' becoming a key organising discourse of contemporary crime prevention, this has become an increasingly unsustainable perspective. Feminist research and activism from the 1970s (building on 19th-century feminism [Mill, 1869; Cobbe, 1878]) chipped away at this hegemonic construction of privacy revealing its role in covering up male abuse/violence in the home, now commonly referred to as 'domestic violence'[1] (Pizzey, 1974; Dobash and Dobash, 1979; Borkowski et al, 1983; Hanmer and Saunders, 1984; Walker, 1984; Maynard, 1985; Pleck, 1987; Mama, 1989). Continuing feminist research and activism have gradually provoked changing and more appropriate responses to 'domestic violence' through policy development and new legislation, although more needs to be done and inadequate funding[2] remains a key problem.

The purpose of this chapter is to look at the historical development of initiatives against 'domestic violence' (which have largely resulted from feminist organising), examining the influence of community safety discourse and activity. During the late 20th century, campaigns and interventions can be analysed (if rather crudely) into two main organisational strands (see Table 4.1): on the one hand, the vital influence of the women's refuge movement (inspired by radical feminism), which has, to some degree, maintained a position of working outside the state and, on the other hand, feminists and others (some with a community safety perspective) organising within and through the state. Throughout this period, crime control strategy was moving towards more generally punitive approaches (Muncie, 2000) but two other relevant strands developed concurrently: one focusing on concern for victims and the other focusing on enhancing safety at the community level. All of these strands have had an impact on responding to 'domestic violence', as we shall see, but this chapter will explore why community safety approaches have been less influential in relation to 'domestic violence' than feminist approaches.

The questions posed here are therefore: how far were community safety approaches extended to women/children experiencing 'domestic violence'? What contradictions were raised in addressing 'domestic violence' using a community safety framework? And, what lessons can be learned from the unfolding development of interventions against 'domestic violence'? First, we will consider feminist theory on the family and women's safety and how this has impacted on feminist initiatives against male violence. This is followed with an examination of community safety initiatives, deconstructing 'community' and 'safety'. Finally, we will examine how Western understandings of 'domestic violence' have led to a focus on state/agency responses, and how this has been underpinned by gendered discourses of caring.

Feminist theory on the family and male violence against women

The notion of 'family' has been, and often still is, deployed as the central motif around which responsibility for women's safety has traditionally been organised. Institutions of state were established by men of property/power to deal with their own public safety and to control the crimes of men of lesser property and little power. Moreover, middle-class male domination was enshrined in legal systems that have been slow to respond to the changing historical position of women in the West and to feminist challenges. In England and Wales, for example, until the decision of the House of Lords in the case of *R v R*[1992] 1 AC 599, rape in marriage was protected from criminal prosecution. As Naffine argues, the reason it took so long to be abolished in all jurisdictions is that its abolition challenged the view of women as the possessions and passive objects of their husbands' desires (Naffine, 1994, cited in Lees, 2000, p 57).

Traditional family discourse constructs women as men's possessions and their safety as in the safekeeping of specific male relatives (varying according to cultural and historical location). This issue was particularly explicit in the second edition of the Home Office booklet, *Practical Ways to Crack Crime: The Family Guide* (Home Office, 1991). Early sections of the booklet, apparently addressed to men, outlined ways of 'keeping your family safe' (here 'family' meant wife and children). Later on, another section added 'men can help too'. In the West, the recent history of state regulation of marriage and the family constructs women's safety as the responsibility of the father until marriage, when responsibility is handed over to the husband (brides are still 'given away' by fathers in the marriage ceremony). In other cultures, responsibility for women's security may be extended to older brothers and uncles. It is important to note that, from this patriarchal perspective, women's 'security' is linked to notions of purity and chastity, which in turn underpin ideas about male/family honour. Security in this context is, therefore, not so much about women's physical safety as about regulating women's sexual behaviour.

Feminist and critical theoretical analyses of the family critiqued the division between public and private spheres (that forms the basis of many policies and services), arguing for the interaction and interdependency of both spheres. 'The public vision ... is deeply involved in our vision of domestic things, and our most private behaviours themselves depend on public actions, such as housing policy, or more directly, family policy' (Bourdieu, 1996, p 25). Traditional concepts of home and family have been developed by white middle-class men, assuming a heterosexual nuclear family (Passaro, 1996) and overlooking the widespread nature of conflict within patriarchal families. The tension between the binary opposites of safety and risk, security and fear, privacy and invasion exist *within* the home for many (Wardhaugh, 1999, p 93). So, feminist research from the late 1970s revealed the family to be a potential place of anxiety and danger for women and children due to male physical, sexual and emotional violence (Stanko, 1988, 1995, 1998).

Finally, there is a problem in conceptualising the family as either totally gender neutral or completely divided along gendered lines, both approaches failing to capture the multiple gendered discourses and practices associated with home and family that are experienced in different ways depending on other social differences – class, 'race' and sexuality spring to mind. We need to be aware of such interconnections if we are to enhance our understanding of 'family' in relation to violence against women by male partners. They help us to understand why a woman cannot 'just leave' a violent relationship and why members of the public rarely suggest the same to an abusive man (Stark, 2004).

Feminist analyses of the family have been enormously influential in opening up to question the whole area of power in gendered relationships. Such analyses, combined with feminist principles of organising, have also been the driving force in setting up and running services for women such as refuges/shelters and rape crisis centres. Moreover, these analyses have been particularly successful in influencing social policy initiatives against 'domestic violence' in Britain, and I now turn to look at these initiatives.

Feminist initiatives against male violence

As we have seen, historically, women's safety was a privatised 'non-issue' as states derogated security responsibilities ostensibly to male members of women's families. As late as the 1970s it was commonly assumed that women faced danger only in public spaces ('stranger danger'), hence police advice on women's safety recommended they take a range of precautions on the streets, putting the onus onto women for their own personal safety. Women are already keenly aware of such public dangers and tend to adjust their behaviour patterns in response to violence as well as the threat of violence (Stanko, 1987).

Violence has been widely viewed in the feminist literature, then, as an effective device for regulating women and the female body. The process of keeping physically safe has been seen as one mode of 'performative femininity' (Stanko, 1997). The threat of invasion or damage to the body through sexual violence restricts many women's uses and perceptions of different spaces (Hanmer and Saunders, 1984; Valentine, 1989). This remains the case, although more recent research on violence has emphasised women's active resistance to violence and

Table 4.1: Key initiatives against 'domestic violence' (DV) since the 1970s

Date	Feminist initiatives 'outside' the state	Feminist/community safety initiatives 'through' the state	Comment
1970s	Women's Aid Refuges	Premises provided by LAs often in poor condition	Refuges overcrowded yet provide safety/support; women's voluntary labour
1974	National Women's Aid Federation (NWAF)		To educate the public and inform women about their options
1975		Government Select Committee on Violence in Marriage	Recommended minimum of one family place in a refuge per 10,000 population. This remains unfulfilled
1980s	'Take Back the Night'; Women against the Cuts'; Miners' Wives groups; Women's Peace Groups etc.	A small number of LA-supported women's centres, Community Safety teams, Women's and Equality Units set up in metropolitan areas	Feminist activist groups raise issues of women's safety, self-defence etc; women members of LA Units raise issues of women's fear of crime, domestic and sexual violence
	Local Women's Aid groups work to forge links with Housing Departments and Social Services	Cooperation mainly women in LA Housing Departments	Scepticism encountered; hard work forging links; cooperation uneven; support at executive levels problematic
1983		Home Office Crime Prevention Unit set up	
1987	NWAF established first dedicated National DV Helpline service		
1988		'Safer Cities', government's crime prevention programme	Funded several DV projects in 1990s
1989	Establishment of the first local multi-agency forums on DV		A noteworthy example being Leeds Inter-Agency Project

contd

Table 4.1: contd.../

Date	Feminist initiatives 'outside' the state	Feminist/community safety initiatives 'through' the state	Comment
1990		Home Office Circulars 14/90 and 60/90	14/90 partnership approaches to crime prevention 60/90 domestic violence units/officers and 'presumption of arrest'
1993		Home Affairs Select Committee Enquiry into DV	Funding to ensure effective provision of refuge services most important action needed
1993-95	WA input to *Brookside* (Channel 4) Jordache family DV plotline		Bringing DV into the public arena via a soap opera drew attention on a larger scale
1994	First DV cinema advertisement distributed by WA and supported by Home Office		
1996	WA lobbied for change to law	Family Law Act 1996 part IV	Improved civil remedies against DV, automatic powers of arrest where violence used or threatened
1996		British Crime Survey	Self-completion module on DV provides a far more complete measure of DV
1998		Crime and Disorder Act 1998	Statutory duty on LA and police to formulate and implement community safety strategy

contd

Table 4.1: contd.../

Date	Feminist initiatives 'outside' the state	Feminist/community safety initiatives 'through' the state	Comment
1999-2002		Home Office Crime Reduction Programme, Violence Against Women Initiative	Funded 33 projects for £7m
1999	National DV website www.womensaid.org.uk and 'The Gold Book'		UK information website and public directory of local refuge and helpline services set up by WA
1999		British Crime Survey	Self-completion module on DV (as 1996)
2001	National DV Helpline		Becomes a 24-hour service
2005		Domestic Violence, Crime and Victims Act 2004	

Sources: Crawford (1998) Crime Prevention and Community Safety; *Women's Aid (2004)* Celebrating 30 years of Women's Aid 1974-2004; *Dodd et al (2004)*

to the social expectation that women will be fearful (Koskela, 1997; Stanko, 1997).

Initiatives against male violence did not, therefore, originate with the state but in women's groups, with women sharing their experiences of male violence and reconceptualising it as an outcome of hierarchically gendered power relations in society. It was feminist women's groups, too, that set up the first refuges/shelters for women, staffed entirely by voluntary labour, which developed into the Women's Aid refuge movement as we know it today. There was, however, some local state involvement even at this early stage in that a handful of local authority housing departments provided women's groups with refuge premises. These premises were often in poor condition but, for the first time, women who had nowhere else to go were offered a place of safety. Importantly, also, the existence of refuge space opened up the possibility for survivors to explore their understanding of what had happened to them. Women frequently saw themselves as personal failures in the relationship, but talking to other women posed an alternative understanding of 'domestic violence' as a *social problem* that could be 'collectively challenged and transformed' (Charles, 2000, p 137). The empowerment of women was a key principle of organising in the women's refuge movement.

In 1974, the Women's Aid Federation England (WAFE) was formed to campaign against 'domestic violence' and to coordinate the work of refuge groups in Britain (Women's Aid, 2004), giving evidence to the Parliamentary Select Committee on Violence in Marriage in 1975. As a result, legislation was called for to provide protection against 'domestic violence' and to make clear local authorities' responsibilities towards homeless women and children who were the victims of such violence (Dobash and Dobash, 1992, p 124)[3]. The Select Committee conceptualised 'domestic violence' primarily in terms of housing, recommending that refuges should be resourced by the local state rather than the central state (Charles, 2000, p 139) and that a minimum of one family refuge place was needed per 10,000 population (this recommendation remains unfulfilled today).

While refuges have been characterised as being organised on radical and socialist feminist principles and women's units and domestic violence forums on liberal feminist principles, the reality on the ground has been far more complex: 'both socialist and radical feminists have engaged with the state, the former via local authorities and the latter through such organisations as refuge groups' (Charles, 2000, p 135). Also feminists do not necessarily locate themselves as either radical or socialist or liberal; many take a more eclectic approach, looking at optimum strategies in particular social and political contexts. Moreover, the later development of post-modern feminist approaches has drawn attention to issues of diversity (such as ethnicity and sexuality) and their intersection with gendered differences, which also must be taken into account.

During the 1980s and 1990s, feminist scholarship was demonstrating growing evidence of the incidence and extent of 'domestic violence' suffered by women worldwide; also male pro-feminist scholars started to research male oppression and violence (notably Jeff Hearn, 1987, 1998). The 'left realist' perspective was also emerging as a distinct criminological paradigm with explicit connections to notions of 'community' and roots in left-inclined local authorities (Lea and Young, 1984). At the same time, refuge workers were starting the long, hard task of forging links with sympathetic individuals in local government, especially in housing departments, and the police, to encourage improved responses to women experiencing/fleeing violence, albeit with mixed results (Women's Aid, 2004). Women's and Equality Units were being established in (mainly metropolitan) local authorities and here women/feminists began to put 'fear of crime', 'domestic' and sexual violence on to local government agendas for the first time (Stanko, 1998, p 54). In 1987, the National Women's Aid Federation established the first dedicated National Domestic Violence Helpline service and by 1989 the first city-wide 'domestic violence' forums came into being (for example, Leeds Inter-Agency Project). It was during the late 1980s and the 1990s that community safety strands of organising intertwined with feminist initiatives and so now we turn to look at the origins and influence of community safety.

Community safety: theory and initiatives

Community safety represented an alternative and more optimistic approach to tackling crime. However, community safety only represented a tiny proportion of the criminal justice system as a whole; in 1993/94, for instance, community safety activities formed just over 1% of the annual criminal justice budget (Crawford, 1998, p 63). Within this small budget, property crimes in public places were over-prioritised with an emphasis on funding situational and environmental projects with social projects playing a relatively minor role. In this case, 'domestic violence' continued to have a fairly low profile.

One reason for this has been the reliance of community safety approaches on rational choice theory, which tends to ignore differently gendered identities and practices, assuming 'unitary rational individuals' whose experiences can be universalised; in other words, a gender-neutral approach and a tendency to perpetuate the status quo in terms of structural inequalities (Henriques et al, 1984). The theory and practice of community safety continued to orient attention towards 'crime on the streets' – 'the community in public' – and away from 'crime behind closed doors' (Walklate, 2001).

Crawford (1998) has identified a range of interrelated developments contributing to the revival of crime prevention (and, within this, community safety) in Britain and we will now examine how these discourses relate (or not) to the 'domestic violence' field. First, he cites the 'growing strain on the criminal justice system, evidenced by the increasing rate of recorded crime and the numbers of people passing through the criminal justice system' (Crawford, 1998, p 33). In terms of 'domestic violence' over the 1980s, although more women reported incidents to the police, the number of 'domestic violence' perpetrators going through the legal system did not vary greatly. Second, there is the question of the 'increased politicisation of crime' and public perceptions that the likelihood of becoming a victim of crime had increased (Crawford, 1998, p 34). Women's fear of crime has always been greater than men's and feminist researchers have argued that this is due to their awareness of the continuum of male violence they face (Kelly, 1988). Adult women's fears are the result not only of first-hand experiences but also of a long process of learning and socialisation that begins in childhood (Goodey, 1999). Third, traditional methods of crime control had 'come to represent an increasing financial burden on the public purse' (Crawford, 1998, p 34). While this may not have been the case in relation to 'domestic violence' and the criminal justice system, it certainly was the case in terms of the economic burden on employment, housing, social services and health. However, in the 1980s, there was no evidence to back this up and it is only in more recent research (Stanko et al, 1998; Women and Equality Unit, 2003) that such costs are being more reliably estimated. Walby's research for the Women and Equality Unit carried out in Leeds into the costs of 'domestic violence' focused only on homicides of women, and estimated the cost of 102 women killed by partners and ex-partners at £112 million (Walby, 2004). Fourth, there has been a growing realisation that most crimes are never reported to the police (Crawford, 1998, p 34). It has long been recognised that 'domestic violence' is one of the most underreported of crimes. Fifth, there is an increasing recognition that the 'formal processes of criminal justice ... have only a limited effect in controlling crime' (Crawford, 1998), an issue that has had a number of consequences for public perceptions of crime. Finally, criminology itself has shifted its focus away from the offender and towards the offence, while also developing a growing interest in the victim (Crawford, 1998, pp 34-35).

Clearly, the discourses Crawford (1998) identifies as contributing to the focus on crime prevention/community safety differ substantially from the discourses that have led to the development of work against 'domestic violence'. Traditionally in criminology, as in wider society, male violence in the private sphere has been relatively ignored, and so there tended to be little if any focus on the 'domestic violence' offender (or victim for that matter). However, this was to change with the new concern for the victim developing out of such discourses, and this began to find common ground with feminist discourses regarding support for female victims.

By the 1990s, many local authorities and police forces as well as the Home Office started to take on board issues of women and violence. The Association of Women's Units in Local Government released *Responding with Authority* (1991) as a call for local authorities to become actively involved in discovering support systems to alleviate all kinds of violence against women, including fear of crime (cited in Stanko, 1995). Edinburgh City Council, for instance, sponsored a highly visible public education campaign, Zero Tolerance, which confronted myths about rape, child sexual abuse, 'domestic violence' and women's safety from a feminist perspective. By the mid-1990s, crime prevention advice was a centrepiece of the Conservative government's campaign against crime but it was still the case that advice to women remained in the crime prevention framework rather than a framework that looked to prevent violence against women (Stanko, 1990).

'Community' and/or 'safety'?

For many, the notion of 'community safety' gained ascendance over the term 'crime prevention' because of its inclusivity, referring not only to crime in the community but also to wider socioeconomic issues. While looking at 'safety' rather than 'crime' was attractive in that it seemed to offer the opportunity to address problems of social disadvantage, the unconsidered use of the concept 'community' (see critiques by Lacey and Zedner, 1995; Young, 2001) in community safety discourse undermined such opportunities. Assuming that people in a community all have the same interests at heart, that intervention(s) should be local or neighbourhood based and developed from the 'bottom up', in partnership and dependent on analyses of local contexts (Crawford, 1998, p 9) may sound well and good, but feminist theory has taught us to be wary of non-structured approaches and gender-neutral language serving to conceal masculinist interests.

Gender is a key idea of late modernity and yet gendered analyses are often missing from, or marginalised in, criminological work on other important ideas of the same period such as risk, globalisation and social control (see, for example, Ericson and Haggerty, 1997; Young, 1999; Garland, 2001). The exclusive nature of such theorising both reflects and constructs our social world as 'masculine'. The community safety/crime prevention literature demonstrates a marked lack of gendered analyses.

As has been argued, we need to critically interpret romanticised notions of 'community'. The idea that they may be more open and democratic, and less subject to inequitable power relations (for example, of dominant masculinity), is simply misleading. As Kelly argues, 'the stress on similarity in definitions of community means that variable experiences of social life that accrue by virtue of gender, class, race, age and sexuality *cannot be acknowledged*, let alone studied' (1996, p 71, emphasis added). It is not that women are not part of the community, as women are clearly involved in the creation and sustenance of communities (Campbell, 1993), but it is often the case that women have to create their own alternative communities and informal networks. Because of their informal nature, such networks rarely form a part of the accepted organisational power structures in a community and therefore have often been overlooked by community safety partnerships.

Taking the view that interests are held in common in the community fosters an assumption that 'we', the community, will band together to defend against 'dangerous' outsiders. This unexamined assumption oriented much community safety action onto *situational* strategies to combat property crime in public places; 'designing out crime'. While some of these actions may be of benefit to some women fleeing violence (target hardening of property against violent ex-partners for example), in general terms this focus is a deeply problematic one as it diverts attention (once more) from violent crimes against women, which for the most part do not take place in public space and which, importantly, are committed by *insiders* in the community; male partners and relatives. In the case of both 'community' and 'safety' partnerships, we need to constantly question 'whose community?' and 'whose safety?' they are in fact addressing.

Notions of both 'community' and 'safety' were taken up by left-oriented workers/activists who saw welfarist strategies as better ways of combating crime than situational crime prevention (Gilling and Barton, 1997). Nevertheless, in most cases, orientation towards 'community safety' and 'fear reduction' tended to focus attention on crime in public spaces, such as that involving young people, while marginalising crime such as 'domestic violence' that occurs in the private sphere (Crawford, 1998, p 27). In the 'domestic violence' field, on the other hand, the focus has been (perhaps understandably) on 'safety', women and children's safety as opposed to 'community' safety. We have much less knowledge about awareness and attitudes to 'domestic violence' among the community at large. Indeed, while there has been a resurgence of interest in community in many fields, this has been singularly missing in relation to 'domestic violence', as Walklate (2002) points out.

The community safety approach fostered a new and different way of tackling crime prevention, moving away from a police focus towards inter-agency partnership and new forms of victim support. At the same time, work against 'domestic violence' was moving *towards* a police focus while also fostering victim support and inter-agency partnerships. This outcome relates partly to the dominant understandings of 'domestic violence' and the consequent focus on agency/state responses to 'domestic violence', and partly to gendered discourses of caring to which we now turn.

Western understandings of 'domestic violence' and the focus on social agencies

Definitions of 'domestic violence' have tended to focus on violence within the intimate, heterosexual couple, hiding the way in which the effects of such violence ripple outwards to impact on children, other members of the family, members of friendship groups and members of the wider community, such as neighbours. Moreover, the focus on more exceptional *incidents* of violence has led to an emphasis on improving the response of social agencies, such as the police. Designed to act on exceptional incidents, social agencies can work intensively with individuals in crisis but for relatively limited periods of time (Kelly, 1999). This in turn unwittingly strengthens the conceptualisation of male abuse of power in the home as a one-off crisis incident rather than as a process, hiding the cumulative effect of seemingly 'minor' infringements of women's emotional and physical integrity over time. The women's refuge movement has worked with feminist principles, prioritising shelter and services to safeguard women and children's safety and survival, and their work too has tended to avoid wider community involvement, primarily for reasons of security, but also due to limitations of funding and resources. By contrast, Southall Black Sisters has argued that state backing can generate more positive responses in the minority ethnic community from its leaders (Gupta, 2004). Yet knowledge of informal and community responses to women experiencing male abuse is relatively limited in the West.

The focus on formal agency work has also inadvertently amplified the separation of public from private, which, as Kelly says (1996), is ironic, considering the original aims and thinking of the women's movement. Moreover, the separation of formal from informal support has hidden the extent to which both aspects of support intersect with each other. Awareness of the interrelated nature of informal and formal support for women trying to stop the violence or have the abusive man leave, and/or trying to leave themselves, is also under-explored.

Gendered discourses of caring

Finally, gendered discourses, through which women construct their social identities as caring, and which assume women's continuing availability as carers, also underpin the relative neglect of informal support for women in the community. Finch (1993) notes a shift away from the problems of institutional care towards a valorisation of the 'healing virtues of communities' at the core of caring discourse in the UK; while this is in itself a problematic discourse, it does not seem to have impacted on responding to violence against women in the home. Twigg (1990) and Ungerson (1990) argue that gendered discourse on caring takes for granted the availability of women as unpaid carers, which raises the question of who does the caring when it is women who are in dangerous and harmful situations.

The feminist literature is itself problematic in dichotomising a distinction between caring on the one hand for dependent persons who are not able to care for themselves and on the other hand for those who can manage well on their own (Leira and Saraceno, 2002, p 62). Clearly, this is meant to distinguish between women caring for able-bodied husbands, who could well look after themselves, and women caring for children. Unfortunately this conceptualisation polarises 'those who are dependent' from 'those who can manage well on their own', failing to recognise the many degrees of dependence in between. Dependence for the adult woman is therefore seen as rather negative and degrading and this results in a problem locating women who are survivors of 'domestic violence'. Hague et al, for example, argue that abused women should *not* be seen as dependent, saying that 'abused women continue to be viewed as dependent, just as they were probably treated during the abuse' (2003, p 16). There is a problem here in that while survivors are not wholly dependent, they have nevertheless been victimised and do need support, help and care. Moreover, they are in need of longer-term support and so varying degrees of dependence *will* exist over varying lengths of time for different women. The need for support is present throughout all our lives but it becomes crucial at times of *transition* like 'leaving' a violent relationship, when, in many cases, women find themselves with severely depleted support networks (Wilcox, 2000a, 2000b).

Conclusion

The philosophy of the community safety approach to some degree attempted to shift social policy away from 'retribution, deterrence and reform towards a concern with prevention, harm reduction and risk management' (Garland, 2001, p 171). So, while community safety approaches were tending to move away from police-focused strategies, it may seem contradictory that a major strand of feminism attempted to tackle domestic violence by involving the police and employing a strategy of criminalisation.

At the same time that this strand of feminism aimed to achieve more effective prosecution of perpetrators and support of victims, this was not without recognition of the deeply problematic nature of working with the state in relation to penality. A key theme in the early literature was that the institutional systems to which women turn for help can reproduce their dependence, and so reinforce their abuse, and prisons were not seen as places that would help in tackling men's violence (Dobash and Dobash, 1979; Stark et al, 1979; Schecter, 1984; Stark and Flitcraft, 1996, cited in Stark, 2004).

At least two things must be remembered, however; first, that this was a struggle for legitimacy, to gain acceptance for the idea that violence in the home is as serious as violence on the streets, and second, that women (and children) were losing their lives. What better route to gain legitimacy than through the traditional and powerful legitimising agency of the legal system? And women are still losing their lives every year. On average two women are killed each week by a current or former male partner[4] (Home Office, 1998, 2003), so safety/security is, therefore, of the utmost priority in any work against domestic violence wherever and however this takes place.

At root the two 'strands' of organising differ along the fault line of defining gender, of acknowledging (or not) the impact of differently gendered lives, and this creates differences in strategies and policies. Responses to violence, through the law, policy and practice, are shaped by choice of definition and this has concrete effects on people's lives. Feminists who conceptualise social life as thoroughly gendered have viewed the patriarchal state as repressive and have tended to maintain some distance from the state. Other feminists, and community safety workers, may envision the state as problematic but open to reform, arguing that it is possible to change conditions of gender inequality by working with/ through the state. There are obstacles and opportunities in both approaches.

Certainly community safety initiatives such as local authority community safety teams provided alternative forums at which to raise violence against women and have expanded the remit of this work. However, the limits of community safety concern precisely a gendered notion of safety, just as gendered conceptions of 'welfare' or 'caring' were themselves key dilemmas for social policy and practice.

Moreover, moving beyond community safety implies grasping issues of both enforcement and support, as the history of work against domestic violence makes abundantly clear.

Notes

[1] Use of the term 'domestic violence' is misleading because of its gender neutrality and broad coverage, but its use is now so commonplace that I use it here, placing the term in inverted commas to indicate its problematic nature. 'Domestic violence' comprises a constellation of behaviours ranging from verbal abuse/threats and coercion, to physical, sexual violence, rape and homicide. In Britain it is estimated that one in four women experiences violence from a known man at some point in her life (British Medical Association, 1998).

[2] One illustration of this is the Home Office national Crime Reduction Programme in England and Wales, from 1999 to 2002, which funded a range of different initiatives. In this programme £150 million was spent on CCTV as compared with £7 million on Violence against Women initiatives (less than 5% of the money spent on CCTV) (Home Office, 2001, pp 9, 11).

[3] The legislation that followed the Parliamentary Select Committee on Violence in Marriage, the 1976 Domestic Violence and Matrimonial Proceedings Act, enabled women who were married or cohabiting to apply for a non-molestation or exclusion order against the abusing partner. The 1977 Housing (Homeless Persons) Act recognised the right of women made homeless as a result of 'domestic violence' to be permanently housed by a local authority, and the 1978 Domestic Proceedings and Magistrates' Courts Act enabled women who were married to an abusing partner to apply to a magistrates' court for an injunction to prevent further abuse (Charles, 2000, p 139).

[4] Leaving a violent relationship does not necessarily bring about an end to violence; it may continue and may even escalate (Binney et al, 1981; Okun, 1986; Smith, 1990; Dobash and Dobash, 1992; Hester and Radford, 1992). Research with survivors in the UK found that violence was committed by an ex-partner in between a third and two thirds of the cases studied (Kelly, 1999; Wilcox, 2000a). Repeat victimisation is common and the British Crime Survey found that over half (57%) of victims of domestic violence are involved in more than one incident (Mirrlees-Black et al, 1998).

References

Binney, V., Harkell, G. and Nixon, J. (1981) *Leaving Violent Men: A Study of Refuges and Housing for Battered Women*, London: Women's Aid Federation England.

Borkowski, M., Murch, M. and Walker, V. (1983) *Marital Violence: The Community Response*, London: Tavistock.

Bourdieu, P. (1996) 'On the family as a realised category', *Theory, Culture and Society*, vol 13, pp 19-26.

BMA (British Medical Association) (1998) *Domestic Violence: A Health Care Issue*, David Morgan (ed), London: BMA.

Campbell, B. (1993) *Goliath: Britain's Dangerous Places*, London: Methuen.

Charles, N. (2000) *Feminism, the State and Social Policy*, Basingstoke: Macmillan.

Cobbe, F.P. (1878) 'Wife torture in England', *The Contemporary Review*, April, pp 55-87.

Crawford, A. (1998) *Crime Prevention and Community Safety: Politics, Policies and Practices*, London/New York, NY: Longman.

Dobash, R.E. and Dobash, R.P. (1979) *Violence against Wives: A Case against the Patriarchy*, London: Open Books.

Dobash, R.E. and Dobash, R.P. (1992) *Women, Violence and Social Change*, London/New York, NY: Routledge.

Dodd, T., Nicholas, S., Povey, D. and Walker, A. (2004) *Crime in England and Wales 2003/2004*, Home Office Statistical Bulletin 10/04, London: The Stationery Office.

Ericson, R.V. and Haggerty, K.D. (1997) *Policing the Risk Society*, Oxford: Clarendon Press.

Finch, J. (1993) 'The concept of caring: feminist research and other perspectives', in J. Twigg (ed), *Informal Care in Europe*, York: Social Policy Unit, pp 5-21.

Garland, D.W. (2001) *The Culture of Control: Crime and Social Order in Contemporary Society*, Oxford: Oxford University Press.

Gilling, D. and Barton, A. (1997) 'Crime prevention and community safety: a new home for social policy', *Critical Social Policy*, no 52, August, pp 63-83.

Goodey, J. (1999) 'Adolescence and the socialisation of gendered fear', in M. Dragan and M.D. Schwartz (eds), *Race, Gender and Class in Criminology*, London/New York, NY: Garland.

Gupta, R. (2004) 'Wake up, activists are pounding on doors of ivory towers', *The Times Higher Education Supplement*, 28 May, pp 20-21.

Hague, G., Mullender, A. and Aris, R. (2003) *Is anyone Listening? Accountability and Women Survivors of Domestic Violence*, London/New York, NY: Routledge.

Hanmer, J. and Saunders, S. (1984) *Well Founded Fear: A Community Study of Violence to Women*, London: Hutchinson.

Hearn, J. (1987) *The Gender of Oppression: Men, Masculinity and the Critique of Marxism*, New York, NY: St Martin's Press.

Hearn, J. (1998) *The Violences of Men*, London: Sage Publications.

Henriques, J., Hollway, W., Urwin, C., Venn, C. and Walkerdine, V. (1984) *Changing the Subject: Psychology, Social Regulation and Subjectivity*, London/New York, NY: Methuen.

Hester, M. and Radford, L. (1992) 'Domestic violence and access arrangements for children in Denmark and Britain', *Journal of Social Welfare and Family Law*, vol 1, pp 57–70.

Home Office (1991) *Practical Ways to Crack Crime: The Family Guide* (2nd edn), London: Home Office and Central Office of Information.

Home Office (2001) *Criminal Justice System Annual Report 1999-2000.*

Home Office (2003) *Safety and Justice: The Government's Proposals on Domestic Violence*, CM 5847, London: HMSO.

Kelly, L. (1988) *Surviving Sexual Violence*, Cambridge: Polity Press.

Kelly, L. (1999) 'Violence against women: a policy of neglect or a neglect of policy?', in S. Walby (ed), *New agendas for women*, Basingstoke: Macmillan.

Kelly, L. (1996) 'Tensions and possibilities: enhancing informal responses to domestic violence', in J.L. Edleson and Z.C. Eisikovits (eds), *Future Interventions with Battered Women and their Families*, Thousand Oaks, CA/London/New Delhi: Sage Publications.

Koskela, H. (1997) '"Bold walk and breakings": women's spatial confidence versus fear of violence', *Gender, Place and Culture: A Journal of Feminist Geography*, vol 4, no 3, pp 301–19.

Leira, A. and Saraceno, C. (2002) 'Care: actors, relationships and contexts', in B. Hobson, J. Lewis and B. Siim (eds) *Contested Concepts in Gender and Social Politics*, Cheltenham: Edward Elgar, pp 55-83.

Lacey, N. and Zedner, L. (1995) 'Discourses of community in criminal justice – locating the appeal to "community" in contemporary criminal justice', *Journal of Law and Society*, no 22, pp 301-25.

Lea J. and Young, J. (1984) *What is to be Done about Law and Order?*, Harmondsworth: Penguin.

Lees, S. (2000) 'Marital rape and marital murder', in J. Hanmer and C. Itzin (eds) *Home Truths about Domestic Violence*, London/New York: Routledge.

Mama, A. (1989) *The Hidden Struggle: Statutory and Voluntary Sector Responses to Violence against Black Women in the Home*, London: The London Race and Housing Research Unit.

Maynard, M. (1985) 'The response of social workers to domestic violence', in J. Pahl (ed) *Private Violence and Public Policy*, London: Routledge and Kegan Paul.

Mill, J.S. (1869) [1970] *The Subjection of Women*, London: Longmans.

Mirrlees-Black, C., Budd, T., Partridge, S. and Mayhew, P. (1998) *The 1998 British Crime Survey: England and Wales*, Issue 21/98, London: Home Office Research, Development and Statistics Directorate.

Muncie, J. (2000) 'Decriminalising criminology', in G. Lewis, S. Gewirtz and J. Clarke (eds) *Rethinking Social Policy*, Milton Keynes: Open University Press.

Okun, L. (1986) *Woman Abuse: Facts Replacing Myths*, Albany, NY: State University of New York Press.

Passaro, J. (1996) *The Unequal Homeless: Men on the Streets, Women in their Place*, London: Routledge.

Pizzey, E. (1974) *Scream Quietly or the Neighbours will Hear*, Harmondsworth: Penguin.

Pleck, E. (1987) *Domestic Tyranny: The Making of American Social Policy against Family Violence from Colonial Times to the Present*, New York, NY: Oxford University Press.

Schechter, S. (1984) *Women and Male Violence: The Visions and Struggles of the Battered Women's Movement*, London: Pluto Press.

Smith, M.D. (1990) 'Socio-demographic risk factors in wife abuse, results from a survey of Toronto women', *Canadian Journal of Sociology*, vol 15, pp 39-58.

Stanko, E.A. (1987) 'Typical violence, normal precaution: men, women and interpersonal violence in England, Wales, Scotland and the USA', in J. Hanmer and M. Maynard (eds) *Women, Violence and Social Control*, London: Macmillan, pp 122-134.

Stanko, E.A. (1990) *Everyday Violence: How Women and Men Experience Sexual and Physical Danger*, London: Pandora.

Stanko, E.A. (1995) 'Women, crime and fear', *Annals of American Academy of Political and Social Science*, vol. 539, May, pp 46-58, .

Stanko, E.A. (1997) Safety talk: conceptualizing women's risk assessment as a "technology of the soul"', *Theoretical Criminology*, vol 1, no 4, pp 479-99.

Stanko, E.A. (1998) 'Warnings to women: police advice and women's safety in Britain', in S.L. Miller (ed) *Crime Control and Women: Feminist Implications of Criminal Justice Policy*, Thousand Oaks, CA:/London/New Delhi: Sage Publications, pp 52-71.

Stanko, E.A., Crisp, D., Hale, C. and Lucraft, H. (1998) *Counting the Costs: Estimating the Impact of 'Domestic' Violence in the London Borough of Hackney*, London: Crime Concern.

Stark, E. (2004) 'Making the Personal Political: Looking Beyond Violence', Paper delivered at Conference on 'Criminalising Gendered Violence: Local, national and international perspectives', 14–15 September, University of Bristol.

Stark, E., Flitcraft, A. and Frazier, W. (1979) 'Medicine and patriarchal violence: the social construction of a "private" event', *International Journal of Health Service*, vol 9, no 3, pp 461-93.

Twigg, J. (1990) 'Models of carers: how do social care agencies conceptualise their relationship with informal carers?', *Journal of Social Policy*, vol 18, no 1, pp 53-66.

Ungerson, C. (ed) (1990) *Gender and Caring: Work and Welfare in Britain and Scandinavia*, Hemel Hempstead: Harvester Wheatsheaf.

Valentine, G. (1989) 'The geography of women's fear', *Area* 21, no 4, pp 385-90.

WAFE (Women's Aid Federation England) (2004) *Celebrating 30 years of Women's Aid 1974-2004*, Bristol: Women's Aid Federation England.

Walby, S. (2004) *The Cost of Domestic Violence*, London: Women and Equality Unit/DTI (available at www.womenandequalityunit.gov.uk/research/, accessed 28 June 2005).

Walker, L. (1984) *The Battered Woman Syndrome*, New York, NY: Springer.

Walklate, S. (2001) 'Community and crime prevention', in E. McLaughlin and J. Muncie (eds), *Controlling Crime: Crime, Order and Social Control* (2nd edn) London: Sage Publications.

Walklate, S. (2002) 'Gendering crime prevention: exploring the tensions between policy and process', in G. Hughes, E. McLaughlin and J. Muncie (eds), *Crime Prevention and Community Safety: New Directions*, London/Thousand Oaks, CA/ New Delhi: Sage Publications, pp 58-76.

Wardhaugh, J. (1999) 'The unaccommodated woman: home, homelessness and identity', *Sociological Review*, vol 47, no 1, pp 91-109.

Wilcox, P. (2000a) '"Me mother's bank and me nanan's, you know, support": women who left domestic violence in England and issues of informal support', *Women's Studies International Forum*, vol 23, no 1, pp 1-13.

Wilcox, P. (2000b) 'Lone motherhood: the impact on living standards of leaving a violent relationship', *Journal of Social Policy and Administration*, vol 34, no 2, pp 176-90.

Wilcox, P. (2006) *Surviving Domestic Violence: Gender, Poverty and Agency*, Basingstoke: Palgrave Macmillan.

Young, J. (1999) *Social Exclusion, Crime and Difference in Late Modernity*, London: Sage Publications.

Young, J. (2001) 'Identity, community and social exclusion', in R. Matthews and J. Pitts (eds), *Crime, Disorder and Community Safety*, London: Routledge.

FIVE

Ethnic minorities and community safety

Marian FitzGerald and Chris Hale

Introduction

The Labour Party 2005 General Election manifesto summarised the key elements of its approach to community safety under the heading 'Safe communities, secure borders'. Citing its record to date, it also set out its view of the issues it would continue to prioritise. These linked measures to address antisocial behaviour and reduce crime with the need to tackle illegal immigration and the threat of terrorism.

> We are giving the police and local councils the power to tackle anti-social behaviour; we will develop neighbourhood policing for every community and crack down on drug dealing and hard drug use to reduce volume crime; we are modernising our asylum and immigration system; and we will take the necessary measures to protect our country from international terrorism. (Labour Party, 2005, p 42)

This chapter explores the implications of these commitments for ethnic minorities in Britain. It starts by charting the development of ethnic diversity, not least in order to unpack some of the complexities often neglected in discussion and largely ignored in available statistics. Next, evidence regarding the effect of 'community safety' issues on the two largest minority ethnic groups up to the election of the New Labour government of 1997 is reviewed as background to developments since then. In the light of this, the impact on minorities of the government's current approach to community safety is considered. The chapter concludes by discussing the implications of continuing to pursue this approach in future.

Ethnic minorities in Britain

Most discussion of ethnic minorities' experience in Britain as victims of crime (and as offenders) has focused on groups with origins in the migration to Britain from its former colonies following the Second World War.

Only in 1962 were restrictions first imposed on Commonwealth citizens coming to Britain; and, although progressively tightened from 1968 onwards, they were applied selectively. Citizens of 'Old Commonwealth' countries (mainly Canada, New Zealand and Australia) were largely unaffected until rights of entry were reframed in the new Nationality Act of 1981. The main targets for control were people from the 'New Commonwealth'; and the largest numbers of these in the post-war period had come first from countries of the Caribbean in the 1950s and 1960s. The balance then shifted strongly towards immigration from India, Pakistan and Bangladesh, with the first arrivals coming mainly direct from the Indian subcontinent, although in the 1970s and 1980s special exceptions were made in order to admit United Kingdom passport holders with origins in the subcontinent expelled from their homes in East Africa.

Hence the groups who were the focus of concern were visibly 'non-white'. On arrival, they tended to cluster in particular urban areas, with London the most important for all groups. Even here, groups of different origins often tended to settle in different neighbourhoods. Inasmuch as sociologists began to pay them attention, however, they often failed to distinguish between the groups or treated them simply as two separate ('black' and 'Asian')[1] categories, despite significant variation within these broad groupings based on national, political and religious distinctions, to say nothing of important socioeconomic differences.

By the time of the 2001 Census, these were still the two largest groups within the 12% of the enumerated population of England and Wales that did not describe themselves as 'white British' (see Table 5.1). Differences in their geographical distribution and their socioeconomic profiles also persisted, with people of Indian origin continuing to outperform the white British on several key indicators, while disadvantage within the black Caribbean group was particularly marked among males, and levels of household poverty were higher among families of Pakistani and Bangladeshi origin than in any other group (Berthoud, 1998). Yet important changes had also been taking place.

While the Indian group has continued to predominate among Asians, however, rates of growth have been much higher among Pakistanis and Bangladeshis, whose age profile is much younger (Figure 5.1). The Caribbean group as such has effectively ceased to grow and now has an age profile that is very similar to that of the white British population. This is in part offset, though, by the rapid growth of a very young 'mixed' group that was largely born in Britain, although the 'black' group as a whole has continued to increase as a result of the growth in the population of African origin, most of whom are immigrants.

Further, in addition to important changes taking place *within* the black and Asian groups, there has been a proliferation of other ethnic minorities as a result

Table 5.1: Ethnic composition and birthplace of population (England and Wales, 2001)

Census category	As % of total population	Of whom % born outside UK	Aggregated group
White British	87.5	1.9	White 90.3
White Irish	1.2	67.6	
White Other	1.6	79.8	
White and Black Caribbean	0.5	6.1	Mixed 1.4
White and Black African	0.2	32.9	
White and Asian	0.4	23.6	
Other Mixed	0.3	33.2	
Indian	2.0	54.1	Asian/Asian British 4.4
Pakistani	1.4	45.2	
Bangladeshi	0.5	53.5	
Other Asian	0.5	69.4	
Caribbean	1.1	42.2	Black/Black British 2.2
African	0.9	66.2	
Other Black	0.2	20.8	
Chinese	0.4	71.7	Other 0.8
Other	0.4	84.5	

Figure 5.1: Proportion of population aged under 16 (selected ethnic groups, 2001)

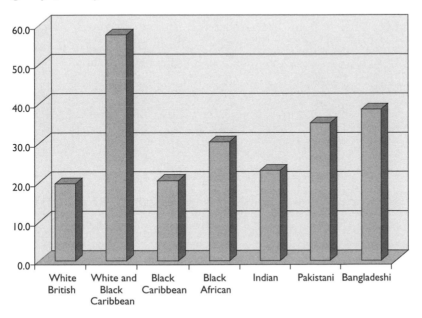

of wider developments since the main post-war migration. Greater access to international travel, the fall of the Berlin Wall, the economic consequences of globalisation and the impact of civil wars have combined to increase significantly the numbers of people entering Britain. Most do so for very limited periods, and by far the largest category of people who enter the country from outside the EU are visitors, but rates of growth have been higher than average among students and work permit holders. While people admitted to settle in Britain account for well under one per cent of all arrivals[2], the numbers who apply for settlement after entering the country and are allowed to remain have also risen markedly, in part reflecting the considerable increase in the number of asylum applications since the early 1990s. While the numbers of illegal immigrants is *de facto* unknowable, it may be assumed that these will also have grown and this will be reflected to some extent in numbers subject to deportation. Table 5.2 brings together figures from different Home Office sources of immigration statistics and illustrates the extent of change over the 15 years until 2003 (the latest date for which figures were available at the time of writing).

Ethnic minorities, crime and community safety to 1997

The first post-war immigrants encountered major overt discrimination and had no specific protection under the law. The problems they faced, including tensions with the indigenous population in the areas where they settled, were largely ignored in national policy until attacks against immigrants from the West Indies escalated into riots on the streets of London and Nottingham in the late 1950s. The subsequent dual response was to set the pattern for several decades. Immigration controls, imposed on Commonwealth immigrants in 1962, were offset by a liberal *quid pro quo* in the form of the first attempt to outlaw discrimination. This legislation was progressively strengthened over the next decade or so, culminating in the Race Relations Act of 1976. This covered indirect as well as direct discrimination; it set up the Commission for Racial Equality and imposed specific responsibilities on local authorities. However, it contained a number of exemptions for key public services – including the immigration service and the police.

Table 5.2: Changing patterns in immigration to Britain (1987 to 2003)

	1987	2003
Numbers entering from outside Europe	7,590,000	12,200,000
Visitors	5,730,000	7,550,000
Students	143,000	319,000
Work permit holders + dependants	26,000	119,000
In-country applications for asylum	3,140 [1988]	35,685
People accepted for settlement	45,980	139,675
Enforcement action initiated to remove people	3,860	57,735 [2002]

By the end of the 1960s, West Indian immigrants had begun to complain specifically of discrimination and harassment by the police, an issue that continued to gain political momentum throughout the following decade (Hunte, 1966; Rose et al, 1969). The police meanwhile began to acknowledge 'tensions' but until the early 1970s explicitly maintained that there were no particular problems of criminality among this group. By 1977, however, in evidence to the Select Committee on the West Indian Community, the Metropolitan Police said that 'from current statistics available, our overall experience of 1971 no longer holds good' (House of Commons Select Committee on Race Relations and Immigration, 1977, p 182). This was the period when larger numbers than previously of the first generation of children of Caribbean immigrants reached the peak age for offending. While this significant, underlying demographic change went largely unnoticed, it was accompanied by two related developments that continue to haunt this generation's descendants and to overshadow their relations with the police.

The first was a moral panic concerning 'black muggers' (Hall et al, 1978) and the second was the increasing use by the police of 'Sus' powers[3], which permitted them to arrest anyone they suspected of being about to commit an offence (Demuth, 1978). In Bristol in 1980, police action against black people triggered the first post-war civil disturbances on the British mainland and this was followed in 1981 by a series of similar disturbances in other parts of the country triggered specifically by a police anti-mugging operation in Brixton. Lord Scarman, charged with inquiring into the causes of the disorders, insisted on widening his remit and focused on their social and economic causes, as well as the accumulated sense of community grievance towards the police, although he did not discover any evidence of systematic bias on the part of the police themselves (Scarman, 1981).

Scarman's report was followed by one from the Home Affairs Select Committee on the general question of 'racial disadvantage' (House of Commons, Home Affairs Select Committee, 1981). Among other things, this called for a more systematic approach to collecting ethnic data. However, the policy response to the disturbances largely avoided being race-specific. It focused on inner-city regeneration and on reforms to the criminal justice process, as codified in the 1984 Police and Criminal Evidence Act (PACE). This took responsibility for prosecutions away from the police and imposed formal recording requirements on many police activities. By now, 'Sus' had been abolished; but section 1 of PACE permitted officers[4] to stop, for the purpose of searching them, anyone they had 'reasonable grounds' to suspect of carrying illegal or prohibited goods; and they were required to make a record of any search undertaken in these circumstances.

However, by 1985, further disturbances had occurred in a number of cities. Again these mainly involved young black people; and this time lives were lost. There was a perceptible hardening of government attitudes; and a recurrent theme in the parliamentary debates of the time was that these events had taken place in local authorities run by 'the Loony Left' of the Labour Party. By implication, a strand within the party actively encouraged anti-police attitudes and, by extension, the Labour Party as a whole could not be trusted to maintain law and order.

Arriving later on the scene and, *as yet*, with no significant youth cohort[5], the Asian groups were still largely seen as unproblematic in terms of offending. Yet by the 1970s they also had begun to raise concerns about the police in two separate contexts. First, tensions had built up around the police's involvement in a number of high-profile 'fishing expeditions' for illegal immigrants; and second, at a time of heightened activity by parties of the far right, the police were seen as failing to protect Asians against ongoing racially motivated attacks and harassment that was commonly referred to as 'Paki-bashing', a particular problem in poor urban areas such as parts of East London.

Given the challenges they already faced in their relations with the longer-established black communities, the police effectively withdrew from any large-scale involvement in immigration control at this time, leaving the responsibility squarely with the Immigration Service. However, the issue of racial attacks and harassment finally reached the national policy agenda in the early 1980s (JCAR, 1981), casting 'Asians' in a stereotyped role as victims just as the riots were setting the seal on a negative stereotype of black young men as offenders.

There had, in fact, been several high-profile cases of group violence by young Asians in the 1970s; but campaigning groups who supported the defendants' claims to be protecting their communities had taken these up as *causes célèbres*. Outbreaks of violence associated with demonstrations against Salman Rushdie's novel *The Satanic Verses* at the end of the 1980s were similarly viewed either as political protest or as examples of 'Muslim extremism' rather than simple criminality; and long-standing rivalries between Asian gangs in Southall[6] were effectively kept out of the national press through a compact between the police and local journalists. By the early 1990s, though, it was becoming increasingly difficult to keep the lid on developments among the poorer groups of Asians as the number of young people reaching the peak age for offending became much larger. The first major disturbances in Bradford, a major area of Pakistani settlement, in 1995 had strong echoes of those in areas with significant black communities 10 years or so earlier.

While ethnic monitoring had increasingly been adopted by local authorities and an ethnic question routinely included in many government surveys throughout the 1980s, information on the experiences of ethnic minorities with the criminal justice system either as offenders or as victims remained relatively rare; and these derived mainly from discrete research studies (FitzGerald, 1993). Prison figures on ethnicity, first collected from the mid-1980s, consistently showed a very significant overrepresentation of black people that was especially marked among prisoners convicted of robbery (see also below); but no national series data were available on earlier stages of the criminal process. From 1985, the police were also supposed to collect figures on 'racial incidents' based on a definition that gave primacy to whether the incident was 'perceived' to have been racially motivated by the complainant, the police or any other party; but the system did not require returns to the Home Office to be broken down by offence type or by the ethnic origin of the complainant.

However, in 1991, a belated amendment to the 1991 Criminal Justice Act (section 95) required the Home Secretary to publish 'information' to people working in the criminal justice system to 'avoid discrimination on race or sex or any other improper ground'. Given criticisms by the Royal Commission on Criminal Justice in 1993 about the lack of ethnic statistics and the inclusion of an ethnic question for the first time in the Census of 1991, section 95 became the peg on which the Home Office hung a requirement for all police forces to adopt a system of ethnic monitoring from 1996. They were to provide an ethnic breakdown to their recorded searches as well as arrests, cautions and homicides (as perceived by police officers) using the four broad aggregated categories of 'white', 'black', 'Asian' and 'other'.

By this time, the British Crime Survey included an 'ethnic over-sample' to boost the numbers of black and Asian respondents. The first detailed analysis, based on the combined numbers from the 1988 and 1992 sweeps, confirmed that both groups were significantly more likely than whites to be victims of crime but that there were important variations between and within the minority groups. Using multivariate analyses to explore the reasons for these, it concluded:

> Demographic and socio-economic factors explain most of the overall difference in victimisation between ethnic groups. This does not, however, mean that ethnicity plays no part in their victimisation. For the Asian groups especially it often remains significant even when other relevant factors are taken into account. Also, *many of the socio-economic factors which contribute to higher rates of ethnic minority victimisation themselves constitute 'racial disadvantage' as defined by the Home Affairs Select Committee in 1981.* (FitzGerald and Hale, 1996, p viii, emphasis added)

Developments since 1997

When it returned to power in 1997, the Labour Party had already proved its determination to shake off its image as being 'soft' on law and order. At the same time, the new government also took a high-profile stance on issues of race equality and one of the earliest symbols of this new approach was the setting up in 1997 of the Macpherson Inquiry. Its terms of reference concerned the murder in 1993 of the black teenager, Stephen Lawrence[7]; but – following the example of Scarman – it chose to expand these to cover the police's relations with ethnic minorities in general and to range wider still. By contrast with Scarman, it concluded that the root of many of the problems it described was 'institutional racism'. This was not confined to the police service and was defined by the inquiry as follows:

the collective failure of an organisation to provide an appropriate and professional service to people because of their colour, culture or ethnic origin. It can be seen or detected in processes, attitudes and behaviour which amount to discrimination through unwitting prejudice, ignorance, thoughtlessness, and racist stereotyping which disadvantage minority ethnic people. (Macpherson, 1999, p 321)

The main factual evidence on which the inquiry based these conclusions came from the first year's figures produced by police ethnic monitoring (see above). These showed that the proportion of searches on black people under section 1 of PACE far exceeded their presence in the population at large. This finding was not only in line with that of earlier research (including Smith, 1983) but also with long-established prison statistics and with police statistics on arrests. However, the search figures were highlighted by the inquiry inasmuch as they provided quantitative corroboration for the evidence from community groups that cited searches as a prime source of grievance.

The government accepted all of the recommendations of the inquiry when it reported in February 1999. It pledged itself to reducing 'disproportionality'; and it adopted the term 'institutional racism' as a concept that would inform the development of its race equality policies generally. It specifically gave a high-profile commitment to:

improving the confidence of the community as a whole, but especially the ethnic minority communities, in the criminal justice system. (Home Office, 1999)

Meanwhile, in pursuit of its wider race relations agenda, the government was instrumental in including a question on religion in the 2001 Census (largely in response to the demands of Muslim groups); and in 2000 it passed the Race Relations Amendment Act. This built on the provisions of the 1976 Race Relations Act but, importantly, lifted the original exemption for the police service. It also placed specific duties on all public bodies, which the Home Office summarised as follows:

... to ensure that they have procedures in place so that all relevant functions and policies meet the general duty to:

• Eliminate unlawful racial discrimination
• Promote equality of opportunity
• Promote good relations between people of different racial groups.

Certain public authorities, including government departments, were specifically required to produce a race equality scheme, containing arrangements for:

- Assessing and consulting on the likely impact of its proposed policies on the promotion of race equality.
- *Monitoring its policies for any adverse impact on the promotion of race equality.* (www.homeoffice.gov.uk/comrace/race/reia/index.html) (emphasis added)

By 2001, when New Labour entered its second term, however, a number of unforeseen events had already begun to pose new challenges to its race relations policies and others were shortly to unfold. Conflicts in other parts of the world continued to add to immigration pressures and, in particular, demands for asylum. This was now further catalysed by military interventions involving British troops – first in Eastern Europe and Afghanistan and, imminently, in Iraq. One of the first ways in which the government tried to respond to the pressures this created was through a policy of dispersal that, albeit voluntary, penalised non-compliance by withholding access to the limited support available under the scheme. Whether the new arrivals dispersed, sustained their increased number at and around ports of entry, or made their own way to the cheaper parts of urban areas that had always attracted new immigrants, their presence was often associated with an increase in racial tensions. By contrast with the situation that faced the post-war immigrants, however, many of these new arrivals were 'other whites' according to the official classification in Table 5.1. They also faced hostility not only from the indigenous white British population in some of the dispersal areas but from indigenous populations in other areas to which they were dispersed or gravitated that were by now a complex amalgam of white, black, Asian and other ethnic groups[8].

Meanwhile, in 2001, further major disturbances broke out in Bradford and a number of other northern towns with significant Pakistani populations. Unlike previous disturbances, these were not triggered directly by clashes with the police but reflected tensions between young Asians and poor whites living in the same areas (Cantle, 2001; Ousley, 2001). Parties of the far right had already begun exploiting the political potential of the divisions between the two communities, as well as capitalising on concerns around immigration and asylum and had begun to gain modest but unprecedented success in local elections[9]. Together these developments prompted the Home Office to set up a new unit in 2002 specifically concerned with developing policies to promote 'community cohesion'.

Shortly after the government returned to power in 2001, the attack on the World Trade Centre and subsequent major terrorist incidents all around the world had a seismic impact on all aspects of policy. In addition to increased military action abroad, the 'war on terror' triggered special legislation at home, an increase in related police activity and heightened concern on the part of the public. Unlike the 1960s and 1970s when the IRA was the main focus of suspicion (and Irish people the object of related prejudice), the enemy was now seen as

'Muslim fundamentalism' and the spotlight fell on sections of the Asian community – in particular, the Pakistani and Bangladeshi groups, over 90% of whom are Muslim[10].

The impact of 'community safety' policies on ethnic minorities

In addition to the evidence that minority ethnic groups tend disproportionately to be victimised, more recent work by the Home Office has also highlighted the fact that perceptions of high levels of antisocial behaviour are much more common among ethnic minorities than among the population at large, at 24% on average compared with 16% overall (Nicholas and Walker, 2004)[11]. So, in principle, it would seem that minorities should disproportionately benefit from community safety initiatives concerned with antisocial behaviour and crime reduction. In practice, however, there is little evidence for this. Rather, a number of indicators suggest that all three strands of 'community safety' policy (that is, addressing antisocial behaviour, crime reduction and tackling illegal immigration and the threat of terrorism) may have adversely affected ethnic minorities.

No data are available on trends in ethnic minorities' experience of victimisation, as reported to the British Crime Survey, since the last in-depth analyses relate to 1999 (Clancy et al, 2001). These broadly replicated the findings of the 1996 report; but the report additionally confirmed that *whites* are victims of the majority of incidents in which victims perceive racial motivation[12]. In the absence of any ethnic breakdown, this makes it very difficult to draw any inferences about minority victimisation from trends in the police figures for recorded racist incidents. The number, however, rose dramatically from 13,151 in 1996/97 to 52,694 in 2003/04[13].

By contrast, time series data on ethnic minorities as suspects and offenders *have* steadily been accumulating; and on two key indicators these suggest that – far from improving – the problem of 'disproportionality' began steadily to get worse during New Labour's second term as the drive for 'community safety' gathered momentum. As Figure 5.2 shows, not only did the overrepresentation of black people in the search figures and among the prison population begin to increase from 2001 onwards, around the same time the Asian group also began to account for a higher proportion of the total.

Although these increases appear more marked in the case of searches, it should be borne in mind that this was in the context of a dramatic *fall* in the overall number of searches. The numbers had begun to rise again but they were still over 25% *lower* in 2003/04 than 1997/98 when the government first came to power. By contrast, over the same period the prison population had grown beyond all expectations, and the growth was particularly marked in the case of black people and Asians. Restricting the comparison to British nationals only, there

Figure 5.2: Black people and Asians as a proportion of section 1 PACE searches and male prisoners (1997 to 2004)

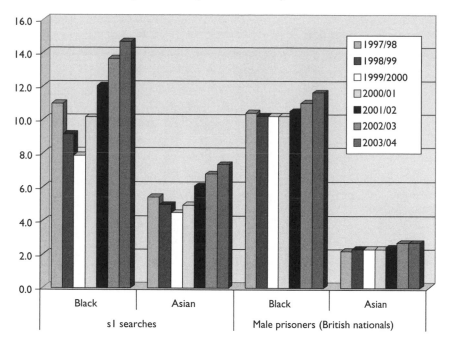

was a 4.8% increase in the white male prison population between 1997 and 2003; but the rise for black men was 21.2% and for Asians it was higher still at 33.3%. Significantly, this was driven primarily by the increase in prisoners of Pakistani and Bangladeshi origin whose number rose by 47%.

More detailed scrutiny of the three strands of community safety policies suggests a number of reasons why each may, on balance, be having an adverse impact on minority ethnic groups. In the case of antisocial behaviour and crime reduction, these reasons may be unrelated to their ethnicity as such but to their socioeconomic and demographic characteristics, including their very uneven geographical distribution. Given that the majority of the black and Asian population of England and Wales lives in just five out of the 43 police force areas (see Figure 5.3), developments in these areas will have a major influence on any national figures for these groups.

In the case of the third strand of community safety policies (tackling immigration and anti-terrorism), the ethnic dimension is more explicit.

Antisocial behaviour

The term antisocial behaviour has been defined very broadly by the government in terms of activities likely to cause '... harassment, alarm or distress' (section 1(a) of the 1998 Crime and Disorder Act). These were summarised by the Home

Figure 5.3: Demographic contribution of selected police force areas to total population aged 10+ by ethnic group (%)

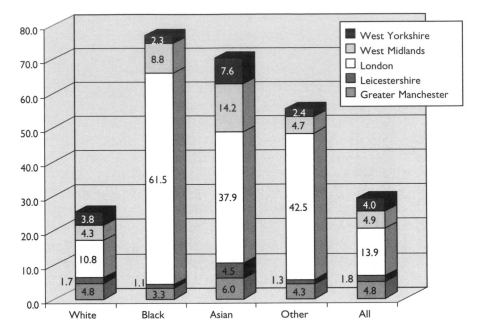

Affairs Select Committee (House of Commons, Home Affairs Select Committee, 2005) under three headings: 'Youth nuisance', 'Antisocial neighbours' and 'Alcohol-related disorder'. Measures to tackle it have consisted largely of either criminalising activities that were not previously illegal by defining new offences or by giving additional new powers to the police, local authorities and the courts[14].

Even though it is only one in a range of new options, the main symbol of this approach is the Anti-Social Behaviour Order (ASBO). Initially, significantly fewer orders were sought than had been anticipated and a further round of new legislation in 2003 explicitly aimed to make it easier to obtain ASBOs, with ministers highlighting the importance they attached to them and citing their increasing use as *de facto* evidence of their success. While 317 were issued in the first two years (from April 1999), by the end of March 2004, 1,813 had been taken out in the previous six months alone. They were very disproportionately used against young people[15]; but the extent to which they were used varied widely between different areas. As Table 5.3 shows, two of the five police force areas that are home to the majority of the minority ethnic population used the power less than average (and these included the London area); but it was higher in the other three.

A wide range of agencies raised concerns when the Home Affairs Select Committee considered the question of antisocial behaviour (House of Commons, Home Affairs Select Committee, 2005). These included the potential for criminalising and increasing imprisonment rates among young people as a result

Table 5.3: ASBOs per thousand of population aged 10+ for selected areas

Greater Manchester	23.5
West Yorkshire	13.6
West Midlands	9.6
London	4.3
Leicestershire	2.1
Average (England and Wales)	6.7

Source: House of Commons (2005b)

of imposing the orders and, in particular, as a result of the high rates of breach (Squires and Stephen, 2005). In addition to general concerns about net widening, those most immediately at risk were young people who had already offended and who might now have an ASBO 'bolted on' to their sentence. References were also made repeatedly to the risk that an overreliance on the enforcement of sanctions would exacerbate the problems of disadvantaged neighbourhoods, groups and individuals.

These adverse effects will impact disproportionately on any groups who are disproportionately young and disadvantaged; but they have particular implications for two minority ethnic groups. Nearly half of the entire Pakistani population lives in the three police force areas that have issued higher than average numbers of ASBOs, including Greater Manchester, which uses the power more extensively than any other area. In the case of black people, their long-standing overrepresentation at all stages of the criminal justice system (see also next section) means that they will disproportionately experience the impact of the 'bolt-on' ASBO.

It is probably no coincidence, therefore, that statistics published by the Youth Justice Board (YJB, 2005) show that while the numbers of young people supervised by Youth Offending Teams rose by 7% overall between 2002/03 and 2003/04, there was a 36% increase in breaches of statutory orders. Importantly for our purposes, in the case of black and Asian young offenders this figure was higher still – at 44% and 51% respectively[16].

In addition, a recurrent theme in the development and enforcement of measures to address antisocial behaviour is the importance of consulting 'the local community' about the problems they most wanted tackled – to the extent of involving them directly in determining the appropriate level and type of punishment for those responsible. Thus the White Paper heralding the Anti-Social Behaviour Act of November 2003 described one of its key aims as 'the community setting clear standards of behaviour' that the police and others would enforce (Home Office, 2003b, p 7). Yet studies of civic participation have persistently shown that most local residents will not become involved in this type of activity and that those who do (and do so effectively) will most likely come from the older, more affluent and better educated sections of the population (see, for example, Verba et al, 1978; Squires, 1998). The Home Office's own citizenship surveys (Munton and Zurawan, 2004) have themselves provided further evidence that only a minority of citizens may be involved either in setting local priorities or in any extension of arrangements for dispensing 'community' justice.

Hence some sections of the local population may effectively set the antisocial behaviour agenda in ways that are inimical to the interests of others; and the most vulnerable ethnic groups in this context may be those on whom no statistics are held. These will include not only the most recent arrivals such as refugees and asylum seekers but also other minorities such as traveller communities.

Crime reduction

The government's increasing focus in its second term on tackling antisocial behaviour in no way diminished its emphasis on crime reduction; and this too has been characterised by the increasing formalisation of enforcement and the use of punitive sanctions (as reflected in the growth in the prison population). Having set specific targets from the outset for all police forces for reducing motor vehicle crime and domestic burglary, the government additionally required five forces to reduce the level of robbery. These included four of the five forces with the highest minority ethnic populations – the Metropolitan Police Service (MPS), West Midlands, Greater Manchester and West Yorkshire[17]. From early 2000, however, the robbery figures began to show a sudden upward trend, driven largely by the rapid expansion in ownership of mobile phones. These robberies were committed disproportionately by young people, in part to supply a ready-made market for stolen phones among their peers (Harrington and Mayhew, 2001; FitzGerald et al, 2003; Smith, 2003).

By March 2002, the government had announced a programme of interventions and additional resources to tackle the problem. The Street Crime Initiative (SCI) covered 10 forces and was overseen by a high-level multi-agency group chaired by the Prime Minister. Not only did the increased resources and proactive policing associated with the SCI disproportionately focus on areas with large minority ethnic populations and on young people within them, but in launching the SCI, the government was also fully aware that young black people would be a prime target, given the long-established pattern of black involvement in this type of offence[18].

Meanwhile, as Figure 5.2 illustrates, the more general trend to proactive, formal interventions to tackle crime and to increased punitiveness in sentencing was also having a disproportionate impact on minorities. Although by 2003/04 section 1 searches had not yet reached pre-Macpherson levels, their number began to rise again in 2001/02. However, almost unnoticed, a much larger increase had already occurred in the police's use of the power of search under section 60 of the 1994 Criminal Justice and Public Order Act. The numbers are much smaller than for section 1 searches but, for limited periods, section 60 permits the police to search anyone in a designated area without needing any grounds for suspicion where they claim to 'anticipate serious violence'. Until recently, the power was used rarely, and only by a small number of forces; but the

Table 5.4: Proportion of section l and section 60 searches on different ethnic groups (2003/04)

	% White	% Black	% Asian	Total (*n*)
s l	74.3	14.7	7.3	738,016
s 60	59.4	23.3	14.0	40,193

numbers have steadily grown and, by 2003, included all five forces that account for most of the minority ethnic groups. Rates are significantly higher than average in the West Midlands and Greater Manchester. Perhaps in part because of this, the representation of black and Asian groups is much higher in section 60 searches than in section 1 searches.

Tackling illegal immigration and the threat of terrorism

By contrast with the evidence regarding antisocial behaviour and crime reduction, this third strand of the government's community safety strategy *de facto* targets minority ethnic communities. Many of those under suspicion in relation to illegal immigration and the threat of terrorism are members of minority communities and may seek to hide among them. So, even though the majority within these communities will legally reside in Britain and have no association with terrorism, it seems inevitable that they will disproportionately bear the brunt of routine inquiries by the authorities as well as speculative interventions and surveillance, including requests to confirm their identity – if only to eliminate them from suspicion. Any cases of mistaken identity in this context will not unnecessarily inconvenience members of the majority population but are likely to fall heavily on particular minority communities.

These developments are again increasingly involving the police in activities related to immigration control from which they preferred to withdraw 30 years ago because of their impact on race relations (see above). Between 1999 and 2003 alone, the total numbers of people already in the country who were actually *removed* as a result of 'enforcement action' increased nearly threefold from 6,440 to 19,630 (Dudley, 2004)[19]. Meanwhile, the draconian anti-terrorism legislation that caused such controversy when introduced in 2005 may, in practice, directly affect only a small number of individuals; but the wider impact of anti-terrorism measures on ethnic minorities may be illustrated by trends in searches under section 44 of the 2000 Terrorism Act. These are authorised personally by the Home Secretary and their use increased more than threefold in the first three full years of the Act to 33,798 in 2003/04. The total number remained insignificant compared with section 1 searches; it was still lower than for section 60 searches (see above), and London accounted for over 80% of terrorism searches on minorities. However, the overall ethnic make-up of these figures is telling, especially when compared with the figures for other searches and, in particular, bearing in mind that the arrest rate is very low (at less than 2%). In 2003/04, black people accounted for 9% of terrorism searches while the figure for Asians was 12%.

Conclusion

Despite the requirement of the 2000 Race Relations Amendment Act, the government does not appear to have produced any race equality impact assessment of its community safety policies. The available evidence, however, suggests that such an assessment would seriously call into question aspects of these policies and would pose two main challenges: one is that of reconciling the government's approach to community safety with other stated aims of Home Office policy; and the other relates to its use of ethnic statistics.

With regard to the first of these, the experience of ethnic minorities provides a stark illustration of the unequal impact of a predominantly enforcement-based approach to community safety. Any net-widening and up-tariffing effects will fall disproportionately on the young, especially where they are poor and living in rundown areas. This has very particular implications for ethnic minorities who fall disproportionately in these categories; but all ethnic minorities are not equally affected[20]. Of the groups for whom relevant data are available, young men of black Caribbean, Pakistani and Bangladeshi origin are currently the most 'at risk' from such policies[21].

These aspects of community safety policies seriously undermine the goal of increasing minorities' confidence in the criminal justice system. In particular, they may actively increase tensions with the police. More specifically, they increase the risk of repeating the problems that occurred with young black people 20 years ago with the equivalent generation within the poorer Asian communities. The 'war on terror' may prove a significant catalyst in this process.

Furthermore, these strategies appear to run directly counter to the aims of the government's race equality policy. For, as the experience of black communities in the US has shown, the economic position of the group as a whole is cumulatively undermined where its young males are not only poorly qualified but where they are also disproportionately removed from the labour market by high rates of incarceration and their prospects of securing gainful, legitimate employment are *de facto* lower still on their release (Tonry, 1995). As yet, these effects have been less evident among the Asian groups; but there are already signs that the poorer communities within this very diverse category are also beginning to be affected.

In addition, these policies may already undermine the government's further stated goal of improving social cohesion, inasmuch as aspects of antisocial behaviour policies and 'community'-led justice may, of themselves, be divisive. The increased criminalisation of some young people may itself exacerbate the growing socioeconomic divisions within society for the reasons given above; and there will be a significant ethnic dimension to these divisions. Meanwhile, the rhetoric associated with the 'war on terror' and, in particular, the portrayal of the arch enemy as the 'Muslim fundamentalist', will further fuel negative stereotypes of British Asians. At the same time, the targeting of muggers under the SCI and the more recent demonisation of 'hoodies' are similarly calculated to conjure up negative stereotypes of black youths.

With regard to the second challenge this analysis poses for the government, the very fact that none of these effects may be *intended* reinforces the argument for a more sophisticated use of ethnic statistics.

Reading specifically 'ethnic' conclusions from crude average differences may be tempting[22]; but it can also be very misleading, if not downright dangerous. On the one hand, it can distort policy development and reinforce divisions by focusing on general problems as though these were *exclusive* to particular minorities (FitzGerald, 2005). On the other hand, it can reinforce negative stereotypes; and figures showing the persistent overrepresentation of black people in the robbery figures have notoriously been used to this end. Yet statistical modelling of patterns of street crime in London (in FitzGerald et al, 2003) was able to demonstrate that the figures do not reflect ethnicity per se but a particular configuration of *general* factors, each of which disproportionately impacts on the black group.

Rather, ethnic statistics can usefully serve to highlight problems that are not peculiar to the minorities they refer to but might otherwise be ignored. The downside of community safety policies as exposed here will not only affect large numbers of the white British population, they will also have implications for many minority ethnic groups for whom no data are available – including some of the smaller, newer and less visible minorities who, in part for these reasons, may be among the most vulnerable. If the government *were* to meet the requirements of the 2000 Race Relations Amendment Act by using its ethnic data as the 'barium meal'[23] for its community safety policies, though, it would almost certainly uncover *prima facie* evidence of institutional racism.

Notes

[1] Accepted usage has changed over time and continues to do so. The first major study to raise concerns about the disadvantage and discrimination suffered by these groups (Rose et al, 1969) collectively refers to them throughout as 'coloured'.

[2] This percentage does not include the much larger numbers admitted as family members.

[3] Section 4 of the 1824 Vagrancy Act was originally intended as a measure of social control following mass demobilisation and unemployment after the Napoleonic Wars. Resurrected in the latter half of the 20th century, it came to be known as the 'Sus' law.

[4] The power was already available under local by-laws in certain forces.

[5] The natural rate of increase in this generation was also constrained by delays in reuniting the primary immigrants with families who might remain for long periods in the Indian subcontinent, especially in the poorer Pakistani and Bangladeshi groups.

[6] Southall was one of the earliest areas of major Indian settlement in London.

[7] These were to inquire into the matters arising from the death of Stephen Lawrence on 22 April 1993 to date, in order particularly to identify the lessons to be learned for the investigation and prosecution of racially motivated crimes.

[8] Unpublished profiles of the 32 London boroughs (FitzGerald, 2003) show that the most deprived, high-crime boroughs are the most ethnically diverse; and whites are in a minority in the youth population. These are also among the boroughs with the highest number of destitute asylum seekers supported by local authorities.

[9] When parties of the far right won large numbers of votes in 1977, the political waves this produced gave rise to a major, national anti-racist movement; but it was never anticipated by the most eminent psephologists at the time that the far right could succeed in winning any seats.

[10] According to the 2001 Census, these two groups alone account for 51% of the total Muslim population.

[11] The main explanation for this is likely to lie in factors other than ethnicity. Higher rates were similarly found among young people, those on low incomes, unskilled workers and people living in rundown areas, in inner-city areas and in London – categories that often overlap and are also characteristic of many minority ethnic groups. We return to this argument later.

[12] The 1988 and 1992 sweeps of the survey had asked this question *only* of black and Asian respondents. The results in 2000 confirmed that these groups *disproportionately* suffered in this way; but whites were still the victims in 63% of all 'racially motivated' incidents.

[13] Some caution is needed in interpreting these figures, however, since the scale of this increase may reflect the much greater political attention given to the problem post-Macpherson. From 13,878 in the year of the inquiry, there were huge annual leaps – to 23,049 in 1998/99, then 47,814 in the following year and reaching 53,092 by 2001/02.

[14] These were summarised in the Select Committee report as follows:

> Since 1997, new laws have introduced or extended the scope of: anti-social behaviour orders, fixed penalty notices, parenting orders, housing injunctions, demoted tenancies, possession orders, selective licensing schemes, closure powers in respect of premises used for Class A drugs and some licensed premises, and dispersal powers. (House of Commons, Home Affairs Select Committee, 2005a, p 12)

[15] While the Select Committee Report cites a figure of 45% between April 1999 and March 2004, a study for the Home Office (Campbell, 2002) showed that by far the largest age range targeted was young people aged 17-18, followed by 15- to 16-year-olds; when the figures for 18- to 21-year-olds are also included, young people actually accounted for 74% of the total.

[16] Considerable caution is needed in interpreting the Youth Justice Board's ethnic statistics because of the high proportion of cases in which ethnicity is not recorded. This fell slightly between the two years but the total still exceeded the number of Asians in both. For a further discussion, see Feilzer and Hood, 2004.

[17] The fifth of the original forces with robbery targets was Merseyside.

[18] For example, according to the Census, black men accounted for 3% of the population in 2001; but, while black British men made up 10% of the sentenced male prison population, in the case of robbery, the figure rose to 19% (Home Office, 2003a).

[19] The majority of these were *not* asylum seekers; but, since no information is available on their countries of origin, it is difficult to know which communities will have been most affected.

[20] Thus the Strategy Unit cites analysis of the 1991 Census showing that over two thirds of 'ethnic minorities' live in the 88 most deprived wards in the country compared with only 40% of the population at large (Strategy Unit, 2003). However, FitzGerald and Hale (1996) draw out the marked differences between groups within this. Of minorities sampled by the 1992 British Crime Survey, 43% of Indians lived in ACORN 'high crime risk areas' compared with 11% of white respondents; but the figure rose to 58% for black respondents and to 61% and 66% for Pakistanis and Bangladeshis, respectively.

[21] The socioeconomic characteristics of the mixed black Caribbean-white group suggest that they may similarly be at risk; but this group is still very young (see Figure 5.1) and the considerable uncertainty over how they are recorded in criminal justice statistics makes it difficult meaningfully to discuss their experience as yet (see Feilzer and Hood, 2004).

[22] Thus, the search figures have continued to be cited as the 'litmus test' of discriminatory police targeting (Bowling and Phillips, 2003) using crude comparisons with local population figures. This is despite the fact that similar 'disproportionality' occurs at all stages of the criminal justice process and that the overall profile of those searched bears little resemblance to that of the resident population anyway (MVA and Miller, 2000; Waddington et al, 2002).

[23] The phrase was first coined with regard to housing policies 40 years ago (Burney, 1967).

References

Berthoud, R. (1998) *The Incomes of Ethnic Minorities*, ISER Report 98-1, Colchester: Institute for Social and Economic Research.

Bowling, B. and Phillips, C. (2003) 'Policing ethnic minority communities', in T. Newburn (ed) *Handbook of Policing*, Cullompton: Willan Publishing, pp 528-55.

Burney, E. (1967) *Housing on Trial: A Study of Immigrants and Local Government*, Oxford: Oxford University Press.

Campbell, S. (2002) *A Review of Anti-Social Behaviour Orders*, Home Office Research Study 236, London: Home Office.

Cantle, T. (2001) *Community Cohesion: A Report of the Independent Review Team*, London. Home Office.

Clancy, A., Hough, M., Aust, R. and Kershaw, K. (2001) *Crime, Policing and Justice: The Experience of Ethnic Minorities Findings from the 2000 British Crime Survey*, Home Office Research Study 223, London: Home Office.

Demuth, C. (1978) *'Sus': A Report on the Vagrancy Act 1824*, London: Runnymede Trust.

Dudley, J. (2004) *Control of Immigration: Statistics United Kingdom, 2003*, Home Office Statistical Bulletin 12/04, London: Home Office.

Feilzer, M. and Hood, R. (2004) *Differences or Discrimination?*, London: Youth Justice Board.

FitzGerald, M. (1993) *Ethnic Minorities and the Criminal Justice System*, The Royal Commission on Criminal Justice Research Study No 20, London: HMSO.

FitzGerald, M. (2003) 'London borough profiles', unpublished report to Metropolitan Police Service, London.

FitzGerald, M. (2005) 'White boys fail too', *Guardian*, 1 June.

FitzGerald, M. and Hale, C. (1996) *Ethnic Minorities, Victimisation and Racial Harassment: Findings from the 1988 and 1992 British Crime Surveys*, London: Home Office.

FitzGerald, M., Stockdale, J. and Hale, C. (2003) *Young People and Street Crime: Research into Young People's Involvement in Street Crime*, London: Youth Justice Board.

Hall, S., Critcher, C., Jefferson, T., Clarke, J. and Roberts, M. (1978) *Policing the Crisis*, London: Macmillan.

Harrington, V. and Mayhew, P. (2001) *Mobile Phone Theft*, Home Office Research Study No 235, London: Home Office.

Home Office (1999) *Criminal Justice System: Strategic Plan 1999-2002 and Business Plan 1999-2000*, London: Home Office.

Home Office (2003a) *Prison Statistics, England and Wales, 2001*, Cm 5743, London: The Stationery Office.

Home Office (2003b) 'Respect and responsibility – taking a stand against anti-social behaviour' (www.homeoffice.gov.uk/docs2/asb_whitepaper.html).

Home Office (2005) *Statistics on Race and the Criminal Justice System 2004: A Home Office Publication under section 95 of the Criminal Justice Act 1991*, London: Home Office.

House of Commons, Home Affairs Select Committee (1981) *Fifth Report of Session 1980-81. Racial Disadvantage*, London: HMSO.

House of Commons, Home Affairs Select Committee (2005a) *Fifth Report of Session 2004-5. Anti-Social Behaviour: Volume 1 – Report*, London: The Stationery Office Limited.

House of Commons, Home Affairs Select Committee (2005b) *Anti-Social Behaviour: Written Evidence*, London: The Stationery Office Limited.

House of Commons Select Committee on Race Relations and Immigration (1977) *The West Indian Community*, London: HMSO.

Hunte, J. (1966) *Nigger Hunting in England*, London: West Indian Standing Conference.

JCAR (Joint Committee against Racialism) (1981) *Racial Violence in Britain*, London: JCAR.

Labour Party (2005) *Manifesto: Britain Forward not Back*, London: The Labour Party.

Macpherson, W. (1999) *The Stephen Lawrence Inquiry*, London: The Stationery Office.

Munton, T. and Zurawan, A. (2004) *Active Communities: Headline Findings from the 2003 Home Office Citizenship Survey*, London: Home Office.

MVA and Miller, J. (2000) *Profiling Populations Available for Stops and Searches*, Police Research Series Paper 131, London: Home Office.

Nicholas, S. and Walker, A. (2004) *Crime in England and Wales 2002/2003: Supplementary Volume 2: Crime, Disorder and the Criminal Justice System – Public Attitudes and Perceptions*, Home Office Statistical Bulletin 12, London: Home Office.

Ousley, H. (2001) *Community Pride and Prejudice: Making Diversity Work in Bradford*, Bradford: Bradford Vision.

Rose, E.J.B. et al (1969) *Colour and Citizenship: A Report on British Race Relations*, Oxford: Oxford University Press.

Scarman, Sir L. (1981) *The Brixton Disorders: 10-12 April 1981,* Report of an Inquiry presented to Parliament by the Secretary of State for the Home Department, London: HMSO.

Smith, D.J. (1983) *Police and People in London. 1. A Survey of Londoners*, London: Policy Studies Institute.

Smith, J. (2003) *The Nature of Personal Robbery*, Home Office Research Study 254, London: Home Office.

Squires, P. (1998) 'Consumerism and the demand for police services: is the customer always right?', *Policing and Society*, vol 8, pp 169-88.

Squires, P. and Stephen, D.E. (2005) *Rougher Justice: Young People and Anti-Social Behaviour*, Cullompton: Willan Publishing.

Strategy Unit (2003) *Ethnic Minorities and the Labour Market: Final Report*, London: Cabinet Office (www.strategy.co.uk).

Tonry, M. (1995) *Malign Neglect: Race, Crime and Punishment in America*, New York, NY: Oxford University Press.

Verba, S., Nie, N. and Kim, J. (1978) *Participation and Political Equality*, Cambridge: Cambridge University Press.

Waddington, D., Stenson, K. and Don, D. (2002) 'Disproportionality in Police Stop and Search in Reading and Slough', unpublished summary report for Thames Valley Police.

Youth Justice Board (YJB) (2005) *Youth Justice Annual Statistics 2003-4*, London: Youth Justice Board for England and Wales.

Section two
Community safety: a contested project?

SIX

The local politics of community safety: local policy for local people?

Matt Follett

Introduction

The role of local authorities in community safety policy development has a long and varied history. The aim of this chapter is to provide an overview of this history, incorporating findings from some recent research fieldwork. The chapter will attempt to show that many local authorities have for some time understood their own contributions to local crime and disorder management, certainly pre-dating the statutory role given them by the 1998 Crime and Disorder Act (CDA). Alongside this review of community safety policy development, from the 1980s to the CDA, consideration will be given to a number of critical criminological approaches to community safety. This is especially important, for it is from these critical perspectives that the greatest criminological illumination of community safety has tended to come. Beyond this, however, the chapter will go on to argue that in order to understand the role of local authorities in community safety, one also has to have a good understanding of the working of local government itself. In turn, this entails incorporating analyses from the field of local government studies into any examination of the role of local authorities in community safety policy making.

Of course, one key issue that has featured in both local government studies and critical criminology regarding community safety is the role of central government itself. More precisely, this refers to the influence of New Public Management (NPM), by which is meant the drive towards economic efficiency utilising accounting procedures such as statistical performance indicators. It is the NPM framework that provides a 'governing context' for much local authority activity in the community safety field. Indeed, this is where much critical thinking has applied itself to debates over new forms of crime management and the 'governance' of disorder. However, this 'governing context' has also brought with it a new role for elected representatives, primarily involving an expansion of central government demands, leaving those at the local level to fill in the details. In this way, rather more space may have been created for local interpretation in local policy making.

Drawing on recent research, this chapter will argue that this 'space' is now being increasingly contested by elected representatives in ways that directly affect the nature and direction of local community safety policies. This local 'space' has important implications for the study of community safety and it is only the more critical criminologies, those prepared to utilise political analyses – including political analyses at the local level – that can really hope to map out how local authorities are playing out their roles in community safety policy making. This is, of course, in stark contrast to those forms of criminology that set out to ignore the political aspects of the question. Before making such assertions more concrete, however, let us remind ourselves of how local authorities came to assume the roles they now have and how critical criminological approaches have tended to view this.

The early years

As others have shown (Crawford, 1998; Stenson and Edwards, 2001; Hughes and Edwards, 2002; Stenson and Edwards, 2003), the history of local authority involvement dates back at least to the mid-1980s. Crawford (1998, p 47) points out that Birmingham, Hammersmith, Islington and Fulham all had local authority 'community safety teams' by this time. This stemmed partly from the Home Office circular of 1984, in which the Conservatives first conceded that crime prevention was not something that should be left solely to the police but was 'a task for the whole community' (Home Office, 1984, p 1). One of the (unintended) consequences, argue Hughes and Edwards (2002), was that local policy actors, like Labour-led municipal authorities and their representative bodies such as the Association of Metropolitan Authorities (AMA, 1990) and the Association of District Councils (ADC, 1990), used this opportunity to 'redefine crime control in terms of community safety' (Hughes and Edwards, 2002, p 7).

Alongside this local authority activity, central government then assisted further. The Home Office had followed up its 1984 circular with another in 1990 (Home Office, 1990), promoting a partnership approach to crime prevention. This combination of central and local direction towards 'partnership' and 'community safety' then found itself articulated in the now landmark report of the Home Office Standing Conference on Crime Prevention, chaired by James Morgan. The Morgan Report (Home Office, 1991) is now acknowledged as being the main springboard for the development of community safety as we find it today.

The Morgan Report, Safer Cities and the 1998 Crime and Disorder Act

A key recommendation of the Morgan Report was that local authorities should be given the leadership role and also statutory responsibility for development of community safety. For Morgan, this meant establishing the capacity to 'encourage greater participation from all sections of the community' (Home Office, 1991, p

3).The significance of this lies in the fact that Morgan had argued that an absence of elected members might restrict crime prevention to the margins of local politics. Consequently, 'any meaningful local structure for crime prevention must be related to the local democratic structure' (Home Office, 1991, p 20).We will see later quite how important this idea was.

The report, however, was not implemented fully by the then Conservative government.The last thing the government wanted was to grant additional powers and resources to the Labour-led local authorities it had spent the past two parliamentary terms fighting. Despite this, the report stimulated the local authorities to initiate relevant policies, and also prompted the development of the first specialist 'community safety' professionals (Stenson and Edwards, 2003).

Indeed, although the national level of debate on how to tackle 'crime' took a punitive turn under the Home Secretary, Michael Howard, the rejection of the Morgan Report did not mark the death of the 'multi-agency community safety approach of the Morgan Report on the local governmental terrain' (Hughes, 1998, p 92). In fact, from the late 1980s through to the mid-1990s, the Conservative government provided funding for the Safer Cities programme following the expressed desire of Prime Minister Margaret Thatcher (in the immediate wake of the 1987 General Election) to 'do something about the inner cities' (Gilling, 1999).Although this was not intended by the Conservatives, the Safer Cities programme entailed a significant movement away from the centralised control of community safety issues (Tilley, 1993; Gilling, 1999).

In what may be the seminal contemporary discussion of this issue,Tilley (1993) argues that there was considerable leeway given to local agents, be they project coordinators or members of steering groups, in the Safer Cities schemes, because, as Tilley notes, 'the Home Office is not equipped for direct service delivery' (1993, p 46). The significance is seen in Tilley's well-observed point that, 'It is likely that with a different party in power a government initiated local crime prevention programme would be subject to local democratic control' (1993, p 47). The government at the time 'lacked confidence in local authorities and was not about to give new responsibilities requiring additional funds to those in whom it lacked trust' (Tilley, 1993, pp 46-7).The ways in which issues of service delivery and central control were reconciled are very similar to what we might find today. Tilley describes this aspect of Safer Cities in the following terms: 'local appointees run projects, subject to a local committee containing a range of representatives from specified agencies, operating with advice from, and ultimately some financial control by, central government' (1993, p 47).

While the Conservative government of the 1990s maintained a wary attitude towards local authorities, with regard to community safety, and much else, local authorities themselves did not stand still. In early 1996, the Local Government Management Board, with the Association of District Councils, the Association of Metropolitan Authorities, and the Association of County Councils, commissioned research into the community safety activities of local government (Gilling, 1999; Squires, 1999). This research found that 90% of local authorities saw community safety as a legitimate policy area, although only about 50% had translated this into policy or personnel decisions (LGMB, 1996). So local authorities had already taken it upon themselves, partly stimulated by central government pushing the idea that issues around crime prevention/community safety should not be the responsibility of the police alone, to stake a claim in this arena. What had prevented them going further was a Conservative government refusing to give any statutory footing or money to local authorities playing this role. In 1997, this was all about to change.

In its manifesto, the incoming Labour government had pledged to introduce the recommendations of the Morgan Report in relation to local authorities being given a statutory duty (Labour Party, 1997). Once in government, the party then put forward the Crime and Disorder Bill. There was, however, a significant change. Despite the Morgan recommendation, the Bill proposed that new statutory duties to coordinate and promote local community safety partnerships be given simultaneously to local authorities and the police (Home Office, 1997). These changes were introduced in response to concerns raised by the police (Crawford, 1998). Part of the reasoning here was that this would ensure that a local community safety strategy would complement the local policing plan, which had been required of the police since the Police and Magistrates' Courts Act of 1994. This also accorded with the new 'principles of partnership' that the government felt it necessary to outline (Newburn, 2003). Section 17 of the resulting 1998 Crime and Disorder Act called on relevant authorities to assess the impact on crime and disorder of *all* the functions of all their departments. Community safety policy was thereby to be embedded in all departments' responsibilities. The local authority contribution to community safety was now truly incorporated in the statutory framework.

Critical criminological approaches

Having considered the historical journey of community safety and local authority involvement in this area, it is also useful to look briefly at some of the critical criminological perspectives on this issue. As mentioned below, it is not to be assumed that there is total uniformity of approach among those considered to be critical criminologists in this field but, for the purposes of this chapter, they can be distinguished by virtue of their position vis-à-vis what has been termed 'administrative criminology' (Young, 1994). This concept refers to the body of work on community safety that has tended to focus on statistically measurable outputs of community safety activity, along with a performance management approach that assumes that community safety can be designed centrally and implemented locally, with a concomitant silence over the political ideologies of decision makers, whether it be decisions by local government, central government or, indeed, by criminologists. This body of work is perhaps most clearly illustrated by the *Safety in Numbers* report by the Audit Commission (1999) and the work of Ekblom (2000). By contrast, work that specifically includes an analysis of the political contexts and modes of decision making, and imputes interests and motivations to those involved is referred to by use of the term 'critical' (see Coleman, 2004). The following discussion will outline some findings emerging from an ethnographic study of local authority involvement in community safety policy development and partnership working in a unitary status authority in the UK that was undertaken as part of a doctoral thesis.

What became clear during this research was that the elected members of the local authority had an increasingly significant role to play, primarily because of their desire to influence local community safety policies. This comes in the wake of legislative developments in local government, most notably the Local Government Acts of 1999 and 2000. The former's significance stems from its insistence on performance indicators and economic efficiency and from the necessity to consult with representatives of those receiving services. The latter's significance derives from the restructuring of the executive functions of elected members and the establishment of a cabinet-style executive comprising councillors of the majority party. Community safety issues fell within the direct purview of those cabinet responsibilities in the case study authority. This directly draws community safety discussions into political decision making at the local level. This is not a new phenomenon. Indeed, earlier critical commentaries on community safety have not overlooked the element of local politics in decision and policy making. Stenson (2002, p 130) notes the significance of political factors in shaping policy and practice, having observed how a change in political control in Wycombe opened up windows of opportunity for progressive policies to be promoted in the community safety arena.

Perhaps inevitably, the politicisation of community safety can involve a series of potentially contradictory pressures. Crawford (1994, 1995, 1997) has explored how the concept of partnership has heralded a new arena of 'hybridisation' between private, public and voluntary sector actors and agents at the local level – a mixed sector. Garland (2001) saw a 'demonopolisation' of crime prevention and attempts to spread responsibility through external agencies other than government. That these new actors are present on the stage is not in question, but how significant are they? How can they influence the political direction? Edwards (2002) talks about 'contingent' and 'necessary' relations governing the shaping of community safety policies at the local level, and how these may differ in differing locales. Authors such as Hughes (1998, 2002a), Stenson (2002) and Edwards (2002) have made note of the importance of locale and local institutional agency regarding the ways in which community safety policies are developed. Within this body of literature lies the implication that to understand the role of local authorities in community safety, one has to understand the local political context, and to understand the local political context, one has to understand the political relationships constituting the local authority, concerning both the officers and the elected members. This, of course, carries certain methodological implications regarding what to actually research and how to go about it. It may also entail some 'neo-pluralist' theoretical assumptions that may not be shared by critical criminologists, working in a more materialist tradition, who see broader economic structures and relations at work in the determination of local policy agendas (Coleman et al, 2002).

That said, there is one overriding concern that the whole of critical criminology has brought to bear on community safety, and this concerns the issue of power. To refer to Edwards' terminology of 'contingent' and 'necessary' relations locally, the power to make decisions and to influence policy change is clearly a necessary relation. It is the exercise of power, by both elected members and officers, and the concomitant power dependence then of central government on local actors that explains the directions chosen for community safety policy in particular local authority contexts. This is not to exaggerate the autonomy at the local level. As will be seen later, there are contexts beyond the local within which these actors also have to operate (for example, within the local authority associations we have already referred to, which were quite fundamental in establishing community safety policy as a field of local government action). However, having considered some issues arising from critical criminological approaches to community safety within the local authority context, it is necessary to gain some further understanding of the processes operating within the local government context itself.

Local authorities and local democracy

The notion of the local authority as a hothouse of power relations also applies to its external relations, such as its 'partners'. As Skelcher (2004) notes:

> The reality is that local authorities are the dominant partners and that the deployment of their political, managerial and financial resources is essential to partnerships. (p 39)

Indeed, local authorities are often prepared to be the accountable body in a partnership, having the responsibility for managing central funding and reporting on the performance of the associated activities. Here it is acknowledged that the other players often rely on local authorities for such resources and, for their part, local authorities are often willing to assume these responsibilities. But the authorities also have an interest in regulating activity occurring within their geographical area, and they also seek to shape how that activity is undertaken (Skelcher, 2004, p 39). It should be added at this point that, for community safety partnerships, this influence might be mediated by virtue of the joint responsibility of the police. So the police may temper the dominance of the local authority. The responsibility of Crime and Disorder Reduction Partnerships (CDRPs) to carry out 'audits' of local crime and disorder in order to formulate a strategy means that, as one of the main data providers, the police are in a key position (Ericson and Haggerty, 1997).

Nonetheless, the influence of local authorities lies here; the question is, how does this actually impact upon community safety policy development? Before being able to answer this question, it is helpful to understand where the power that local authorities exercise comes from. Ostensibly, this derives from them being the site of recognised local democracy. However, what one might expect to find regarding 'local democracy' may not be that 'pure' in terms of actual democratic practice. Jones (1995) neatly summarises the situation by explaining that accountable local government occurs where citizens elect representatives who then enact policies that are implemented by public agencies; this is called 'overhead democracy'. There are two aspects to this – electoral accountability, whereby citizens control elected members, and bureaucratic accountability, whereby elected members control bureaucrats. Neither is well reflected by reality (Jones, 1995, pp 74-5).

One of the explanations given for this by some authors is that democracy is increasingly deprioritised compared with efficiency in local government. Wolman (1995) has described the purpose of local government as follows:

- as a counterweight to national government as a form of pluralism,
- in terms of developing democratic participation, and
- efficient provision of services. (p 139)

Yet he goes on to argue that it is clearly the last that takes precedence (Wolman, 1995, p 146). Indeed, the Widdecombe Committee, established by the then Conservative government to look at a range of issues concerning local government, concluded that 'clearly the three attributes of local government – pluralism, participation and responsiveness – provide a strong case for its continued existence as the principal means of local service delivery' (1986, p 53).

Wolman suggests, however, that in recent history provision of services has taken precedence over values of democratic governance (1995, p 140). This dilemma, the basic difficulty facing officers of any community safety partnership when confronted by councillors with very different perspectives on what is necessary to promote community safety, is essentially the problem of merging participatory democratic ideals with the managerial aspects of service provision (Pierre, 1995). This brings us to a vital aspect of local authority provision of community safety, the political and economic context within which they operate. While there is much statutory responsibility given to local authorities, they have to operate under conditions not set by them. One such condition or context is provided by the discourse of NPM.

The managerialist context

Managerialism is another building block in the understanding of how community safety operates at the local authority level. It is to these 'managerial aspects' that we can now turn for further illumination. Hansen (2001) provides an interesting view of how managerialism has occurred in local government in Denmark, and suggests that there is much here that is applicable to England. For Hansen, local government is in a state of change across Europe due to pressures arising from governments seeking to implement what has become known as NPM. For Hansen, there are various modes of NPM in play across Europe, but certain key features are identifiable in comparative studies. One feature pertinent to this discussion concerns the new forms of decision making within which councillors find themselves operating.

Hansen clearly feels that there is a move from government to 'governance' (as defined by Rhodes, 1997, 2000; Stoker, 2000), where authority goes from one formal centre of decision making towards a multitude of autonomous entities networking within their areas (Hansen, 2001, p 110). Hansen suggests that this model of new governance is influenced by NPM. It consists of three elements, with the third and most relevant for this discussion being that of 'central' goal steering and economic frame regulation. This means that much of the implementation detail is delegated to administrative and service delivery institutions. Regulations handed down from above, the national level, represent broad goals and policy objectives set by the centre. The more micro-steering by local government takes place in conjunction with autonomous (non-governmental) agencies and institutions through dialogue and agreed procedures. The local government/municipality interacts with the centre (nationally) regarding the goals and economic frames (Hansen, 2001, p 112).

This would seem to reflect relatively accurately how the partnership worked in the case study. However, the roles of the councillors, on the one hand contributing to localised, micro-goal steering, also involved questions of the democratic legitimacy of the partnership. Local government may well be variously 'improved' though its engagement with a wide diversity of partnership associations, but questions of legitimacy still remain (Jessop, 2000).

Local legitimacy

In the case study authority, the councillors based their claims to legitimacy on being 'recognised representatives of the public'. This appeared especially marked in the case of those councillors who seemed not to support the recommendations of officers working for the partnership or concerning proposals emanating from other partnership agencies. Their claims achieved further potency by virtue of the fact that the strategy documents produced by the partnership very much identified the involvement of councillors, both town and parish, as a way of illustrating the democratic accountability and representative nature of the overall policy development process.

However, there are some contrasting questions for councillors who may be elected at differing levels of local government. In 1997, the function of local (as in parish and town) councils was extended to include community safety (Coulson, 1999). This opens up a question of legitimacy if some officers did not accept that parish and town councillors in particular have much of a mandate, due to the small numbers voting them in. As one community safety practitioner observed:

> I don't think they're representative at all, it's easy to get voted on to a parish council because no one votes in those elections. (Case study research notes)

This, then, raises questions as to why and how these forms of representation are impacting on the development of community safety policies by local authorities. These are questions of democratic representation and legitimacy that cannot easily be answered here, although they do seem to suggest that the local authority cannot be seen quite so clearly as the sole source of claims to representative legitimacy. These necessarily complicated relations of legitimacy, responsibility and representation constitute aspects of the process by which government is replaced by governance, as Crawford and others have already noted (Crawford, 1995, 1997; see also Rhodes, 1997, 2000).

Government and governance

This clash of legitimacy arises from the new governance arrangements where there is no longer a single central authority but a network of institutions working together. As Rhodes (2000) puts it, 'as networks obscure formal accountability so they create opportunities for diverse interests to influence policy and the micro politics of the city challenges representative democracy'. In areas where there are parish councillors also, this creates extra problems due to the obvious dilemma of local decisions unpopular at parish level being taken ostensibly by town or city councils for the benefit of the wider community (Coulson, 1999, p 247). In the case study research, there were examples of this, where parish councillors utilised their perceived legitimacy as elected representatives to try to block certain actions that they felt the 'local residents' would not want. This elicited the following comment from a community safety practitioner:

> She (parish councillor) is only trying to play power games for her parish. We have to think about the city as a whole. (Case study research notes)

Such issues suggest that criminologists might usefully employ governance theory in understanding local authority community safety policy development. For example, Rhodes (1999) claims that the 1980s and 1990s saw 'partnerships and networking rivalling the unified departments as effective mechanisms for integrated action in the emerging local governance' (p xvi). The implications of utilising a governance approach for those studying local sites are clear. 'To an appreciation of the limits to command and control, we can add an understanding of the repertoire of networking; of management by trust and diplomacy' (Rhodes, 1999, p xvi).

It is interesting to see the community safety manager/officer as performing this role of managing and diplomacy, but achieving this for the benefit of the real centre, national government. In the case study, central government (in the form of a regional government representative) relied to a certain extent on the local manager to get national initiatives 'pushed through' locally, and this is a process that has to be 'managed', not just stated and demanded. So the manager is inseparably part of a political process, both in terms of the ideological politics underpinning government demands and of the pragmatic politics of getting things done locally, working with and through local interests. For example, at one partnership meeting in the case study research, a community safety officer had been asked to provide a presentation on the newly arrived Anti-Social Behaviour (ASB) Act of 2003. He presented it thus:

> This Act is rather a mess. We should be utilising ASBOs [Anti-Social Behaviour Orders] as a last resort rather than a main mechanism.... Mediation is part of an ASB Act that should have appeared. It should have been part of a checklist, have we considered mediation? Before going on to more punitive measures? It is neutral, stroke, independent [sic] from council, police, health, etc. (Case study research notes)

This, then, makes the broader point that local authorities are key, not just because councillors have become new players in this field, but also because a new cadre of community safety 'professionals' is now firmly located within this 'extended local government' responsibility. Indeed, authors like Hughes and Gilling (2004) have examined the role of community safety managers, with Hughes (2002b) offering a variety of potential future roles for such officers in terms of the future development of the community safety agenda. Again, this assumes that such local actors have the space to undertake such varied roles. As we have already noted, there are differing views on this within critical criminology.

There is, however, a need for some reflection on how we can have such a complex multilayered form of governance in the first place, especially as regards community safety. If interdependence is an aspect of governance (Rhodes, 1999, p xvii), then it is not easy to claim that anything especially new is occurring. In the case study, interdependence exists in terms of the statutory duties of the police and council. Actions are discussed in multi-agency settings and are then incorporated into public documents such as the published community safety strategy. There are examples of genuine multi-agency working, but this need not reflect any principle of equal responsibility on the part of the various partners. For example, in the case study area, there is a Safer Communities Unit where the police have a seconded officer to look at ASBOs, but the other aspects of the unit (abandoned vehicles, traveller management, wardens, dog fouling, litter, graffiti) are all the responsibility of the council. So while not a unified department, it is nonetheless a network of predominantly council departments (waste and resources, environment services, and so on). The police officer seconded to the community safety team, although playing a role in liaising with the parishes, effectively carried out some fairly conventional 'community policing' activities.

A good example here could be schools liaison: visits by police officers to schools are familiar as part of a 'personal and social responsibility' strategy. They involve police officers going along to classes and talking to children about safety issues and about 'how crime doesn't pay'. Putting it this way is not to denigrate the effectiveness of such activities for their purpose, but in pure 'partnership' terms this is largely an activity the police undertake anyway, and requires no other agency, apart from schools, to take part. Of course, that is not to say that local authorities are dominant over the police, but that new notions of 'networked governance' that might conjure up an array of fully engaged and significant institutions is maybe going too far. Perhaps Hughes (2004, p 16) is more accurate when he speaks of 'duopolies led by the police and local council'.

How these issues have played out in the particular case study may not have much bearing on what happens elsewhere. This brings us to a final important element concerning modern local governance. This concerns recognising the importance of local context. Hansen (2001) notes how, in Denmark, NPM has not really caught on at local level in a purely managerial way. The managerial elements have been mixed with 'historically developed traditions' and norms of 'rather open government at the local level' (2001, p 114), which has conferred opportunities on local actors, a point also made about community safety by Edwards (2002).

With this in mind, it is now necessary to ask how the local actors, primarily councillors, but also officers and a potentially diverse array of local partners, can exercise their influence at the local level and have some impact on the shaping and implementation of community safety policies.

Elected members and the significance of local politics

There has been a considerable critical literature on the political or ideological direction of community safety partnerships (Hughes and Edwards, 2002), but most of this has been concerned with how authority officers utilise their agency for pragmatic or 'resistance' ends (Gilling and Hughes, 2002). However, during the research on the case study, what emerged strongly was the potential and actual impact of elected members. In the case study partnership, it appeared that the local elected members had firmly grasped the significance of community safety, and were not content for it to be 'steered' solely by officers of the council or the police. Recalling the legislative context of the Local Government Acts of 1999 and 2000, local councillors in the case study authority had recognised that community safety could and did include 'doorstep' issues such as graffiti, neighbour nuisance and general 'antisocial/quality of life' elements, which were often referred to them by their constituents. This then meant that councillors were, to a degree, emboldened to intervene. As we have seen, a key aspect of the legitimacy of their interventions concerned the notions of representation and accountability.

Elected members in the case study seemed very cognisant of the fact that the accountability for decisions came from them. It was they who represented the people and therefore the officers had to take account of their views. On many occasions, an intervention by a councillor could mean that a certain proposed activity would not receive the resources that officers had wanted for it. At one senior meeting of the partnership, an officer gave a presentation on drug taking and what the partnership could do to offer support to people with drug addiction problems as a means of preventing offending. A councillor remarked at the end of the presentation that this was 'not the world I live in'. The attempt by the officer to obtain more resources or prioritisation of such activities was foiled.

This is not to say there are no occasions where officers are unable to block the desires of some elected members, but the point is that both types of local authority political infighting also now apply to community safety. This is equally the case with town and parish councils, not just the city councillors of unitary authorities. The research suggests a significant development in the role of local authorities in community safety, one that reinforces the earlier suggestion that, when we talk about local authorities from a critical criminological viewpoint, we cannot just refer to the authority as part of an extended state form, and we cannot just think about the community safety *operatives* – we have to take account of the other significant actors. This is a significant development from the days when such partnerships were seen as almost entirely 'officer-driven' (Hughes, 1996, pp 238-40). This goes further than Stenson (2002), who recognised how such actors can change or provide a context for community safety work to take a certain political direction. Rather, councillors are themselves also pushing certain agendas; they are now having a say in the actual work, rather than just confining themselves to the broader political directions. Of course, in keeping with recognising the importance of local contexts, this development may be occurring quite unevenly across the country precisely depending on local factors.

Indeed, the research has found examples of this in one particular meeting. A councillor with a strategic role in the partnership asked, with regard to prioritising offenders for a variety of interventions, 'how do we justify prioritising offenders over law-abiding people waiting for housing?'. This is a prime example of an elected member concerned about how something will 'play' with the public, the local electors. At the same meeting, a different councillor remarked, 'agencies don't often talk to the man in the street. I wish they could give these presentations to my communities. I think that if the officers talked to the communities they wouldn't agree with it'. Here we see a claim about representation invoked by an elected member with a view to moving the partnership away from a particular policy or activity.

However, as we saw earlier, if such interventions were really not accepted as legitimate, a question arises as to why there was so little obvious response by officers. Part of the reason, and again this may be a significant factor that the criminology of community safety needs to acknowledge, concerns local party politics. When this question was put to a senior officer, he replied that 'you have to look at the numbers, 24 and 27'. When I correctly surmised that he was talking about the small majority held by the ruling administration, he continued, 'if such a councillor defected there would be a majority of one. It's not in the interest of the current leaders of the administration or the officers for that to happen'.

Such factors have a significant influence on the ways in which community safety is decided and developed by local authorities.

Conclusion

It is clear that there has been a great deal of academic work on the politics of local government and concerning local governance in recent times (Rhodes 1997, 1999, 2000; Stoker, 1999, 2000; Stewart, 2003; Stoker and Wilson, 2004). One of the reasons these areas of study are now overlapping with criminology is that, through partnerships, crime and disorder management is now an increasingly important aspect of local governance. This requires us to change our perspective and look at community safety from a critical criminological perspective and, in effect, to begin studying local governance *through* crime and community safety.

The significances for community safety are manifold. One issue is that this creates dilemmas for partnerships, as councillors become increasingly involved in community safety governance. It also means that those analysing community safety from the vantage point of local authority involvement need to have a firm understanding of local politics, local government and other local contextual elements when looking at community safety planning, crime and disorder management and the prevention of antisocial behaviour. This, arguably, then brings into question the usefulness of a criminology that ignores those factors, a criminology that seeks to look at methods of crime prevention regardless of the governance contexts that will affect how they are applied. This is a criticism that applies especially to some 'administrative criminology approaches' that imply that some kind of 'scientific' force field protects the projects from being affected by governance decisions. Such a critique might apply especially to the notion that 'successful' crime and disorder projects, perhaps tried and tested in one area, can simply be 'rolled out' in another area and expected to work. On the contrary, one size seldom fits all.

Finally, we need to be careful in assuming that partnership really means partnership and that governance networks have truly replaced local government. Looking to the study of local politics will certainly help us and, arguably, this is now a key task for truly critical approaches to community safety. It is essential to incorporate an analysis from the field of local government studies and from political science, in order to develop critical analyses that go beyond both the grand narratives that overlook the importance of political relations at the local level (see Stenson, 2002), as well as the supposedly apolitical 'administrative criminologies' that presume to reduce community safety and crime prevention to mere technique. At a time when so-called new 'crime science' approaches appear to be suggesting that politics can be safely ignored in the management of crime and the further development of community safety, it is important to recognise that politics is everywhere in community safety, but especially so in local authorities.

References

ADC (Association of District Councils) (1990) *Promoting Safer Communities: A District Council Perspective*, London: ADC.

AMA (Association of Metropolitan Authorities) (1990) *Crime Reduction: A Framework for the Nineties*, London: AMA.

Audit Commission (1999) *Safety in Numbers: Promoting Community Safety*, London: Audit Commission.

Coleman, R. (2004) *Reclaiming the Streets: Surveillance, Social Control and the City*, Cullompton: Willan Publishing.

Coleman, R., Sim, J. and Whyte, D. (2002) 'Power, politics and partnerships: the state of crime prevention on Merseyside', in G. Hughes and A. Edwards (eds) *Crime Control and Community: The New Politics of Public Safety*, Cullompton: Willan Publishing, pp 86-109.

Coulson, A. (1999) 'Town, parish and community council: the potential for democracy and decentralisation', *Local Governance*, vol 24, no 4, pp 245-48.

Crawford, A. (1994) 'The partnership approach to community crime prevention: corporatism at the local level?', *Social and Legal Studies*, vol 3, no 4, pp 497-519.

Crawford, A. (1995) 'Appeals to community and crime prevention', *Crime, Law and Social Change*, vol 22, pp 97-126.

Crawford, A. (1997) *The Local Governance of Crime*, Oxford: Clarendon Press.

Crawford, A. (1998) *Crime Prevention and Community Safety*, London: Longman.

Edwards, A. (2002) 'Learning from diversity: the strategic dilemmas of community based crime control', in G. Hughes and A. Edwards (eds) (2002) *Crime Control and Community: The New Politics of Public Safety*, Cullompton: Willan Publishing, pp 140-67.

Ekblom, P. (2000) 'The conjunction of criminal opportunity', in S. Ballintyne, K. Pease and V. McLaren (eds), *Secure Foundations: Key Issues in Crime Prevention, Crime Reduction and Community Safety*, London: Institute for Public Policy Research, pp 30-67.

Ericson, R. and Haggerty, K. (1997) *Policing the Risk Society*, Oxford: Clarendon Press.

Garland, D. (2001) *The Culture of Control*, Oxford: Oxford University Press.

Gilling, D. (1999) 'Community safety: a critique', in M. Brogden (ed) *British Criminology Conferences: Selected Proceedings. Volume 2* (www.britsoccrim.org/v2.htm).

Gilling, D. and Hughes, G. (2002) 'The community safety profession', *Community Safety Journal*, vol 1, no 1, pp 3-12.

Hansen, K. (2001) 'Local councillors: between local "government" and local "governance"', *Public Administration*, vol 79, no 1, Spring, pp 105-23.

Home Office (1984) *Circular 8/84: Crime Prevention*. London: Home Office.

Home Office (1990) *Circular 44/90: Crime Prevention; The Success of the Partnership Approach*, London: Home Office.

Home Office (1991) *Safer Communities: The Local Delivery of Crime Prevention through the Partnership Approach*, Report of the Standing Conference on Crime Prevention ('the Morgan Report'), London: Home Office.

Home Office (1997) *Getting to Grips with Crime: A Framework for Local Action*, London: Home Office.

Hughes, G. (1996) 'Multi-agency crime prevention and community safety strategies in Britain', *Studies on Crime and Crime Prevention*, vol 5, no 2, pp 221-44.

Hughes, G. (1998) *Understanding Crime Prevention: Social Control, Risk and Late Modernity*, Buckingham: Open University Press.

Hughes, G. (2002a) 'Plotting the rise of community safety: critical reflections on research, theory and politics', in G. Hughes and A. Edwards (eds) *Crime Control and Community: The New Politics of Public Safety*, Cullompton: Willan Publishing, pp 20-46.

Hughes, G. (2002b) 'Crime and Disorder Reduction Partnerships: the future of community safety', in G. Hughes, E. McLaughlin and J. Muncie (eds) *Crime Prevention and Community Safety: New Directions*, London: Sage Publications, pp 123-42.

Hughes, G. (2004) 'Straddling adaptation and denial: crime and disorder reduction partnerships in England and Wales', *Cambrian Law Review*, vol 35, pp 1-25.

Hughes, G. and Edwards, A. (eds) (2002) *Crime Control and Community: The new Politics of Public Safety*, Cullompton: Willan Publishing.

Hughes, G. and Gilling, D. (2004) 'Mission impossible: the habitus of the community safety manager', *Criminal Justice*, vol 4, no 2, pp 129-49.

Jessop, B. (2000) 'Governance failure', in G. Stoker (ed) *The New Politics of British Local Governance*, London: Macmillan, pp 11-33.

Jones, B.D. (1995) 'Bureaucrats and urban politics: who controls? Who benefits?', in D. Judge, G. Stoker and H. Wolman (eds) *Theories of Urban Politics*, London: Sage Publications, pp 72-96.

Labour Party (1997) *Because Britain Deserves Better*, London: Labour Party.

LGMB (Local Government Management Board) (1996) *Survey of Community Safety Activities in Local Government in England and Wales*, Luton: LGMB.

Newburn, T. (2003) *Crime and Criminal Justice Policy*, Essex: Pearson.

Pierre, J. (1995) 'Comparative public administration: the state of the art', in J. Pierre (ed) *Bureaucracy in the Modern State*, Aldershot: Edward Elgar, pp 1-17.

Rhodes, R. (1997) *Understanding Governance*, Buckingham: Open University Press.

Rhodes, R. (1999) 'Governance and networks', Foreword, in G. Stoker (ed) *The New Management of British Local Governance*, London: Macmillan, pp xii–xxiv.

Rhodes, R. (2000) 'Governance and public administration', in J. Pierre (ed) *Debating Governance*, Oxford: Oxford University Press, pp 54–90.

Skelcher, C. (2004) 'The new governance of communities', in G. Stoker and D. Wilson (eds) *British Local Government into the 21st Century*, Basingstoke: Palgrave Macmillan, pp 25–43.

Squires, P. (1999) 'Criminology and the community safety paradigm: safety, power and success and the limits of the local', in M. Brogden (ed) *British Criminology Conferences: Selected Proceedings,* Volume 2 (www.britsoccrim.org/v2.htm).

Stenson, K. (2002) 'Community safety in Middle England – the local politics of crime control', in G. Hughes and A. Edwards (eds) *Crime Control and Community: The New Politics of Public Safety*, Cullompton: Willan Publishing, pp 109–40.

Stenson, K. and Edwards, A. (2001) 'Crime control and liberal government: the Third Way and the return to the local', in K. Stenson and R. Sullivan (eds) *Crime, Risk and Justice: The Politics of Crime Control in Liberal Democracies*, Cullompton: Willan Publishing, pp 68–87.

Stenson, K. and Edwards, A. (2003) 'Crime control and local governance: the struggle for sovereignty in advanced liberal polities', *Contemporary Politics*, vol 9, no 2, pp 203–17.

Stewart, J. (2003) *Modernising British Local Government*, Basingstoke: Palgrave Macmillan.

Stoker, G. (ed) (1999) *The New Management of British Local Governance*, London: Macmillan.

Stoker, G. (ed) (2000) *The New Politics of British Local Governance*, London: Macmillan.

Stoker, G. and Wilson, D. (eds) (2004) *British Local Government into the 21st Century*, Basingstoke: Palgrave Macmillan.

Tilley, N. (1993) 'Crime prevention and the Safer Cities story', *The Howard Journal of Criminal Justice*, vol 32, no 1, pp 40–57.

Widdecombe Committee (1986) *The Report of the Inquiry into the Conduct of Local Authority Business*, London: HMSO.

Wolman, H. (1995) 'Local government institutions and democratic governance', in D. Judge, G. Stoker and H. Wolman (eds) *Theories of Urban Politics*, London: Sage Publications, pp 135–60.

Young, J. (1994) 'Incessant chatter: recent paradigms in criminology', in M. Maguire, R. Morgan and R. Reiner (eds) *Oxford Handbook of Criminology* (1st edn), Oxford: Clarendon Press, pp 69–125.

SEVEN

The police and community safety

Barry Loveday

Introduction

As a range of current policing strategies now demonstrate, the traditional law enforcement role of the police is in the process of being overtaken by initiatives based on a combination of intelligence-led policing and a commitment to the implementation of effective crime reduction programmes based on sharing information and intelligence throughout England and Wales. Currently, all police forces are now required to introduce and use the National Intelligence Model (NIM) as identified within the 2002 Police Reform Act. As its title suggests, the NIM requires the collection and more effective use of local (and other) sources of information that together form the basis of the work of police intelligence analysts. This, along with the analysis of offender patterns at various geographical levels on a regular basis, now provides a much more comprehensive picture of crime patterns and quality of life problems to which the police can respond.

The application of NIM has also coincided with the recognition that the police can expect to gain much from the 'partnership' approach that constitutes the central element of current community safety strategies developed out of the Morgan Report of 1991 and the 1998 Crime and Disorder Act (CDA). Indeed, post-Morgan, there has been a strong commitment, particularly at the police operational level, to supporting the successful implementation of community safety strategies by way of Crime and Disorder Reduction Partnerships (CDRPs) (Police Superintendents Association, 2004). The movement towards preventative policing is now also reflected in the adoption by the police of the 'reassurance agenda', designed to reduce levels of crime concern by targeting 'signal crimes' (incivilities and signs of disorder) that can generate feelings of insecurity and danger within local communities (Tilley, 2005). Most recently, the police service has made manifest its long-term commitment to community safety within the Neighbourhood Policing initiative, designed to address local crime and disorder priorities in conjunction with other local agencies (Tilley, 2005).

1998 Crime and Disorder Act

It was, arguably, the implementation of the CDA that proved to be the most significant driver in terms of reorienting policing strategies. By making the police and local authorities jointly responsible for crime reduction, the CDA provided formal recognition that the police as law enforcers could never, in the absence of support from local public services, be expected to significantly impact on crime and disorder. Indeed, such was the recognition of the significance of the local authority that, as originally conceived, local authorities were to be identified as 'lead authority' within the planned CDRPs. This proposal was, however, to be successfully challenged by police associations, which refused to accept that the police should 'follow anyone' (Povey, 2000). As a result, the CDA was to assign to local police forces and local governments joint responsibility for community safety strategies.

The linkage between police and local authorities should have been enhanced, at least in theory, by the earlier arrival of Basic Command Units (BCUs) in the early 1990s. Originally conceived as a means of reducing police bureaucracies by ending the two-tier divisional and subdivision structure, the BCU as a policing unit was planned to provide local policing with an establishment of around 150 to 200 police officers (O'Byrne, 2001, p 125). By 'flattening' police hierarchies within the BCU, it was also argued that these units could be more effectively managed by the local commander (a police superintendent). There may also have been an expectation that the BCU boundary could be made coterminous with that of local governments, so facilitating cooperation and potential partnership arrangements (O'Byrne, 2001, p 133).

The potential benefits of the BCU structure were to be highlighted by the CDA, under which the Home Office was to make every local authority a 'responsible authority' and which was to lead to the creation of 376 CDRPs. This very large number of CDRPs only reflected the reality of local government arrangements within which, along with unitary authorities, county councils and metropolitan districts, 236 non-metropolitan districts are made responsible for the delivery of local services in the non-metropolitan counties (Wilson and Game, 1998, p 60). A further factor not perhaps sufficiently appreciated within the Home Office was the significance of the 'two-tier division' (and tension) between county and district that has characterised the relationship since the emergence of the 'reformed' local government system in 1974 (Alexander, 1982). This often difficult local authority relationship has inevitably contributed to the problems surrounding the development and management of successful partnerships and the ability of local police commanders to encourage effective cooperation between local authority tiers (Loveday, 2005a).

Police BCU boundaries and CDRPs

The potential problems overlooked by the Home Office in relation to local government structure were to be matched by not altogether dissimilar tensions within police forces. Here the problem was to be quickly identified within some police headquarters as relating almost entirely to the operation of BCUs and the management challenge they appeared to represent. The concept of the BCU as originally identified was to be sustained and expanded by way of delegation of budgets to local commanders. However, many police headquarters were in fact to delegate only a fraction of budget responsibility to these officers. As an enlightening survey conducted by the Police Superintendents Association in 2003 revealed, local commanders could expect to be made wholly responsible for 'office equipment' and 'overtime' payments but not police manpower, the most significant budget item (Police Superintendents Association, 2003; Loveday, 2004). This interesting feature of non-delegation of budgets, while reflecting internal strains within a number of police forces, also served to further highlight the problem of centralised bureaucratic control of police budgets identified earlier by Bayley in many US police departments (Bayley, 1994). It also reflects a view emanating from the Association of Chief Police Officers (ACPO) as to the importance of 'corporacy' and the perceived dangers of BCU commands identifying too closely with local authorities, not least in relation to the loss of control this might represent for ACPO leadership. This perception appears to be entirely shared by Her Majesty's Inspectorate of Constabulary (HMIC), which was to raise the dangers of this development in relation to Cleveland Police and the management of its BCUs. Cleveland's management was to be severely criticised for allowing BCUs to go 'native' (HMIC, 2002/03).

Problems surrounding the role of BCUs did not, however, extend to budgets alone. Police professionals were to also challenge the 'ideal' size of BCUs. As noted by O'Byrne, while, in the early 1990s, the ideal number of officers required for establishing a BCU was calculated to be between 150 and 200, by the end of the decade that number had risen to between 250 and 350 officers. Indeed, in some forces, BCUs were to comprise more than 400 officers, while at least one BCU commander (Bristol Central) is now responsible for over 1,000 officers (O'Byrne, 2001, p 125). The establishment level of the BCU can be significant not just in terms of raising the issue of effective internal management, but also in relation to coterminosity or boundaries shared with the local authority. As BCUs have been enlarged, this has often been at the cost of ending shared boundaries (Loveday, 2005b). Yet it is commonly accepted that the absence of coterminous boundaries can prove to be problematic for the development of effective partnerships, particularly with the local authority the other 'responsible authority' under the CDA.

To date, however, local chief officers have not been required to ensure that BCU boundaries are aligned to those of the local authority. Frequent reorganisation of BCUs in a number of forces has been implemented on 'police operational' grounds, with apparently little consideration being given to the likely impact of this on partnership arrangements. Ironically, and despite the development of sophisticated police performance measures, HMIC has not identified coterminous boundaries as a measure of performance and does not retain information on this matter in relation to local forces.

Yet the real problems generated by the lack of coterminosity have been frequently highlighted by the Police Superintendents Association, whose members constitute the majority of BCU commanders in the field. The association has argued that:

> The requirement to engage in partnership working makes coterminosity the single most critical factor in determining whether a BCU is likely to deliver effective local policing. We believe that the more closely aligned are the respective partners' boundaries then the more effectively the partners combine in delivering community safety. Where BCU commanders are required to negotiate with multiple partnerships that, in turn, are required to work with more than one BCU commander, an inevitable confusion follows in respect of resourcing and responsibility. It is not unknown for a BCU commander to have to work with two or more partnerships whose strategic aims are at best misaligned and at worst conflicting. (Police Superintendents Association, 2004, p 4)

The acknowledged problem surrounding the role of BCUs might have been expected to be resolved as a result of an important HMIC 2002 evaluation of the work of BCUs. Ironically, this report was to refer to debate about future structures for policing delivery 'posited around BCUs with a high degree of self-sufficiency, capable of tackling all but the most serious and organised crimes' (HMIC, 2002, p 8). The same report was also to relate that 'learning points from the first BCU inspections' included 'co-terminosity of partnership and BCU boundaries' (HMIC, 2002, p 23).

Given the perceived centrality of shared boundaries to successful partnerships, it is particularly instructive to discover that as late as 2005 it was still felt necessary by the Home Secretary, Charles Clarke, at the ACPO summer conference of that year to emphasise the need for coterminosity in relation to police and other agency boundaries. As he was to argue in relation to the police role in building a safer and more secure community, while it was 'perhaps the most controversial' issue to raise with them, he stated that he gave 'great priority to making the basic command units and the local districts coterminous'. He also raised what he described as the 'difficult question' of 'empowering local police at BCU level' by increasing delegation to BCU commanders to increase their capacity to respond to local needs (Clarke, 2005). The Home Secretary's growing concern about police failure to develop shared boundaries was subsequently reinforced by a letter sent to the President of ACPO. This requested that officer to raise the issue with over 12 police forces where there was little or no evidence on their part of any commitment to establishing BCU boundaries that were coterminous with local district authorities (Police Superintendents Association, 2004).

The two-tier system and CDRPs

Pressure from the Home Secretary could provide the impetus for both ACPO and HMIC to reaffirm the importance of aligning BCU boundaries with those of local authorities. Yet one further problem remains. This revolves around the structure of local government within the non-metropolitan counties and can be expected to have a direct impact on the overall effectiveness of CDRPs. Thus, the division of functions between counties and districts can mean that it is difficult to develop the level of cooperation and consensus that partnership arrangements demand. The potentially fatal consequences of dividing service responsibilities between local authority tiers made in 1974 were highlighted many years ago.

As was to be argued by Alexander in relation to service delivery where, for example, social services and housing departments exist in separate authorities, much would ultimately depend on 'liaison and cooperation' between the tiers (Alexander, 1982, p 53). Yet the very tensions that characterise the relationship between county and district make such liaison extremely difficult, particularly when this is suffused with such issues as 'autonomy', independence and 'amour propre', which, when combined, can undermine effective partnership arrangements.

Additional problems arise in relation to the attendance of county officers at local district CDRPs. This can be problematic anyway when there are many district CDRPs within one county. Ironically, this absence can become the source of further acrimony at district level between ostensible partners. One consequence of these tensions was to be graphically described by a local BCU commander in a non-metropolitan district, who noted that in his experience of local district CDRP meetings 'no county council representative had ever attended' and that there had often been 'more apologies than attendees at partnership meetings' (Loveday, 2005a, p 5). The same commander was to summarise his experience of CDRPs as one in which there had been 'an absence of cohesion in relation to membership; a lack of enthusiasm and an absence of leadership' (Loveday, 2005a, p 5). Nor is the experience of this officer outside of either unitary or metropolitan districts likely to be that unusual. It is on to these rather fragile structures that the Home Office has, however, regularly loaded responsibility for achieving national targets set for reducing local crime rates.

Going local or going central?

Although, as initially planned, the CDA was identified as a means of establishing greater local responsibility for community safety strategies, this has failed to materialise. Indeed, as with many other public services, CDRPs have been subject to a growing avalanche of centrally set targets and initiatives that have served to circumscribe local responsibility. Most recently, a report from the Committee of Public Accounts was to question the impact on CDRPs of no less than 14 different Home Office crime reduction initiatives over the past six years, each bringing its own 'grant fund, application and monitoring procedures' (House of Commons Committee of Public Accounts, 2005, p 6). The 'nationalisation' of what was ostensibly a commitment to a local responsibility model established by way of local CDRPs, local authorities and police BCUs appears to have been a deliberate policy on the part of the Home Office. This significant change in orientation was to be identified in a National Audit Report that clearly picked up current perceptions of the national dimension that now characterise community safety. As was noted:

> The Home Office told us that from 2005–06 there will be a national target of a 15% reduction in crime and more in high crime areas and (regional) government Offices will be taking a much more pro-active role in setting CDRP targets with the help of central Home Office guidance that are [sic] deliberately designed to ensure that targets set at local level will sum to the desired national outcome. (NAO, 2004, para 3.11)

Home Office intervention has been reflected in a variety of ways. This has ranged from the decision to amalgamate local CDRPs with Drug Action Teams (DATs) to the Home Office plan to make the Prolific and Priority Offenders scheme a specific CDRP responsibility following limited consultation with local authorities. Indeed, the pronounced lack of regular consultation conducted by the Home Office with local government representatives was to be highlighted by the Local Government Association (LGA). It noted in 2004 that it had been disappointed that the Home Office had failed to consult with it before the publication of its Five Year Strategy for community safety and crime reduction. As this strategy also included the proposed movement to Local Area Agreements (LAAs), fundamentally altering funding streams for CDRPs and police BCUs, this could be viewed as something of an oversight. The LGA also expressed concern that within the strategy document little reference was made to the role that local authorities played in community leadership. It also expressed concern about the apparent imbalance between punitive and long-term measures in relation to the further use of Anti-Social Behaviour Orders (ASBOs) (LGA, 2004/05, p 4).

Indeed, in respect of ASBOs, it was made clear by Home Office minister, Hazel Blears, in 2005, that the success of this measure was to be determined within the Home Office largely by how close local authorities and the police had come to reaching nationally set ASBO targets. In 2005, it was discovered that the target of 5,000 ASBOs was close to being reached, with 3,600 orders being issued by the courts by June of that year (Loveday, 2005c, p 1). It remains unclear, however, as to whether the single-minded pursuit of an ASBO target can be expected, of itself, to curb the apparent rise in antisocial behaviour that now appears to plague many towns and cities in England and Wales and generates deep concern about crime and disorder within many communities.

The evidence to date might reinforce a view that the traditional 'non-operational' role and lack of contact and knowledge within the Home Office of local government has been clearly revealed in its approach to the implementation of the CDA. The potential problems of the two-tier local government system for partnerships and apparent Home Office lack of awareness of this matter has been most recently evidenced by the decision to make county councils lead authorities for LAA funding. Predictably, this was to raise deep concern at district level and within CDRPs, where the decision was viewed as a means of diminishing their role in community safety work (LGA, 2004/05, p 2). The subsequent experience of community safety officers in relation to reduced county funding of CDRPs at district level was to fully justify that concern (LGA, 2004/05, p 7). Additionally, the Home Office decision to make CDRPs responsible for the Prolific and Priority Offenders scheme might fall at the first hurdle. This is because CDRPs are not corporate bodies and Home Office proposals could as a result be declared *ultra vires*.

Police and CDRPs

Although the National Audit Office (NAO) in its 2004 report was to comment that local police commanders were generally positive about the effectiveness of their local partnerships, it was noted that the determinant of success was whether there was 'synergy' among the partners and a commitment to tackle crime. The same report did, however, go on to stress that 'issues of genuine local concern were more likely to generate such commitment among partners' (NAO, 2004, para 3.10). This feature identified by the NAO, regarding the dynamics of local CDRPs, provides some insight into the problems that have undoubtedly confronted local BCU commanders in terms of encouraging and managing the work of CDRPs. As was to be rather vividly highlighted within a survey conducted for the Police Superintendents Association in 2003, local commanders could be confronted by the requirement to achieve nationally set priorities even when they had little application or relevance within the BCU area (Police Superintendents Association, 2003, p 97).

As the survey noted, police commanders could find national targets frustrating, 'especially if Home Office priorities did not match local needs'. An example of this was the earlier push towards reductions in street crime when this was not an issue in the BCU but where resources needed for local problems were diverted into street crime to fulfil central targets. Where national priorities corresponded with local crime problems in the BCU area, then providing greater resources to reach set targets offered evidence to the Home Office and HMIC that the BCU was performing well (Police Superintendents Association, 2003, p 97). BCU performance as measured and monitored by the Home Office has now assumed a salience that could serve to further remove policing from its local context. Thus, the power given to the Home Secretary by the 2002 Police Reform Act to directly intervene in BCU performance was to be fully exercised by David Blunkett when he was Home Secretary in pursuit of his policy of 'driving up the police performance'. Then, as now, BCU performance data provided by HMIC are circulated to weekly meetings of the Police Performance Steering Group within the Home Office, which is responsible for identifying 'failing forces'. These forces can in turn be inspected by the Police Standards Unit that has responsibility for improving BCU (or police force) performance (Loveday, 2005a). As the first casualty in the detection of poor performance by HMIC will very likely prove to be the local BCU commander, this process places great pressures on these officers to conform to centrally set targets and priorities.

One irony of this approach to performance measurement was to be identified within the 2003 Police Superintendents Association survey. This was the requirement placed on all BCU commanders to reduce crime rates even in areas with low crime. Many BCU commanders with low recorded crime rates believed that the requirement to reduce crime still further 'did not make sense'. As was to be argued:

> Commanders in this position were particularly perplexed over the judgement that they were poorly performing if they failed to reduce what were already low crime rates, which could be a very challenging task. (Police Superintendents Association, 2003, p 98)

The same survey found that local commanders favoured local targets if only because they matched the needs of the BCU area. Evidence of professional frustration was very clearly communicated when their preference for local targets did not seem to fit with the government's approach 'in spite of the emphasis on CDRPs and local strategies' (Police Superintendents Association, 2003, p 98). It was for this reason that local commanders strongly favoured an orientation where local rather than national agendas had priority. Interestingly, in relation to BCU performance, police commanders were also to question the underlying assumption that they had control over all the factors that affected performance when, as a result of limited budgetary freedom and the local environment, 'commanders themselves felt they did not always have the power to make a difference' (Police Superintendents Association, 2003, p 5).

Police and partnerships

The challenges surrounding the successful operation of partnerships have not, however, significantly diminished police commitment to the partnership process. Indeed, the 2003 Police Superintendents Association survey was to prove extremely reassuring on that point. It was to discover that a high proportion of local commanders saw liaison with local partner agencies as an important aspect of the role of BCU commanders (Police Superintendents Association, 2003, p 9). It was apparent, however, that there was a significant variation in commitment exhibited by partners within CDRPs. BCU commanders were to identify a number of local authority departments as not being sufficiently 'on board' (see Table 7.1 below).

The data identify the police perception of the extent to which partners have fulfilled their role within CDRPs. This view may not, of course, be shared by other partners. Yet the reality of partnership work as evidenced within some 2004 crime audit reports suggests that the commitment to CDRP work may be less than wholehearted within a number of local authorities (Loveday et al, 2004). Concern about the variable nature of commitment exhibited by member agencies and local services is, of course, not a recent issue. In its 2004 report, the NAO found that BCU commanders and the chairs of partnerships 'typically rated their

Table 7.1: Police perceptions of the extent to which CDRP members were fulfilling their commitments

	Base:	Completely (%)	Partly (%)	Not (%)
Local Authority Chief Executive's office	210	58	38	2
Fire Service	174	40	53	5
Police Authority	146	40	53	6
Victim support	124	39	52	6
Local Authority Housing department	173	34	60	4
Probation services	192	26	60	11
For two-tier authority areas: County Council	81	26	69	5
Local Authority Youth Services department	183	25	67	7
Community groups and voluntary agencies	139	25	69	3
Social Landlord/Housing Association	123	24	63	12
Local Authority Environmental Health department	134	22	64	9
Local Authority Social Services department	170	22	61	15
Local Authority Leisure and Amenities department	114	18	70	11
Religious body	68	16	57	25
Local Authority Planning department	103	15	69	15
Local Authority Education department	182	15	70	13
Parish/Community Council	75	15	68	13
Business group or group promoting business interests	118	14	68	18
Health services, including Primary Care Trust	195	11	60	26
Crown Prosecution Service	81	11	47	40
Transport provider	49	10	43	43
Court Service	93	8	56	32
Other	21	33	52	5

Source: Police Superintendents Association (2003)

local probation service and local health service as less active than other statutory partner agencies' (NAO, 2004, para 3.15). This assessment was in fact far less damning than that reached by an earlier report from the Audit Commission, which, in examining partnerships, was to conclude that health services, social services, probation and education services were often not full partners (Audit Commission, 2002).

Some explanation for the significant discrepancies in commitment to the partnerships was to be made apparent, however, in the 2004 local crime audit process. This was to reveal in stark terms the impact of the performance management approach adopted by the government on the delivery of individual services (Loveday et al, 2004). It became clear that by identifying performance targets for each public service these centrally set targets rather than partnership priorities would always be given precedence. Performance targets set centrally dictated priorities for local partnership members. Specific targets for health services were found rarely if at all to coalesce with those of CDRPs. Within education, the impact of school performance on national league tables could mean that school targets might actually work against CDRP objectives. Pupils deemed to be underperformers academically could be sidelined while school league tables meant that schools were now far less prepared to respond to the needs of likely offenders (Loveday et al, 2004). School exclusions were increasing but did not tell the whole story. There was an increasing acceptance within schools of regular non-attendance by difficult pupils who 'were not excluded but just not counted' (Loveday et al, 2004).

This suggests that an unintended consequence of the government's commitment to performance measurement could undermine the partnership approach it wishes to establish at CDRP level. Ironically, performance regimes effectively isolate service providers where separate performance targets can be expected to circumscribe any activity not aligned to national targets set for service providers.

A further problem for partnerships relates most immediately to finance. Thus, despite the prominence the government gives to community safety and despite the recognition of 'fear of crime' as a major blight for many communities, no core funding for community safety is automatically provided by many local authorities. In the absence of any central government assistance in funding (of greater potential value than the cascade of centrally set targets), community safety within the local government world remains a Cinderella service. The very limited funds made available to CDRPs may explain the limited value attached to the work of the partnership by some partner members and chief executives. The noticeable feature of low-level funding was indeed to be rather starkly revealed anyway with the decision to amalgamate CDRPs with DATs. DAT budgets currently dwarf those of the partnerships, while also highlighting how much is expected from CDRPs on what remains a very limited funding base.

This situation is not helped by the equally limited budget delegation provided to BCU commanders by police force headquarters. This problem has only been compounded by the continuing impact of the Crime Fighting Fund (CFF), which requires the employment of more police officers. A reflection of 'party political' competition, police establishments are now seen as a kind of virility symbol within which it is important to be able to claim that police officer numbers exceed those employed by the predecessor administration. Yet, it is evident that the CFF impedes the ability of BCU commanders to provide the service they believe is required and could benefit from the expansion of employment of a variety of police staff rather than just police officers (Police Superintendents Association, 2003, p 8).

Section 17 CDA and enforcement

The CDA contains explicit guidance on enforcement matters among partners and other authorities. Section 17 of the Act states that 'it shall be the duty of each authority to exercise its various functions with due regard to the likely effect of the exercise of those functions on, and the need to do all that it can to prevent crime and disorder in its area'. Section 17 therefore represents a critical element within the armory of CDRPs to ensure compliance with crime reduction strategies. It is fair to say that following the passage of the CDA much was expected from section 17. Some commentators were, for example, to observe that section 17 was 'arguably the most radical part of the Act and that it was difficult to conceive of any decision that would remain untouched by Section 17 considerations' (NACRO, and LGA, 1999, p 2). Section 17, described by some commentators as a 'wolf in sheep's clothing', would mean that narrow compliance exhibited by authorities would be seen as 'no change' and would leave them open to legal as well as governmental intervention or local challenge. Authorities needed to act immediately, it was stated, 'as the meter was running on section 17' (NACRO and LGA, 1999, p 18).

While enforcement powers are clearly necessary to encourage compliance among numerous service providers, it is evident that the early optimism surrounding the application of section 17 may have proved to be misplaced. Within one authority subject to local crime audit, police perceptions of the value of section 17 were clear (Loveday et al, 2004). While it was recognised that section 17 should have provided a means of ensuring conformity with the local crime reduction strategy, 'it had not always been invoked'. Moreover, the application of section 17 could prove to be a real challenge 'when staff at the local council were not aware of the relevant section' (Loveday et al, 2004, p 106). Indeed, police perception of the limited value of section 17 was reinforced by the absence of its enforcement by the courts. No cases had arisen from non-compliance with section 17 and there 'was a feeling that as with much of the law section 17 could be safely ignored at times'. Yet without the exercise of its enforcement powers it was felt that 'there was little justification in keeping section 17' (Loveday et al, 2004, p 107).

Most recent evidence of the very limited impact of section 17 enforcement can be found in a report on antisocial behaviour from the House of Commons

Home Affairs Committee (2005). In its assessment of the impact of the 2003 Licensing Act, it noted that the development of the night-time economy in many towns and cities was a consequence of local authority planning decisions that had encouraged the establishment of numerous pubs or clubs, often in close proximity to each other. One result of this had been the creation of a massive problem of binge drinking and associated violence that police forces found increasingly difficult to tackle. While the Home Affairs Committee was to argue for the incorporation of crime reduction principles in town and city centres, it also noted that:

> Under section 17 of the CDA 1998 local authorities already have the duty to consider the effects of their decisions on crime and disorder. We have heard however that this has been ineffective in leading to the type of planning that would be necessary if a major impact was to be made on alcohol related matters. In addition (the committee) has been told that the courts are not bound by section 17 in their considerations. (House of Commons Home Affairs Committee, 2005, p 354)

One consequence of the non-application of section 17 had been the creation of a drinking culture among predominantly young people in town and city centres where it was rare in practice to have the necessary facilities to cope with the night-time economy (House of Commons Home Affairs Committee, 2005, p 351). Now, however, even where the local authority sought to refuse a further late night drink-led entertainment application in a particular area, the decision was likely to be appealed and would go to court. Evidence from the local authority would be very likely to include the fact that it was a policy approach driven in part by section 17. Yet as the Home Affairs Committee was to discover, in the statutory guidance for the Licensing Act 'the courts were not bound by that' (House of Commons Home Affairs Committee, 2005, p 323).

Conclusion

To date, CDRPs have had to struggle with a range of challenges that have served to limit their impact on crime reduction. It is also clear that many CDRPs may as yet have failed to evaluate the impact of those crime reduction strategies on which they have embarked (House of Commons Committee of Public Accounts, 2005, p 5). While, for example, it was claimed by government that over £1 billion was spent through CDRPs over the previous five years (2000–05), less than half of the partnerships considered that their work had contributed to a measurable reduction in crime (House of Commons Committee of Public Accounts, 2005, p 5). In evidence to the Committee of Public Accounts, a senior Home Office official commented that the extent to which partnerships had contributed to the reduction in crime was in the nature of things 'inherently unknowable'. Yet that would not in any way impede the Home Office from setting yet further crime reduction targets over the next three years for every CDRP starting in 2005/06 (Oral Evidence to Committee of Public Accounts, 2005).

Although problems arise in relation to the work of CDRPs, it is also the case that local police commanders overwhelmingly support the partnerships. Clear evidence of this positive perception of the CDRP process has come from the Police Superintendents Association, whose members have closest contact with local partnerships. Most recently, the association has commented in relation to CDRPs, for example, that:

> Many BCUs have been singularly successful through their CDRPs in identifying even the most hard to reach groups within their communities and giving them a voice and the opportunity to participate in BCU objective setting. (Police Superintendents Association, 2004, p 6)

The association has also argued that to give the local BCU democratic legitimacy there is now a need to establish a mechanism that enables locally elected representatives to share responsibility for police services within the locality with the BCU commander. Locally elected representatives should, the association believes, also be closely involved in the selection of local BCU commanders (Police Superintendents Association, 2004, p 6). This would perhaps also put a brake on the rapid circulation of officers of this rank. The former Home Secretary himself recently identified the need for greater continuity at commander level (Clarke, 2005).

The future role of CDRPs is also likely to be enhanced by the commitment to the recently launched Neighbourhood Policing strategy linked to 'reassurance policing'. For these reasons among others, there must be an expectation that the work of CDRPs in developing appropriate community safety strategies will continue. Alongside that could go closer police and local authority links that together are likely to provide both more effective and locally accountable policing in England and Wales.

References

Alexander, A. (1982) *Local Government in Britain since Reorganisation*, London: Allen and Unwin.

Audit Commission (2002) *Community Safety Partnerships*, London: Audit Commission.

Bayley, D. (1994) *Police for the Future*, Oxford: Oxford University Press.

Clarke, C. (2005) 'Address to ACPO Conference', Birmingham, July.

HMIC (Her Majesty's Inspectorate of Constabulary) (2002) *Getting Down to Basics. Emerging Findings from BCU Inspections in 2001*, London: Home Office,

HMIC (2002/03) *Cleveland Police Inspection Report*, London: Home Office.

House of Commons Committee of Public Accounts (2005) *Reducing Crime: The Home Office Working with Crime and Disorder Reduction Partnerships*, HC 147, London: The Stationery Office.

House of Commons Home Affairs Committee (2005) *Anti-Social Behaviour*, Fifth Report of Session 2004-05, HC 80-1, London: The Stationery Office.

LGA (Local Government Association) Community Safety Advisers Group (2004/ 05) Minutes of Meetings, August 2004, February and May 2005 at Local Government House, Smith Square, London, Internal Briefing Paper.

Loveday, B. (2004) 'Police reform and local government: new opportunities for improving community safety arrangements in England and Wales', *Crime Prevention and Community Safety: An International Journal*, vol 6, no 2, pp 7-19.

Loveday, B. (2005a) 'The challenge of police reform', *Public Money and Management*, vol 25, no 5, pp 275-81.

Loveday, B. (2005b) 'Learning from the 2004 crime audit. How effective are local partnerships proving to be?', Paper presented to the Strategic Leadership Development Programme Community Partnership Conference, Centrex Bramshill, Hook, Hampshire, 23-24 June.

Loveday, B. (2005c) 'Performance management: threat or opportunity? Current problems surrounding the application of performance management on public services', *The Police Journal*, vol 78, no 2, pp 97-102.

Loveday, B., Button, M., Fletcher, R. and Blackbourn, D. (2004) *Isle of Wight Safer Communities Partnership Board 'Crime and Drugs Audit'*, Portsmouth: University of Portsmouth.

NACRO (National Association for the Care and Resettlement of Offenders) and LGA (Local Government Association) (1999) *Crime and Disorder Act 1998 – Section 17: A Briefing Paper for Local Authorities on the Implementation of Section 17 of the CADA 1998*.

NAO (National Audit Office) (2004) *Reducing Crime: The Home Office working with Crime and Disorder Reduction Partnerships*, Report by Comptroller and Auditor General, HC 16, London: The Stationery Office.

O'Byrne, M. (2001) *Changing Policing; Revolution not Evolution*, Lyme Regis: Russell House Publishing.

Police Superintendents Association (2003) *Factors that Impact on BCU Performance*, Pangbourne: Police Superintendents Association.

Police Superintendents Association (2004) *Moving Policing Forward – Proposals for the Future*, Pangbourne: Police Superintendents Association.

Povey, K. (2000) 'Policing Public Order', Seminar Series at European Centre for the Study of Policing, The Open University, Milton Keynes.

Tilley, N. (2005) 'Crime reduction: a quarter century review', *Public Money and Management*, vol 25, no 5, pp 267-74.

Wilson, D. and Game, C. (1998) *Local Government in the United Kingdom* (2nd edn), London: Macmillan.

EIGHT

Community safety and the private security sector

Mark Button

Introduction

The growing role of the private security industry in policing and the criminal justice system has been recognised by academics across the globe (South, 1988; Johnston, 1992; Rigakos, 2002). Studies have illustrated the expansion of the role of private security and the greater number of security personnel employed than the public police in most industrialised countries (Jones and Newburn, 1998; De Waard, 1999). Research has also highlighted the ability of private security firms to operate core state functions, such as prisons, custody suites and tagging schemes (James et al, 1997; Button, 2002). There are very few activities in the broader criminal justice system and policing that private security is not undertaking or is not capable of doing (Forst and Manning, 1999). This research, however, has so far neglected a specific overview of private security firms' contribution to community safety. In part, this is because the contribution to policing and criminal justice more broadly overlaps community safety. Nevertheless, such is the growing importance of community safety as a concept and as a strategy that an assessment of the contribution of the private security sector in this context is timely.

Before we embark on this, however, it is important to examine the concept of 'community safety'. Its origins lie in politicians from the left seeking to widen the ownership of the problem of crime to organisations other than the police (Hughes, 1998). There was much evidence to show crime was the product of a wide range of factors, many of which were beyond the control of the police. Many agencies, both public and private, and most notably local authorities, carried out functions that could impact on crime, but were not fully mobilised in this role. The situational and social crime prevention measures that could be pursued, when targeted within a specific community by organisations working in partnership to pursue them, has become the essence of what is meant by the term 'community safety' (Gilling, 1997). However, for many, the use of safety would seem to encompass a much broader range of issues, including accidents, food hygiene, risks from dangerous products and pollution, to name a few; but when the activities of community safety partnerships are explored, however, they tend to focus predominantly on crime-related risks and therefore what most would describe as 'security'. In the UK, 'community safety' is used rather than 'community security', but in France, our separate English notions of 'security' and 'safety' are combined in the single noun *sécurité* (Gill, 1996). For these and other reasons, Johnston and Shearing (2003) have argued for the 'governance of security'. There is not the space here, nor is it the intention of this chapter, to become embroiled in these debates. However, the use of 'community security' could be equally applicable and is probably more appropriate than 'community safety'.

Before we embark on an assessment of the contribution of the private security sector to community safety, however, it would be useful first to examine the scope and activities of this sector. There are many different conceptions of what constitutes the private security industry (see Manunta, 1999; George and Button, 2000). This chapter, however, uses George and Button's (2000) definition of private security, which comprises manned security services (static manned guarding, cash-in-transit services, door supervision and stewarding services, close protection services); private sector detention services; security storage and destruction services; professional security services; and the security products sector. Many of these sub-sectors are not directly or significantly engaged in community safety. Therefore, for the purposes of this chapter, the main focus of the private security sector will be on the contribution of manned guarding sectors and specifically security guards (or officers) and door supervisors (or bouncers). Some of the other sub-sectors also contribute to community safety, such as private investigators providing witness statements on antisocial behaviour and security consultants advising on crime prevention. Nevertheless, the rationale will be to focus on those sectors providing some of the most significant contributions to community safety that also provide the most issues for debate.

It is also very timely to undertake this review for a number of reasons. First, in the UK the most reliable measures of crime indicate a continuing and overall falling trend, yet there is still significant insecurity among the public. This paradox has led to opportunities for the private security sector to fill this 'gap'. Second, and partly linked to the former, there has been a growing commodification of security. Third, there have been a number of statutes that have recognised and given scope to enhance the role of the private security industry in the delivery of community safety. These include the 1998 Crime and Disorder Act, the 2001 Private Security Industry Act and the 2002 Police Reform Act. Fourth, the Labour government has been keen to continue with the privatisation agenda of the last Conservative government and the policy of 'contestability' has emerged, providing further opportunities for the private security sector in community safety. Finally, the nature of the spaces where we live as communities and pursue our leisure activities is increasingly moving from the public to the quasi-public and private domains. All of these issues warrant further consideration before we examine in greater depth the role of the private security sector.

The paradox of falling crime but rising insecurity

Despite regular recent good news about the reduction of crime from the annual crime statistics drawn from both the recorded crime statistics and the British Crime Survey (BCS), public anxieties over crime and antisocial behaviour (ASB) remain high. Since reaching a peak in 1995, crime rates recorded in the BCS have fallen by 39% and the risk of being a victim of crime is the lowest since the BCS began in 1981 (Dodd et al, 2004). Set against this fall in crime, however, is a belief that crime is rising. Indeed, in the 2003/04 BCS, 65% of those surveyed thought crime had increased in the previous two years and one third thought crime had increased 'a lot'. Alongside this, a high proportion of adults are still worried about crime and various forms of ASB, although this is falling (Dodd et al, 2004). These issues have emerged at the micro-level in many local crime audits and resulting strategies (House of Commons Home Affairs Committee, 2005; and, for example, Safer Portsmouth Partnership, 2005).

It is not surprising in this context that surveys of the public have consistently shown a high demand for the reassuring presence of a police officer on the street. In a poll conducted for the Police Federation, 80% of people wanted more police patrolling their area (Police Federation, 1995). The same research found that only one person in a hundred wanted less patrolling. In research conducted for the Audit Commission, the only area of police work where there was significant public dissatisfaction was the level of foot patrol at minus 20% (Audit Commission, 1996). That same research also found that 72% of people are always reassured by the sight of a patrol officer and a further 16% are reassured if they feel vulnerable. However, there is much evidence that police patrol has limited impact on crime. Indeed, research has illustrated that a constable on patrol is only likely to pass within 100 yards of a burglary every eight years (Police Foundation and Policy Studies Institute, 1996). Furthermore, in a typical police constabulary, only one in 20 police officers are likely to be on the beat at any given time, with the rest on other shifts, training, in court, sick, in specialist roles, and so on (Audit Commission, 1996). Thus expanding the numbers of police officers on patrol would require either significant reform of police working practices or substantial resources, set against the knowledge of police managers that such radical proposals would have a limited impact on crime. It is therefore not surprising that other policy initiatives – including those from the private sector – have emerged to fill this gap, a point that will be considered later (Button, 2002; Crawford and Lister, 2004).

The commodification of security and safety

Linked to the paradox of falling crime and rising insecurity is the increasing commodification of security (Loader, 1997; Johnston and Shearing, 2003). In addition to the usual consumer durables, people want security to protect themselves, their possessions and their family. Security has become openly traded like any other commodity, with products and services available, ranging from simple intruder alarms to rapid armed response units in some countries (Singh, 2005). Combined with this, an increasingly dominant neo-liberal thinking has encouraged individuals and organisations to take responsibility for a wider range of functions, including security (Garland, 1996; O'Malley, 1996). The important implication of these factors, however, is that if the state (either nationally or locally) fails (or, more importantly, is perceived to fail) to supply the appropriate level of security, many of those who can afford to will therefore purchase additional security. This is most visible in cases where residents pay security firms to patrol their communities, even when they do not have the sanction of the police (Noaks, 2000; Sharp and Wilson, 2000). Residents may also choose to live in gated communities or to shop, work and pursue leisure activities in locations where the level of security is felt to be appropriate (Atkinson et al, n.d.). Therefore, failing to recognise the growing demand for security combined with encouraging the public to take on more security responsibilities for themselves opens up communities to the marketisation of security and all the imbalances, injustices and other problems that that may involve.

Legislative developments

During the past 10 years, there have been some major legislative developments that not only shape the community safety infrastructure, but also define, enhance and legitimise the role of the private security sector. The 1998 Crime and Disorder Act created a new statutory framework for the establishment of Crime and Disorder Reduction Partnerships (CDRPs) and the establishment of a cycle of audits (Loveday, 1999). This legislation does not directly deal with the private security sector. However, what it does do is recognise that community safety is not the responsibility of one agency but rather a partnership of bodies that should work together. This includes the private sector and therefore private security. Indeed, many CDRPs have embraced this by making representatives from the private security sector and other private bodies members of CDRP sub-groups and even the main boards. It marks the end of the myth of a monopoly or near monopoly of control of the public police, which had really disappeared many decades ago (Johnston, 2000).

The 2001 Private Security Industry Act did more than introduce a statute to regulate the private security industry (Button, 2003). Among its aims was to reduce crime and disorder, drive out criminals from the private security industry, and raise the standards of the industry (*Hansard*, 28 March 2001, col 967). The legislation recognised that many private security services and products have a 'crime prevention' role and that by improving their standards (which were generally perceived to be low) there could be a positive impact on reducing crime and increasing security at limited cost to the taxpayer. Hidden in the regulating agenda for the security firms was a recognition and hope that regulation would bring greater legitimacy, more opportunities and ultimately increased profits.

If the 2001 Private Security Industry Act did not formally set out a greater role for the private security industry, then the 2002 Police Reform Act was unambiguous in this respect. The legislation covered a wide range of provisions but most significantly set out a regime for the contracting out of various police functions and the granting of special legal powers to such personnel. Most significantly, the legislation created a system whereby chief constables can accredit community safety schemes that may in return provide access to various powers. These include the power to issue fixed penalty notices relating to road traffic offences, dog fouling and disposal of litter; to require an address from a person acting in an antisocial manner; and to confiscate alcohol and tobacco being consumed in public places; and powers relating to the removal of abandoned vehicles. Such powers cover many (but not all) of those that community support officers were to receive in the same legislation.

These three pieces of legislation are therefore very important in formalising the mixed economy in community safety, in particular recognising the legitimacy of the private security sector in carrying out many of these functions and in formally identifying a variety of specific tasks they can undertake.

From privatisation to contestability

Another development that has influenced the expansion of the private security sector has been the privatisation agenda. Many aspects of the criminal justice system have been subjected to privatisation, of which the contracting out of police and prison services has enabled the private security sector to expand (Johnston, 1992; Button, 2002). More recently, with the advent of the National Offender Management Service (NOMS), contracting out has been replaced by the new term 'contestability' (NOMS, 2005). Whatever the current 'buzzword', the principle of identifying services which can be undertaken by the private or voluntary sector seems set to remain and expand under the current Labour government. Many of the services delivered by the public community safety infrastructure could, and probably will, face the expanding policy of contestability. Indeed, many security companies are now actively promoting such services, for example, Group 4 with its 'community safety officers' (Group 4, 2005).

Spatial developments

There have also been spatial developments surfacing that have enhanced the contribution of private security in providing community safety, but also pose challenges to creating community safety. At one level, there has been a growth of so-called 'gated communities'. These are housing developments on private land where access to the public is restricted. Such developments have expanded massively in countries such as the US, South Africa and Brazil (Blakely and

Snyder, 1999; Huggins, 2000; Singh, 2005). However, even in the UK, over 1,000 such schemes have been identified, some of which are guarded by security officers as well as being fitted with physical and electronic security devices (Atkinson and Flint, 2004). Such communities are largely driven by a desire for exclusivity and security (Atkinson et al, n.d.).

The security officers and devices that protect these communities have significant implications for community safety. First, they create segregation in communities, whereby those residents living in secure areas have an interest in and commitment to their own safety rather than the safety of the community as a whole. Second, as these communities do not seek to address underlying causes of criminality and ASB, they may merely displace these problems elsewhere. Third, the majority of people outside the gated communities are left with the problems and the 'bog standard' security infrastructure to deal with these. Increasingly, this is not enough to satisfy the community's need for security. Finally, an essential element of community safety is partnership between agencies and residents to confront common problems. Gated communities represent the model of opting out from such cooperation. As one of the police officers interviewed in a study of gated communities by Atkinson and Flint (2004, p 17) noted: 'Overall, there has been a negative impact. It is very much a separate community whose residents use their own [private] schools and shops.... There is very little interaction with other local residents, and it has not brought social or economic benefits'.

Linked to the development of gated communities is the expansion of shopping and leisure facilities in purpose-built private space. In some towns and cities, private shopping malls have replaced high-street shops and leisure facilities have become the main focus of entertainment. As such places are built on private land, landowners (and their agents) can make use of an impressive range of rights in relation to their property, including the right to determine who has access and the conditions on which they remain on site. Therefore access to many outlets that provide essential goods and services, such as post offices, is at the whim of the landowner. There is a concern that the private security officers who enforce order in such locations will use their powers to arbitrarily exclude, among others, 'down-and-outs', the unemployed, teenagers and certain ethnic minorities, creating what Charles Reich feared would be an 'internal exile' (cited in Gray, 1994, p 175).

These sites have become the subject of legal debate and some have argued that they should be legally treated as 'quasi-public' or 'hybrid' spaces, where, for example, access should be based on a reasonable rather than an arbitrary basis (Gray and Gray, 1999a). However, as the decision in *CIN Properties v Rawlings* [1995] 2 EGLR 130 shows, this is not yet the case. In this case, CIN, the leaseholder of a shopping centre, sought to indefinitely ban a group of unemployed youths from the precincts of the centre after unsubstantiated allegations of misbehaviour. The ban was subsequently re-enforced with a court injunction. CIN argued that as it was the owner of the property it did not have to show any good cause for denying them entry. The Court of Appeal upheld this decision and the European

Commission of Human Rights was unable to intervene because the UK – at the time – had not ratified the guarantee of liberty of movement. This decision has effectively given property owners unprecedented power to regulate citizens' freedom of movement, assembly, association and speech. However, the implementation of the 1998 Human Rights Act, Gray and Gray argue:

> ... will result in a significant curtailment of the estate owner's right in respect of quasi-public property. The incorporation of Convention freedoms will effectively impose on landowners a duty to demonstrate that any exclusion from privately owned areas of quasi-public space is justified on reasonable grounds which do not contravene the guaranteed liberties of the citizen. (1999b, p 50)

Whether such a situation will arise in the UK is open to legal debate. Whatever the result, the expansion of such space creates further challenges for those responsible for community safety. Given that people are expected to spend increasing amounts of shopping and leisure time in such spaces, they will do so in accordance with landowners' safety regimes. These may or may not be undertaken in partnership. And even if they are, it means that the security of significant public locations is subject to the negotiations of the partnership and the landowner, rather than the democratic will of the community. Take, for instance, the recent decision to ban people wearing hooded tops at the Bluewater Shopping Centre in Kent (BBC News, 2005). Even if we were to accept that people in hooded tops are at a higher risk of misbehaving (which is unproven), their exclusion would merely divert them elsewhere, where the much less well-resourced public infrastructure would have to deal with them. Further, could this mark the 'thin end of the wedge', leading to social cleansing of other 'stigmatised groups' under wider discriminatory criteria and ultimately suggesting more sinister undertones?

Now that some of the most salient developments influencing the expanding role of the private security sector in community safety have been considered, it would seem appropriate to examine some examples in more depth. The next section will therefore discuss the mixed economy of community safety, exploring some of the most prominent contributions of the private security sector.

The mixed economy of provision in community safety

The delivery of community safety services has become a mixed economy of the public, private and voluntary sectors. A number of attempts have been made to classify this 'mixed economy', which has also been termed the 'extended police family', the 'pluralisation' and the 'fragmentation' of policing (Bayley and Shearing, 1996; Johnston, 2000; Button, 2002). One of the clearest attempts to deconstruct this mixed economy so far is Crawford and Lister's (2004, p 21) typology of policing initiatives, which includes:

- *Additional public policing* – full-sworn police officers supplied for an additional fee.
- *Additional civilian policing* – additional non-sworn police personnel, such as community support officers.
- *Municipal policing* – Neighbourhood Warden schemes or other local authority/ registered social landlord-employed policing.
- *Civilian policing* – voluntary resident patrols or varieties of neighbourhood watch.
- *Commercial policing* – private security patrols.

Crawford and Lister's focus on *commercial policing* is on those private security patrols created through the state by contractisation. However, commercial policing has also emerged through the processes identified above, for example, the changing context of space, such as the growth of nightclubs, shopping malls, and so on. It has also flourished in areas where there is a disparity in state provision and consumers are willing to pay to fill the gap, most notably through provision sold directly to communities by entrepreneurial providers. The contribution of private security in these different areas will now be examined.

Private patrols

The growth of patrols by private security firms has been difficult to gauge, although there have been a number of attempts based on different and sometimes questionable methodologies. In 1993 Birch (1993) estimated that there were over 1,000 private patrols in existence in the UK, although this figure was not based on any formal research. In research conducted for the government's initiative on Neighbourhood Wardens, Jacobson and Saville were able to collate information from 50 schemes covering a wide range of different models, although this encompassed local authority-employed patrols as well (Jacobson and Saville, 1999). Coming from another angle, that of the providers, Crawford and Lister (2004) in a limited survey of private security-manned guarding firms were able to identify 47 – relatively small firms – that offered mobile patrol services. It is therefore difficult to gauge the actual size of this sector.

Probably the most accepted form of private patrol are security officers contracted by local authorities and housing associations to patrol specific public areas. Crawford and Lister (2004) cite a number of examples of this type of patrol. For instance, in York, 19 of the city's 22 council wards purchase Community Ranger patrols supplied by a private security firm. In another example, in the small market town of Rothwell, the local council purchased 25 one-hour patrols per week from a security firm. Jacobson and Saville (1999) also examined patrols provided by security firms contracted to local authorities. In Southwark, the local authority employed a private security firm to patrol the Aylesbury estate. The scheme was developed to combat fear of crime, and tackle antisocial behaviour, graffiti and drug nuisance among more general crime problems. The scheme was managed by a neighbourhood office and was put out to tender each year (Jacobson and Saville, 1999). Stockport's Town Wardens are another example of a contracted-out patrolling force that was originally funded by a £100,000 grant from the Single Regeneration Budget.

Perhaps the most extreme model of private security patrols in housing estates – private albeit not gated – is the example of Intelligarde in Toronto, Canada. The work of this security company has been the subject of detailed research by Rigakos (2002). He illustrates how in housing estates at the bottom of the socioeconomic spectrum where there was endemic antisocial behaviour and crime and drugs problems, and where the public police had largely withdrawn, Intelligarde filled the gap by providing tough enforcement-based policing – termed 'parapolicing' – that increased the residents' security to their satisfaction.

There have also been a variety of 'entrepreneurial patrols' that have emerged in residential areas operated by private security companies funded by subscriptions from local residents. These tend to have 'lukewarm' support from the police and in some cases even invoke hostility. Household Security of Doncaster provides an example of this type of initiative. Founded by an ex-offender, Malcolm Tetley, the company provided uniformed patrols funded by a weekly fee of £1 per week from residents. In 1996, it had an estimated 3,000 customers (Sharp and Wilson, 2000). Residents received a sticker in their windows stating, 'Warning, these premises patrolled by Household Security', and Household Security officers patrolled the streets night and day on foot and in vans. Sharp and Wilson encountered a positive attitude to Household Security for the service provided. Many residents were satisfied with the more proactive attitude to crime of Household Security compared with that of the police. There was also a belief that Household Security would be more likely to use informal methods to settle problems, such as a 'kick up the backside'. The local police were very 'lukewarm' towards the whole venture in their public pronouncements and there was a belief by Malcolm Tetley that the police were actually harassing his staff and publicly 'rubbishing' them.

Another study of an 'entrepreneurial' private patrol involved the private security firm Merryside (Noaks, 2000). As in the Doncaster example, Merryside (comprising a managing director and five guards) provided a patrolling service to an estate of 4,000 homes for a fee of £2 per household per week (pensioners paid £1). Noaks's research found a high degree of satisfaction among the subscribers; 92% were either satisfied or very satisfied with the service and over three quarters thought that crime had declined in the area as a result of the patrol. Of the non-subscribers, only 25% were dissatisfied with the service. As in Doncaster, there was a degree of hostility towards the company from the local police, such that they were even excluded from the local partnership under the 1998 Crime and Disorder Act. These two examples of research on 'entrepreneurial' patrols illustrate the general positive regard among residents for these types of initiatives, something McManus (1995) also found, but also the negative response of the police to 'entrepreneurial' initiatives.

Quasi-public space

There have been a number of studies that have explored private security in quasi-public space, which probably reflects the most significant growth in private security activity. Wakefield (2003) undertook a study of three shopping/leisure facilities employing 56 security officers with strong working relationships with the police and significant policing roles. In a study primarily about surveillance, McCahill (2002) also investigated security officers and found widespread evidence of the exclusion from the facilities of certain groups of people based on judgements that they might be 'troublesome'. Hutchinson and O'Conner (2005) also investigated a shopping mall, illustrating the importance of security officers in surveying and sanctioning the mall's rules. Button (2005) has conducted a detailed analysis of a retail/leisure complex employing 31 security officers, illustrating their significant role in policing and their involvement in exclusion, quelling disorder and apprehending shoplifters to name just some of their key activities. Table 8.1 below illustrates the security context and the characteristics of Pleasure Southquay at the time of the research. Above all, it illustrates how such a sizeable place is policed largely by private patrols backed up by various security devices and strategies, leaving the public police a role only in high-risk periods (Friday and Saturday nights when pubs and nightclubs close), or on occasional visits to provide a police presence.

There is much in these studies that requires further debate and consideration. In the context of this chapter, however, it is worth noting the following:

- security officers assuming the primary roles in policing this 'new' space;
- strong partnerships developing between the public and private sectors at the micro-level, involving cooperation in dealing with incidents and the sharing of intelligence;
- security officers making active use of the legal tools available to them;
- varied mechanisms for the governance and accountability for the security officers operating in these places.

Table 8.1: Policing Pleasure Southquay

NODAL CONTEXT	SECURITY CONTEXT
33 acres of former MoD land; 65 shopping outlets; 20 restaurants, bars and coffee shops; 11-screen cinema; bowling complex.	31 security officers, additional security officers and door supervisors employed in shops/bars
1,450 parking spaces	Limited entrances/exits linked to access control policy
100,000 square feet of office space	CCTV
310 homes: further expansion of all of above	Design, image and reputation
5,000+ visitors at peak times	Ad hoc police presence on demand and at high-risk times
116 incidents of crime recorded in first year of opening	

The night-time economy

The other significant arena of community safety where the private security sector is involved is in the night-time economy (NTE). Hobbs et al (2005) found that on a typical Friday or Saturday night in Manchester around 130,000 people are attracted to the area. During this period, typically there will be only 40 police officers engaged in public order duty, compared with an estimated 1,000 door supervisors undertaking the primary policing role. The ratios are similar throughout the country in NTE centres (Hobbs et al, 2005). Research has illustrated that the peak time for violent offending is weekend nights around pubs and clubs (Finney, 2004). Indeed, in one case study, it was found that 45% of all logs for violence were made between the hours of 9pm and 3am (Hobbs et al, 2003). In many towns and cities, the problems of violence and disorder in the NTE have become major concerns for the community safety infrastructure (Squires et al, 2004; Home Affairs Committee, 2005). This concern, however, must be reconciled with the fact that the main agents for policing the NTE are door supervisors, not the public police. Door supervisors have therefore assumed a significant role in ensuring public safety, and no effective strategy to deal with disorder can be pursued without them. As Hobbs et al (2005, p 169) argue:

> Consequently, control strategies and regulatory attempts to incorporate the night-time population rely heavily upon intimidatory devices in the form of commercial security staff such as bouncers or door staff.

Conclusion

The private security sector is assuming a growing role in the delivery of services that are central to community safety. There are numerous forces at work that have influenced this expansion. These include the paradox of falling crime but rising insecurity, the increasing commodification of security, legislative changes, the pursuit of privatisation (or contestability) and the changing nature of space. These developments have combined to create an increasingly fragmented mixed economy of policing, of which the private security sector has assumed an expanding and increasingly important place. Patrolling public streets, policing shopping malls and leisure facilities and the security of the NTE have become major places of operation for private security. This mixed economy of policing is posing many challenges for policy makers, but it is in the field of community safety that we shall restrict the concluding comments.

Perhaps the biggest challenge is in developing effective partnerships with the private security sector. The status and influence of private security in CDRP partnerships varies significantly and their growing role suggests that they need to be effectively represented in some manner. Linked to this is the major challenge of coordinating and controlling (in an accountable fashion) the contributions of the private security sector. The growing role and size of this sector is complemented by an increasingly diverse and fragmented contribution. Ensuring that this resource works to the same agenda and does not pursue a purely sectional interest is a significant challenge (see Coleman, 2004 for a critique). Failure to achieve this may exacerbate further the growing inequities in security provision, creating havens of security for the rich and privileged, with the rest excluded and left with basic and inadequate state provision. Finally, with the expanding role of the private security sector comes the need to ensure appropriate accountability and governance and there remain question marks over the effectiveness of the structures that have been created. Ultimately, the forces unleashing the expansion of private security in community safety are largely unstoppable. The challenge will be to attach reins to it, so at least there is some control and influence over where the 'beast' goes.

References

Atkinson, R. and Flint, J. (2004) 'The fortress UK? Gated communities, the spatial revolt of the elites and time space trajectories of segregation', ESRC Centre for Neighbourhood Research Paper 17 (www.bristol.ac.uk/sps/cnrpaperspdf/cnr17pap.pdf, accessed 3 June 2005).

Atkinson, R., Flint, J., Blandy, S. and Lister, D. (n.d.) 'The extent and neighbourhood impacts of gated communities' (www.bristol.ac.uk/sps/cnrpapersword/report_gated12.doc, accessed 20 June 2005).

Audit Commission (1996) *Streetwise – Effective Police Patrol*, London: HMSO.

Bayley, D. and Shearing, C.D. (1996) 'The future of policing', *Law and Society Review*, vol 30, no 3, pp 585-606.

BBC News (2005) 'Mall bans shoppers' hooded tops' (news.bbc.co.uk/1/hi/england/kent/4534903.stm, accessed 3 June 2005).

Birch, G. (1993) 'The security sham', *Police Review*, 19 February.

Blakely, E.J. and Snyder, M.J. (1999) *Fortress America – Gated Communities in the United States*, Washington, DC: Brookings Institution Press.

Button, M. (2002) *Private Policing*, Cullompton: Willan Publishing.

Button, M. (2003) 'Private security industry law in Europe: the case of Great Britain', in S. Outer and R. Stober (eds) *Recht des Sicherheitsgewerbes*, Cologne: Heymanns, pp 93-103.

Button, M. (2005) 'Big fish in little ponds: private security officers and the policing of private and hybrid space', Unpublshed PhD thesis, London School of Economics and Political Science.

Coleman, R. (2004) *Reclaiming the Streets: Surveillance, Social Control and the City*, Cullompton: Willan Publishing.

Crawford, A. and Lister, S. (2004) *The Extended Policing Family*, York: Joseph Rowntree Foundation.

De Waard, J. (1999) 'The private security industry in international perspective', *European Journal of Criminal Policy and Research*, vol 7, no 2, pp 143-74.

Dodd, T., Nicholas, S., Povey, D. and Walker, A. (2004) 'Crime in England and Wales 2003/2004', Home Office Statistical Bulletin 10/04 (www.homeoffice.gov.uk/rds/pdfs04/hosb1004chap123.pdf, accessed 6 June 2005).

Finney, A. (2004) 'Violence in the night-time economy: key findings from the research', Findings 214 (www.homeoffice.gov.uk/rds/pdfs04/r214.pdf, accessed 6 June 2005).

Forst, B. and Manning, P.K. (1999) *The Privatisation of Policing*, Washington, DC: George Washington University Press.

Garland, D. (1996) 'The limits of sovereign state: strategies of crime control in contemporary society', *British Journal of Criminology*, vol 33, no 4, pp 445-71.

George, B. and Button, M. (2000) *Private Security*, Leicester: Perpetuity Press.

Gill, M. (1996) 'Risk, security and crime prevention: an international forum for developing theory and practice', *International Journal of Risk, Security and Crime Prevention*, vol 1, pp 11-17.

Gilling, D. (1997) *Crime Prevention Theory, Policy and Politics*, London: UCL Press.

Gray, K. (1994) 'Equitable property', *Current Legal Problems*, vol 47, no 2, pp 157-214.

Gray, K. and Gray, S.F. (1999a) *Land Law*, London: Butterworths.

Gray, K. and Gray, S.F. (1999b) 'Private property and public propriety', in J. McLean (ed) (1999) *Property and Constitution*, Oxford: Hart Publishing, pp 11-19.

Group 4 (2005) 'Security and safety services: community safety officers' (www.group4.co.uk/index.asp?PageID=30, accessed 21 June 2005).

Hansard (2002) 28 March, col 967.

Hobbs, D., Hadfield, P., Lister, S. and Winlow, S. (2003) *Bouncers: Violence and Governance in the Night-time Economy*, Oxford: Oxford University Press.

Hobbs, D., Winlow, S., Hadfield, P. and Lister, S. (2005) 'Violent hypocrisy governance and the night-time economy', *European Journal of Criminology*, vol 2, no 2, pp 161-83.

House of Commons Home Affairs Committee (2005) *Anti-Social Behaviour*, Fifth Report of Session 2004-05, HC 80-I, London: The Stationery Office.

Huggins, M.K. (2000) 'Urban violence and police privatisation in Brazil: blended invisibility', *Social Justice*, vol 27, pp 113-34.

Hughes, G. (1998) *Understanding Crime Prevention*, Buckingham: Open University Press.

Hutchinson, S. and O'Conner, D. (2005) 'Policing the new commons: corporate security governance on mass private property in Canada', *Policing and Society*, vol 15, no 2, pp 125-44.

Jacobson, J. and Saville, E. (1999) *Neighbourhood Warden Schemes: An Overview*, CRRS Paper 2, London: Home Office.

James, A.J., Bottomley, A.K., Liebling, A. and Clare, E. (1997) *Privatizing Prisons: Rhetoric or Reality*, London: Sage Publications.

Johnston, L. (1992) *The Rebirth of Private Policing*, London: Routledge.

Johnston, L. (2000) *Policing Britain: Risk, Security and Governance*, London: Longman.

Johnston, L. and Shearing, C.D. (2003) *Governing Security*, London: Routledge.

Jones, T. and Newburn, T. (1998) *Private Security and Public Policing*, Oxford: Clarendon Press.

Lister, S., Hobbs, D., Hall, S. and Winlow, S. (2000) 'Violence in the night-time economy; bouncers: the reporting, recording and prosecution of assaults', *Policing and Society*, vol 10, pp 383-402.

Loader, I. (1997) 'Private security and the demand for protection in contemporary Britain', *Policing and Society*, vol 7, no 2, pp 143-62.

Loveday, B. (1999) 'Tough on crime or tough on the causes of crime? An evaluation of Labour's crime and disorder legislation', *Crime Prevention and Community Safety: An International Journal*, vol 1, pp 7-24.

Manunta, G. (1999) 'What is security?', *Security Journal*, vol 12, no 3, pp 57-66.

McCahill, M. (2002) *The Surveillance Web*, Cullompton: Willan Publishing.

McManus, M. (1995) *From Fate to Choice: Private Bobbies, Public Beats*, Aldershot: Avebury.

Noaks, L. (2000) 'Private cops on the block: a review of the role of private security in residential communities', *Policing and Society*, vol 10, no 2, pp 143-61.

NOMS (2005) 'Corporate plan 2005-2008' (www.noms.homeoffice.gov.uk/downloads/NOMS_Corporate_Plan_2005-2008.pdf, accessed 20 June 2005).

O'Malley, P. (1996) 'Risk and responsibility', in A. Barry, T. Osborne and N. Rose (eds) *Foucault and Political Reason*, London: UCL Press, pp 189-207.

Police Federation (1995) *Survey of Public Attitudes to Policing*, Surbiton: Police Federation.

Police Foundation and Policy Studies Institute (1996) *The Role and Responsibilities of the Police*, Independent Inquiry, London: Police Foundation and Policy Studies Institute.

Rigakos, G.S. (2002) *The New Parapolice*, Toronto: University of Toronto Press.

Safer Portsmouth Partnership (2005) 'Crime, disorder and substance misuse audit 2004' (www.portsmouth.gov.uk/media/Safer_Portsmouth_Partnership_Audit_summary.pdf, accessed 11 June 2005).

Sharp, D. and Wilson, D. (2000) '"Household security": private policing and vigilantism in Doncaster', *The Howard Journal of Criminal Justice*, vol 39, no 2, pp 113-31.

Singh, A. (2005) 'Private security and crime control', *Theoretical Criminology*, vol 9, no 2, 153-74.

South, N. (1988) *Policing for Profit*, London: Sage Publications.

Squires, P., Cunningham, L. and Fyvie-Gauld, M. (2004) *Perceptions of Anti-Social Behaviour in the London Borough of Sutton*, Brighton: Health and Social Policy Research Centre, University of Brighton.

Wakefield, A. (2003) *Selling Security – The Private Policing of Public Space*, Cullompton: Willan Publishing.

NINE

Outreach drug work and Crime and Disorder Reduction Partnerships: square pegs in round holes?

Adrian Barton

Introduction

Some social problems are predictable, allowing, in theory at least, a proactive and structured policy response: for example, the age ranges of the population can be measured via the use of demographics. This enables the clear identification of time periods when more resources will be needed by primary schools, pension funds and so on. Equally, in many of these policy areas, there is a clear and unambiguous 'lead' agency that will structure the nature of the response. Other forms of social problem often emerge from the need to respond to changes in behaviour. In those cases, the fluid and relatively immediate nature of the problem precludes planned responses, creating conditions where reactive policy is necessary and service provision responds to the problem in a relatively unstructured and sometimes ad hoc manner. In some of these policy areas, there may well be shared or disputed ownership of the problem, leading to mixed and often competing policy responses.

The latter scenario is clearly the case in the state's response to the rise in illicit drug use. Since the 1960s, when the use of illicit drugs for recreational and experimental purposes started an upward rise that continues today (Bean, 2002) to a level whereby some commentators (Parker et al, 1998) have claimed that illicit drug use is normalised among certain sections of the population, we have seen the health and criminal justice wings of the state, coupled with sections of the private sector, struggle to provide a response to the various problems associated with the use of illicit drugs. However, the era of unstructured and uncoordinated drug policy appears to be coming to an end, due in no short measure to New Labour's fixation with audit, the managerialist imperative to produce quantifiable criteria of 'success' and New Labour's particular obsession with crime and disorder (Power, 1994; Barton, 2003).

Taken together, these three factors have had an impact on drug services, largely because they have sought to merge the criminal justice and welfarist approaches to dealing with problematic drug use and users. While in many respects this makes sense – in the majority of cases the criminal justice and welfare teams will be dealing with the same person – the manner in which the managerialist changes have been made and the degree to which the needs of community safety have been moved to the forefront of drug work has had an impact on some of the 'weaker' members of multi-agency teams. Accordingly, this chapter examines the impact of New Labour's restructuring of drug services, paying special attention to the effects of the three factors cited above on voluntary sector, outreach-type agencies.

The account begins with a brief review of the growth of the drug–crime link, audit and best value under New Labour. It then examines the changes to drug services. From there, the chapter considers the nature of outreach work, highlighting the inherent problems such work has in terms of management, audit and closeness to the criminal justice system. It then moves on to discuss some empirical research and concludes with a discussion of the findings and their implications for policy and service provision.

Restructuring drug services: New Labour writ large?

This is not the place in which to provide a detailed history of service provision for drug users in the UK, the subject having been dealt with elsewhere (Blackman, 2004). Suffice to say that the state's response to the rapid rise in drug use over the past 40 years can be seen as either ad hoc or knee-jerk, depending on one's perspective. Service provision in that time has been a mixture of law and order-based criminal justice responses, highly specialised health responses, statutory social work-based welfarist provision and enthusiastic, often ex-user-founded, voluntary sector interventions. These have been variable in terms of both quantity and, more importantly for the client, quality, as well as exhibiting a distinct lack of coherent ideology across the agencies – at one and the same time, the same person could have been a criminal, patient and client, been punished by the criminal justice system, treated by the medics and receiving all manner of help and support from the non-statutory sector. Clearly, the problems generated by these approaches involve a lack of coordination between services and professional groups, inadequate or imbalanced resource allocation and the absence of structured and formalised training for staff (McGregor et al, 1991).

This uncoordinated response could not continue, especially given the political interest in the 'drug problem'. The roots of the current restructuring lie in the 1993 document *Across the Divide* (Howard et al, 1993) and the three major policy documents that followed – the Conservatives' 1995 *Tackling Drugs Together* (HM Government, 1995), New Labour's 1998 *Tackling Drugs To Build A Better Britain* (HM Government, 1998) and the *Updated Drugs Strategy* document (HM Government, 2002), all calling for a more 'joined-up' approach to service provision. Reflecting New Labour's recognition of the links between acquisitive crime and some forms of drug use, and resonating with Blagg et al's (1988) 'criminalisation of social policy' thesis, central government's drug policy is Home

Office-led, putting the needs of the criminal justice system – and community safety more generally – at the centre of drug work.

At the heart of this issue is the belief held by central government that crime is the major attendant problem of illicit drug use. It is not so much the primary criminality of possession that taxes the government and law enforcement agencies, but the secondary criminality associated with some drugs and drug users. As Bean (2002, pp 7-8) notes, on a *prima facie* level 'the links are clear: drug users require large amounts of money to support their habit and … they need to commit crime'. However, while causality may not be as clear-cut as politicians would have us believe, the fact remains that there is a core of users, mostly of heroin and crack cocaine, that is clearly committing a high volume of offences. On a common-sense level, addressing their drug use could lead to a reduction in crime and a concomitant increase in community safety, thus linking the outcomes of structured drug treatment programmes with the reduction of criminality. In essence, under New Labour this has become the rationale for drug policy and it has impacted on the direction of all drug work and all drug workers.

At the same time, New Labour has been equally keen to implement a 'modernisation' agenda, which Newman (2001) argues only serves to legitimate change, placing a stronger emphasis on collaboration and partnerships and widening the incorporation of voluntary sector agencies within forms of social provision. The problem for central government in this approach lies in the dilemma of needing to increase competition between agencies and sectors in order to provide 'best value' but still retain a politically driven managerial control structure over the direction of policy in the face of a group of professions jealously guarding their autonomy. Newman (2001) suggests that New Labour employed the following tactics to ensure that central control is retained across organisations, workers and projects: measuring outputs; specifying practices; introducing quality assurance and standards; and the use of audits and inspection to issue sanctions and threats. When she summarises the implications of this, Newman (2001, pp 93-4) neatly encapsulates the themes of the remainder of the chapter:

> … encouraging a greater conformity with an expected norm…. [T]hey may have significant consequences in terms of organisational isomorphism squeezing out the diversity of practice within a particular sector. Such diversity is an important source of innovation and, ultimately, of new models of policy and practice for the future.

All of the elements outlined above are visible in the most recent set of changes, which are led and directed nationally by the National Treatment Agency (NTA), and administered locally by Drug Action Teams (DATs). The former is a special health authority, created by the government in 2001, with a remit to increase the availability, capacity and effectiveness of treatment for drug users in England. The stated aim of NTA is to double the number of people in treatment from 100,000 in 1998 to 200,000 in 2008 and to increase the proportion of people completing or continuing treatment, year on year, in line with UK drug strategy targets (NTA, 2003). These changes are to be overseen locally by DATs working in conjunction with, and taking responsibility for, the commissioning of services by providers from all sectors. Service provision is organised around a four-tier system, itself based on a mental health model of intervention (NTA, 2003). The four-tier system comprises:

- Tier 1: Non-substance misuse specific services requiring interface with drug and alcohol treatment.
- Tier 2: Open access drug and alcohol treatment services.
- Tier 3: Structured community-based drug treatment services.
- Tier 4: Residential services for drug and alcohol misusers.

In addition, and fitting the pattern of audit and evaluation, great store is placed on measurement and monitoring of services. NTA is keen to stress that monitoring of the process of each tier in terms of activity, cost and outcome is only part of a wider evaluation that focuses on the effectiveness, efficiency and acceptability of a planned intervention in achieving stated objectives and to aid the identification of ways to improve and modify service provision. Moreover, NTA states that client/service user satisfaction is central to effective services (NTA, 2003).

These issues are clearly seen in relation to the focus of this chapter – outreach work. NTA demonstrates a clear recognition that the flexibility of outreach work raises issues for 'management structure, functioning and accountability' (NTA, 2003).

However, while the section of the NTA document specifically concerned with measurement and evaluation notes the importance of process, it is largely devoted to outcome measurement and, unsurprisingly, raises issues of cost and value for money. In turn, this is reflected in the suggested set of performance indicators (PIs) for outreach services, which are:

- the number of new clients contacted in a four-week period (that is, not seen by any other service in the past three months);
- the number of clients remaining in contact with the worker longer than three months;
- the number of clients referred per month to other services for help with drug misuse problems;
- the cost per new client contacted.

In addition, it is incumbent on all aspects of drug service delivery to include client satisfaction as part of any measurement (NTA, 2003).

While these PIs are commendable and ask outreach services to answer key questions about their performance, they also set parameters for the nature of what is and what is not done in relation to work – in short, work becomes that which is defined by, and can be measured in respect of, the PIs. It may be the case that the requirement of outreach workers and their managers to adhere to these PIs creates problems for the outreach workers in relation to their standard operating procedures (Hill, 1984), especially in terms of their relationships with their clients.

The overall result is an attempt to restructure outreach drug services in the now familiar New Labour manner, with clear organisational hierarchy, management structures, PIs and clear pathways to 'best value' service provision, with the ultimate aim of getting outreach work 'on message' and tailoring their approach to fitting a community safety-led paradigm. In some respects, this approach to the good husbandry of public monies is to be applauded. However, there is a nagging doubt in some minds (Barton, 2005; Gilling and Barton, 2005) that PIs become drivers of organisational provision, and work that falls outside of the parameters of the target, or work that is not susceptible to measurement and costing, either falls by the way or creates changes in work practices in order to better fit outcome and process indicators. The problem is that changes in working practices can lead to gaps in services by virtue of changes to an existing set of arrangements, thereby creating problems where they formerly did not exist. One such area of concern is the future of outreach drug work in a criminal justice-driven system.

Outreach work, managerialism and the criminal justice system

In 1996, the Task Force to Review Services for Drug Users (DH, 1996) noted the need for a much greater degree of research into outreach work and highlighted the inherent difficulties of managing and evaluating such work, a point further endorsed by the NTA (2003). This mirrors the view across the whole of the European Union with the European Monitoring Centre for Drugs and Drug Addiction noting that data collection in outreach work is 'in its infancy … evaluation instruments are often invented ad hoc …' (EMCDDA, 1999). Many of the concerns are due to the fact that outreach work is often fluid, based on the need to build trust with hard-to-reach groups, often over a series of fleeting contacts with the client.

Moreover, outreach workers often provide their services in a twilight world that falls between agencies and the street in an arena that is not susceptible to detailed information gathering. However, and somewhat paradoxically, outreach work is also noted as having a key place in services for drug users because of the very flexibility its 'closeness' to hard-to-reach groups and its distance from officialdom provides (NTA, 2003). The dilemma facing outreach work, and importantly those charged with managing and evaluating its performance, is how to retain its street-based 'shadowland' essence while at the same time conforming to the evaluative and management culture demanded by service commissioners working within a Home Office-driven paradigm. Much of the essential nature of outreach work stems from its origins and it is to those the chapter now turns.

Outreach work has been defined as 'any community orientated activity aiming to contact individuals and groups not regularly in contact with existing services' (Rhodes et al, 1992, pp 12-14), or in reference to the difficult and challenging nature of the task as 'the difficult art of reaching the very fringes of society' (Coppel, 2002). Rhodes et al (1992, pp 25-6) identify three types of outreach work: *detached outreach*, where work is undertaken outside any agency contact; *domiciliary outreach*, where work is undertaken in the homes of the target population; and *peripatetic outreach*, where work takes place in community-based agencies. Services provided in all three types of work range from condom distribution and the distribution of various types of literature, including health education and literature on referrals, to mobile needle exchange facilities and screening for sexually transmitted disease and HIV infection.

As noted above, there is recognition that outreach work can, and does, provide a useful and integral part of many types of social intervention programmes. Buning (1993) identifies four key elements of outreach work that typify the impact it can have on hard-to-reach populations: reaching the unreached; survival help; links to other organisations; and field observations as sources of information. Yet, any praise for outreach work is often accompanied by caveats such as: 'It is important to note that outreach work *may not easily fit with traditional ways of assessing outcome*' (Scottish Executive, 2002, emphasis in original) or 'outreach projects ... [can] cause hierarchy and supervision to break down' (Broadhead et al, 1995).

Turning attention to the nature of outreach work, it is the case that the work often takes place in an unstructured and ad hoc fashion away from any agency base. As such, outreach workers have considerable autonomy and can be away from management or colleague supervision for long periods of time. In some cases, the outreach worker will be engaged in productive work; in others, they may simply be 'hanging out' in ways that might fall outside of the planned aims and objectives of the project. Thus time management becomes an issue and a source of conflict for the worker and the managers of the project inasmuch as it can become difficult to distinguish between non-effective 'hanging out' and the very necessary task of gaining client trust and confidence.

Equally, it is very difficult to monitor and evaluate the impact of outreach work; this is a problem shared by a number of 'social' intervention projects in a wide range of fields. Essentially, it is very difficult to measure the effect of educative interventions aimed at changing individual behaviour within hidden populations (Hughes, 1998). For example, it may be that a fleeting contact with an outreach worker prevented a recreational dance drug user from moving on to heroin use. However, there can be no accurate measurement of this either by the worker or the agency. Equally, clients may be reluctant to even provide a false name or address, making follow-up difficult – and in many cases, the outreach worker would lose the trust of the client if they asked for one.

Some of this is due to problems of selection and recruitment. As Pates and Blakey (1992) note, there are no formal qualifications for outreach work at present, meaning that applicants can be from the professions or become what are know as indigenous outreach workers (IOWs) – meaning they can be drawn from the population the project seeks to aid. Where that is the case, Pates and Blakey (1992) make the salient point that the credentials of IOWs are often those that are used to preclude selection elsewhere – ex-drug user, criminal record, poor work record and so on. Paradoxically, these are attributes that can be vital in making a good outreach worker: whether the worker is a professional or an IOW, local knowledge of the street scene is vital (Pates and Blakey, 1992). This assumes some form of prior contact with, and respect from, hard-to-reach groups, which in turn often requires the outreach worker to 'fit in' or, as Rhodes et al (1992, p 36) put it, gain the '*trust, respect* and *credibility*' of a client group who will often make contact in 'environments characterized by *mistrust* or *suspicion*' (emphasis in original).

This is important in relation to outreach drug workers' lack of closeness to state agencies. Bean and Billingsley (2001) note that the drug world is 'imbued with treachery', with users who are chaotic and desperate willing to exchange information with the police. The same authors continue to ask the very pertinent question of how any police force can play a serious part in any multi-agency rehabilitation scheme when it uses informers, who are clearly encouraged to break trust and betray other users (and in all probability use any money given to them to buy their drug of choice). Building trust in this environment is difficult enough; being seen as close to the criminal justice system makes it practically impossible for outreach workers to conduct their business.

To summarise this section, it is evident that outreach drug work succeeds because it is flexible, often occurs in naturalist settings, is non-judgemental and requires a low level of commitment to the project by the client, who, in the short term, often does not become a 'client' in the formal sense, thus challenging established forms of management and evaluation. In addition, outreach workers must be able to maintain a 'shadowland' presence that allows them to maintain a distance from state agencies in order to engender trust in an untrusting environment. The key, it seems, is to devise a management and evaluation strategy that allows the outreach worker to retain the aspects of their work that make it successful, yet at the same time protects the 'right to manage' so integral to New Labour's approach. The following section of this chapter draws on some empirical research that seems to suggest that this has yet to be achieved.

The colonisation of outreach drug work by Crime and Disorder Reduction Partnerships

The PIs for outreach drug work outlined above effectively issue a requirement that outreach work fit into a management and evaluation structure that, hitherto, has been absent in most cases. Again, while reiterating the point that certain aspects of the need to fit into a structure can be seen to be positive, the question remains as to whether fitting into the NTA system damages the aspects of outreach work that makes it so important to the range of services for drug users. In short, is the need to conform to what is essentially a law and order, evaluation-based approach resulting in a lack of diversity in services for drug users, diversity that has long been seen as an important factor in their effectiveness in the manner highlighted above by Newman (2001)? In order to provide an answer to this question, the next section of this chapter turns to some work that the author has recently undertaken (Barton, 2005)[1] examining the effect of evaluation, management and the demands of Crime and Disorder Reduction Partnerships (CDRPs) on outreach drug work.

The work focused on an audit of drug services for a CDRP that was conducted in conjunction with the local DAT. It was noted that the statutory agencies working with drug users collected a wealth of data on clients, often as part of a mandatory requirement. These data were collected in a structured manner, using a plethora of 'official' forms. This allowed the statutory agencies to feed into the crime audit using quantitative information that the CDRP and DAT saw as 'accurate' and 'valid' in terms of painting a picture of the local drug 'scene' and thus 'useful' in developing community safety strategies. This type of information became the benchmark for all other drug data. In many ways, the audit-wise state agencies, well versed in constructing practice that produces quantifiable data, set parameters for the voluntary sector agencies that fell outside the latter's established methods of working.

This was clearly the case where outreach workers were dealing with clients in a fleeting contact, or working with current drug users who hold local knowledge of specific drug 'scenes'. This aspect of outreach work is clearly very different from that performed by the statutory agencies as it requires the worker to 'fit' into the local drug milieu, which, in turn, depends on the worker cultivating trust within the client group. Moreover, the impressionistic and qualitative nature of much of the data reflected the unstructured manner in which they were collected and certainly did not fulfil reliability tests in the same way as the quantifiable working practices of the state agencies. Accordingly, the demands of CDRP for data 'like the statutory agencies provide' were seen as threatening by some outreach agencies and workers, generating clear concerns about changing the nature of their agency and shifting the workers' understanding of their tasks away from their client-centred, educative approach and more towards a formalised and managerialist model.

The research provided some data to support this. It was noted that, in one example, outreach workers had located concentrations of heavy crack use among a group of users that had yet to be picked up by the statutory agencies. The outreach workers were busy trying to address the problem, yet had little in the way of 'hard data' to support their findings. For the CDRP, this type of data failed to comply with the Drugs Prevention Advisory Service criteria of being '… credible and reliable … accurate, consistent and timely' (DPAS, 2002, p 14), yet, arguably, it is perhaps only a matter of time before a cluster of problematic crack users creates problems for the wider community.

The CDRP needed to be informed of this development but because of the informal nature of the data, and the impossibility of collecting structured data without compromising the position and the methods of the outreach workers, it was impossible to feed quantitative, structured information into any strategic group. The dilemma the agency faced was that in order to remain credible to the DAT and the CDRP, it needed to change working practices, yet paradoxically changing practice might have given the impression that the agency and its workers were moving too close to the criminal justice system. If this happened, it would have effectively removed the agency from the environment where the outreach workers achieved their best results.

Finally, the research (Barton, 2005) noted that every worker from the outreach-based agencies made comments about their lack of capacity to resist the transformative pressures of the CDRP audit process. They were all aware that in terms of resources, location in the DAT's hierarchy of agencies and degrees of influence, their respective agencies were located firmly at the weaker end of the power continuum. Moreover, some of these agencies were dependent on DAT commissioning or referrals from state agencies for large parts of their budgets. Finally, all had been promised much-needed technical support and resources in return for agreeing to take part in the CDRP audit. All the managers and staff interviewed were clearly aware that overt resistance could threaten the very existence of their agency.

Most were resigned to making the changes required by the DAT and the CDRP, thus fitting into the needs of the criminal justice-dominated CDRP and NTA evaluation culture. Yet all agreed that, in so doing, gaps in service provision would appear and 'hard-to-reach' clients would be further marginalised from accessing services. This, in the eyes of the outreach workers, reduced one of the key values of outreach work, namely that of being able to 'reduce the pressure of drug use turning into drug *problems*' (Awiah et al, 1990, p 8, emphasis in original) and came about as a direct result of being asked to tailor their work to fit the needs of the CDRP.

One size fits all: a too simple solution to a complex problem?

In Barton's (2005) example, the demands of the DAT and the CDRP for 'good' community safety-based data 'responsibilised' outreach agencies into adopting the requirements of a community safety discourse as part of their work. In short, the CDRP audit imposed a change in the nature of the work conducted by outreach workers and their host agencies. This was predicated on the demands of the CDRP for work that is auditable in order that the data being fed into the CDRP 'fit' other types of data collected by a variety of (mostly) statutory, crime-based agencies. For outreach drug workers, this translated into a clamour for more data, collected in a structured and routine manner and recorded and presented in a manner that reflected (and, arguably, complemented) drug-related data emanating from the statutory sector. Thus, 'good practice' in working with drug users became benchmarked by what the statutory agencies did, leaving little room in the process for the 'difficult' working practices of outreach workers.

In turn, the need to be part of the CDRP process, with all the implications for commissioning and funding this carries with it, placed pressures on outreach managers to at least consider their priorities when thinking about work and what constitutes 'good practice'. However, the need for auditable data, itself a top-down priority, is skewing the nature of outreach work against the better judgement of the outreach workers and managers. Nevertheless, such is the colonising and transformative dynamic of the audit process that these concerns are taking second place to the agency-based need to be 'in the loop' as far as CDRP audits are concerned. This clearly underscores the agency requirement to include aspects of crime prevention in its work, regardless of whether it 'fits' the ethos or working practices of the agency concerned.

It would seem that the solution New Labour has chosen to 'cure' the problem of uncoordinated drug services is to use the power of evaluation and audit to create a one-size-fits-all approach to ensure that addressing the consequences of problematic drug use is viewed through a Home Office-dominated lens that sees the criminal justice system as the vehicle for accessing treatment and the main beneficiary of drug policy. In one respect, however, placing outreach work under greater scrutiny could be seen as a positive move. It does force outreach workers and their managers to open all aspects of their work to wider view and provides them with a focus beyond 'helping' the client, thereby allowing all agencies working with drug users to contribute towards 'safer communities'.

However, this rather misses the point about the complex nature of drug work and certainly marginalises the needs of the vast majority of drug users who fall under the recreational and experimental users umbrella – the groups from which tomorrow's problematic drug users will most likely emerge. Paring the policy approach down to a criminal justice-led, treatment-based approach only conforms to the one-dimensional need of satisfying the seemingly incessant need to control, thus ensuring that individuals and organisations remain 'on message' (Rawnsley, 2001). In turn, this is leading to the creation of a one-size-fits-all approach, marshalled by criminal justice-dominated needs. The problem is that 'difficult' working practices, such as those used by outreach workers, can quickly look out of place and thus redundant.

It is arguable that outreach work does serve a useful purpose and needs to be included in the wide range of social provision, especially where there is reluctance by client groups to access more formalised services. Placing pressure on agencies to remove, or at least reduce the level of, such service provision has two negative consequences. First, it has the potential to reduce service provision in areas by transforming the work of the outreach team to better fit the requirements of a CDRP audit. As an example, the inappropriate use of data recording and collection can act to distance the outreach worker from reluctant or disillusioned clients, leaving a gap in provision. Second, this transformative dynamic is led by the colonising instincts of an insatiable criminal justice discourse. There is clearly a case to be made that recognises that not all social problems or indeed aspects of social provision need to be defined and understood in terms of their contribution to crime prevention.

The worry for outreach-type agencies and outreach workers is that the nature of the CDRP audit, and the pressure that the voluntary sector agencies are under to be seen to be credible in order to continue to be included in the crime prevention loop, may radically change the nature of their work. Should this happen, many more so-called 'hard-to-reach' groups and individuals will feel the effects of a local crime audit-driven, one-size-fits-all approach to social provision. A perverse consequence of this, then, may be that the criminal justice system's apparent audit and control needs will overrule real community safety benefits. This is not, of course, the only time we have been pushed towards such a conclusion (Squires and Measor, 2005). Perhaps, above all in community safety policy, our concern should be with overall outcomes: quality of life, reduced crime and rates of victimisation, indicators that cannot necessarily be reduced to audit process outcomes.

Note

[1] The author would like to thank the British Academy for supporting this work.

References

Awiah, J., Butt, S. and Dorn, N. (1990) 'The last place I would go: black people and drug services in Britain', *Druglink*, vol 5, no 5, pp 14-15.

Barton, A. (2003) *Illicit Drugs: Use and Control*, Routledge: London.

Barton, A. (2005) 'Working in the margins: shadowland agencies, outreach workers and the crime audit process', *Drugs: Education, Prevention, and Policy*, vol 12, no 3, pp 239-46.

Bean, P. (2002) *Drugs and Crime*, Cullumpton: Willan Publishing.

Bean, P. and Billingsley, R. (2001) 'Drugs, crime and informers', in R. Billingsley, T. Nemitz and P. Bean (eds) *Informers: Policing, Policy, Practice*, Cullompton: Willan Publishing, pp 25-7.

Blackman, S. (2004) *Chilling Out: The Cultural Politics of Substance Consumption, Youth and Drug Policy*, Open University Press: Milton Keynes.

Blagg, H., Sampson, A., Pearson, G., Smith, D. and Stubbs, P. (1988) 'Inter-agency co-operation: rhetoric and reality', in T. Hope and M. Shaw (eds) *Communities and Crime Reduction*, London: HMSO, pp 204-20.

Broadhead, R., Heckathorn, D.D., Grund, J.-P., Stern, L. and Anthony, D.L. (1995) 'Drug users versus outreach workers in combating aids: Part I. Agency problems in traditional outreach interventions' (www.drugtext.org/library/articles).

Buning, E. (1993) 'Outreach work with drug users: an overview', *International Journal of Drug Policy*, April, pp 78-82.

Coppel, A. (2002) 'The outreach method: the difficult art of reaching the very fringes of society' (www.drugtext.org/library/articles).

DH (Department of Health) (1996) *Report of an Independent Review of Drug Treatment Services in England (Task Force Report)*, London: HMSO.

DPAS (Drugs Prevention Advisory Service) (2002) *Communities Against Drugs*, Bristol: DPAS, South West Region.

EMCDDA (European Monitoring Centre for Drugs and Drug Addiction) (1999) *Final Report Outreach Work Among Drug Users in Europe: Concepts, Practice and Terminology*, Brussels: European Union.

Gilling, D. and Barton, A. (2005) 'Dangers lurking in the deep: the transformative potential of the crime audit', *Criminal Justice*, vol 5, no 2, pp 163-80.

Hill, M. (1984) *The Policy Process in the Modern State*, London: Prentice Hall.

HM Government (1995) *Tackling Drugs Together – A Strategy for England 1995-1998*, London: HMSO.

HM Government (1998) *Tackling Drugs to Build a Better Britain: The Government's Ten Year Strategy for Tackling Drug Misuse*, London: HMSO.

HM Government (2002) *Updated Drugs Strategy* (www.drugs.gov.uk/drugsstrategy/overview).

Howard, R., Beadle, P. and Maitland, J. (1993) *Across the Divide: Building Community Partnerships to Tackle Drug Misuse*, Report to the Department of Health, London: Department of Health.

Hughes, G. (1998) *Understanding Crime Prevention: Social Control, Risk and Late Modernity*, Buckingham: Open University Press.

McGregor, S., Ettorre, E., Coomber, R. and Crozier, A. (1991) 'Paradigms and practices in drug services in England', *International Journal of Drug Policy*, March.

Newman, J. (2001) *Modernising Governance: New Labour, Politics and Society*, London: Sage Publications.

NTA (National Treatment Agency) (2003) *Models of Care for the Treatment of Adult Drug Users: Framework for Developing Local Systems of Effective Drug Misuse Treatment in England*, London: NTA.

Parker, H., Aldridge, J. and Measham, F. (1998) *Illegal Leisure: The Normalization of Adolescent Drug Use*, London: Routledge.

Pates, R. and Blakey, V. (1992) 'What should we be looking for in outreach workers?', *International Journal of Drug Policy*, March, pp 130-4.

Power, M. (1994) *The Audit Explosion*, London: Demo.

Rawnsley, A. (2001) *Servants of the People*, Harmondsworth: Penguin.

Rhodes, T., Holland, J. and Hartnoll, R. (1992) 'Innovation and constraint: management of an outreach intervention', *International Journal of Drug Policy*, vol 3, no 3,

Scottish Executive (2002) *Evaluating Outreach Services*, Effective Intervention Unit Evaluation Guide 8, Scottish Executive: Edinburgh.

Squires, P. and Measor, L. (2005) 'Below decks on the flagship: evaluating youth justice', in D. Taylor and S. Balloch (eds) *The Politics of Evaluation*, Bristol: The Policy Press, pp 21-40.

Section three
Community safety:
a flawed project?

TEN

Community safety and corporate crime

Steve Tombs and Dave Whyte

Introduction

It has been well documented that corporate crime has enormous economic, physical and social costs. Yet despite this, such crimes remain almost entirely absent from 'crime, law and order' agendas. One might have been forgiven for thinking, however, that with the noises emanating from the Home Office around the introduction of the 1998 Crime and Disorder Act (CDA), and the requirement for local crime and community safety audits in particular, such offences may have received some local community, regulatory and policing attention. If the CDA represented the UK government's legislative endorsement of 'community safety' as the driving force behind new strategies of crime control, this agenda was supposedly more 'open': '[c]rucially the Act does not prescribe in any detail what the agenda for the local partnership should be ...' (Home Office, 1998b, Foreword). Thus, '[t]he Crime and Disorder Act deliberately avoids attempting to define the terms 'crime' or 'disorder' within this context. Nor does it impose any list of particular topics which every strategy must address.... Within reason, nothing is ruled out and nothing is ruled in' (Home Office, 1998b, para 1.43).

The institutionalisation of community safety by New Labour, then, in rhetorical terms at least, appeared to open up new spaces in local debates on harm and crime. However, the argument of this chapter is that some of the more specific, recent processes associated with community safety, and the wider problematic of which, for us,[1] it is a part – namely, 'governing through crime' – have played key roles in rendering corporate crime less rather than more visible. What follows is an attempt to describe and understand those processes.

Corporate threats to community safety

'Corporate crime' covers a vast range of offences of omission and commission with differing types of *modus operandi*, perpetrators, effects and victims. In order to appreciate the range of harms encapsulated by the term 'corporate crime', it is worth thinking of such crimes in terms of four broad categories, or types, of offences.

One such category covers various financial crimes, including: illegal share dealings, mergers and takeovers; various forms of tax evasion; bribery; and other forms of illegal accounting. Enron is a classic example of the latter and the company has joined a list of offenders – including Guinness (involved in illegal share dealings in the 1980s; see Punch, 1996, pp 167-80) and BCCI, a global bank that was systematically involved in fraud, money laundering and bribery (Punch, 1996, pp 9-15) – as symbols of what we mean by the term 'financial crime'.

A second general area of corporate crime is that committed directly against consumers. Examples include illegal sales/marketing practices; conspiracies to fix prices and/or carve up market share among different companies; false/illegal labelling or information; the fraudulent safety testing of products; and the sale of unfit goods, such as adulterated food. A classic example of the last category was the outbreak of *E. coli* among Lanarkshire residents in November 1996, resulting in 18 deaths and almost 500 people ill. The poisoning was traced back to a local butcher that was eventually fined £2,500 for failing to ensure that equipment was kept clean and that food was protected against contamination.

Third, we can identify crimes arising out of the employment relationship. These include cases of sexual and racial discrimination and other offences against employment law (including equal opportunities legislation); violations of wage laws; violations against rights to organise and take industrial action; and a whole range of offences against employee occupational health and safety. Such offences are widespread. For example, of the two million school-age children working in the UK (more than a quarter in food preparation and sales), around 75% are thought to be employed illegally – employed without permits, in dangerous work, or in breach of working hours regulations (Whyte, 2004a).

The fourth category of offence, crimes against the environment, includes illegal emissions to air, water and land; the failure to provide, or the provision of false, information; hazardous waste dumping; and illegal manufacturing practices. In 2002, the Environment Agency prosecuted 1,712 successful charges against businesses for a range of environmental offences (Environment Agency, 2003). This is an agency hardly known for a prosecutorial ethos. For example, a 2001 Greenpeace report calculated that between 1999 and 2001 there were 533 *known* breaches of licences by 10 municipal waste incinerators operating in England. Most were likely to be emissions of dioxins – highly toxic, known cancer-causing substances – but only one of these breaches had been prosecuted (Brown, 2001).

Beyond identifying the range of offences that fall within the general rubric of 'corporate crime', there are several observations, based on the available research evidence, that we can make with confidence regarding its prevalence and its deleterious impact on communities.

Collectively, corporate crimes entail enormous, if incalculable, costs. Many forms of corporate crime have physical costs – deaths, injuries, ill health – arising out of dangerous workplaces, polluted environments, unsafe goods and services, and so on. But even if we confine ourselves to considering the economic costs of corporate offending – costs borne by governments, taxpayers, consumers, workers and other companies – the best available evidence indicates that these far outweigh those associated with 'conventional' or 'street' offending, a conclusion difficult to contest even while recognising the difficulty faced by attempts to estimate the 'costs' of any form of crime. Even studies of 'single' examples or groups of corporate crime – such as the illegal activities of pensions companies in the so-called mis-selling cases of the 1990s, collectively said to have involved a sum of 'up to £11 billion' involving 2.4 million victims (*Guardian*, 13 March, 1998) – are enough to support this general conclusion.

Second, the range of work that now exists around corporate crime, such as case studies either of particular offences or categories of offences by type or industry, as well as the more limited efforts at quantifying the scale and ubiquitousness of such crimes, indicates clearly that such offending is not a peripheral activity carried out by a marginal group of individuals and organisations, the so-called 'bad apples' of the business world. Rather, it is endemic within economic activity: corporate crimes are not simply widespread; they are routine and pervasive (Slapper and Tombs, 1999, pp 36-84).

Finally, and crucially in terms of the discourses that have emerged around the idea of community safety, corporate crimes also have corrosive and regressive social costs. In general, their economic and physical costs fall on those in society who are already relatively disadvantaged: low-paid workers are most likely to work in dangerous workplaces; poorer people are least able to relocate from polluted neighbourhoods; those on the tightest budgets are most vulnerable to purchasing goods and services that may lead to them becoming victims of corporate crime, such as the cheaper cuts of 'fresh' or processed meat, or cut-price electrical items. A further effect of corporate crime is a diminution of social trust in the corporations on whom we increasingly rely for the food we eat, the clothes we wear, the services we access, the financial products we purchase, and, indeed, any order and security that we may enjoy through our purchasing power in the marketplace. Then, by implication, social trust in governments is diminished for their failure to regulate effectively the activities of these corporations.

Thus, as Croall has sought to document (1998, 1999), individuals may fall victim to corporate crime in the home, their local neighbourhoods, at work, as consumers, when travelling, using health and welfare services, or at leisure. Yet Croall and other scholars working in this relatively neglected area of offending also note the relative absence of corporate crime from law and order agendas. In general, to explain this absence, we need to recognise that there are an array of social processes that contribute to removing such offences from dominant definitions of 'crime, law and order' (Slapper and Tombs, 1999). At every stage of the legal process – framing, enforcement and sanctioning – law tends to operate quite differently with respect to corporate crimes than in the context of 'conventional' crimes. Beyond the nature of law and legal regulation, there are other social processes that seek to render corporate crimes relatively invisible. These include: the focus of formal politics; the poverty and paucity of official corporate crime data; the nature and significance of ideologies surrounding business, and the difficulties these pose for naming corporations as potential offenders; representations of crime through various media that converge to produce 'blanket' conceptualisations regarding 'law and order' that reinforce dominant stereotypes of crime and the criminal; and the victim–offender relationship in many corporate offences. None of the various mechanisms whereby corporate crimes are rendered relatively invisible is particularly remarkable in isolation. What is crucial, however, is their mutually reinforcing nature – that is, they all work in the same direction and to the same effect, removing corporate crime from 'crime, law and order' agendas.

These processes of relative invisibility are of particular significance in terms of public perceptions of policing priorities – precisely one of the key rationales for the local community safety audits mandated by the CDA. A survey of the second generation of those audits in an area where there were high-profile and controversial instances of crimes against the environment found that local authorities failed even to mention those crimes, far less include those types of crime in their local consultations or surveys (Whyte, 2004b). Yet a key point that is commonly made by corporate crime writers is that when people are actually *asked* about corporate crime, they tend to report surprising levels of victimisation (Pearce, 1990). Thus, for example, respondents in the US National White-Collar Crime Survey, conducted between January and April 1999, found that, during a 12-month period, one in every three households (36%) was victimised by a form of white-collar crime (www.nw3c.org/publications.html).

With regard to perceptions of the seriousness of white-collar crime, the survey dispels early work that indicated that members of the public were not concerned about fraud and white-collar crime affecting them. Instead, the research shows that the public now views certain white-collar crime offences as equal to, or more serious than, certain traditional street crimes: for example, they were much more likely to agree than disagree with the statement that 'allowing tainted meat to be sold which results in one person becoming ill is a more serious offence than armed robbery' (Rebovich and Lane, 2000). Those findings are derived from a US survey and, while they may not necessarily be reflected in UK public sentiment, there is no obvious reason why popular concerns should differ here. The important point to grasp, however, is that there are a large number of questions that local crime surveys and crime and disorder audits fail to even ask.

Corporations, responsibilisation and neo-liberalism

To some extent, asking such questions has become more rather than less likely in a community safety landscape that is dominated by neo-liberal crime control strategies. Corporate crime control has always been relatively ineffective (see, for example, Snider, 1993, pp 120-4). Indeed, as we have indicated above, both historically and contemporaneously, even documenting corporate harm or corporate crime has been beset by a range of obstacles (Tombs and Whyte, 2003).

Thus it is unsurprising that there has been a virtually complete absence of criminal justice focus on corporate threats to community safety within the work of local crime prevention and Crime and Disorder Reduction Partnerships (CDRPs) (Coleman et al, 2002) – the prevalence and mitigation of local crimes such as environmental pollution offences, product safety or mortgage and pension fraud have remained almost invisible issues. Crime prevention – despite the claims of Home Office functionaries that community safety and crime prevention agendas were to be locally defined and broadly interpreted to include as wide a range of criminal and social harms as deemed appropriate by local partnerships (Hall and Whyte, 2003) – has remained focused on the dominant concerns of authoritarian and punitive populism: the problem of street crime, increasing police detections and targeting criminal populations with intensive surveillance, swift prosecution and tougher sentences. The dominant mode of operation for local criminal justice systems has increasingly become a 'technical concern with managing the effects of targeted categories of action or event rather than a political or moral concern with faults or causes ...' (O'Malley, 1996, p 191). Crime prevention strategies have thus targeted the poor and relatively powerless.

At the level of the individual, neo-liberal crime prevention encourages privatised responsibility for security, often resulting in what has been termed a 'fortress mentality', in which forms of sustainable social prevention are displaced by technocratic, highly individualised prevention efforts. Now, for us, in the case of corporate crime prevention, such a comparable (and regressive) uncoupling of social intervention is not inevitable. Indeed, there are several reasons to expect the *reverse* to be the case (see also Alvesalo et al, 2006).

First, attempts to control corporate crime are likely to experience the opposite of the 'fortress mentality' effect. The involvement of state institutions and other agents in new forms of monitoring of organisational practices is likely to make more public, rather than private, the mechanisms of prevention. Second, situational crime prevention applied to corporations is more likely to entail a move away from the responsibilisation of the individual towards re-responsibilisation of the state by local publics, workers groups or social movements. Using apparatuses of crime control to redirect the preventative gaze back towards corporations is therefore likely to entail a reconnection of collective social action to the local state. A third reason for expecting corporate crime prevention to be socially *reconnective* can be found in the experience of campaigns that seek the criminalisation of offending corporations: social movements around corporate crime tend to be connected to wider projects of social justice or equality. If those represent preliminary reasons for imagining that, theoretically, corporate crime prevention provides an opportunity for mobilising communities in more progressive and social connective modes of collective action, the question at the centre of situational crime prevention remains: is the emphasis on 'place' or location of the event likely to improve or hinder corporate crime prevention?

However, it is a consequence of the wider contours of neo-liberal capitalist social order that the chances of establishing forms of corporate crime control within community safety partnerships has become less rather than more likely. As an extensive, recent criminological literature on crime prevention has documented, neo-liberal rule has in most liberal democracies ushered in an active role of corporations in the *delivery* of criminal justice. A key thematic of this literature has been neatly encapsulated by Ericson and Haggerty's (1997, p 169) description of the 'police–corporate quid pro quo'. Here, a series of private–public common interests is consolidated by the corporate funding of public sector prevention efforts in exchange for advertising, or the provision of, a specialist service. The latter point is illustrated with reference to a shopping mall's financial contribution to the updating of a police suspect database. The authors also note the proliferation of corporate logos on police hardware and publicity materials. Exchange of intelligence and expertise is now commonplace between police and corporate specialists, whether this relates to the design of 'crime-free' spaces or the historical analysis of patterns of offending (Ericson and Haggerty, 1997, pp 167-76). And the literature points to the colonisation of public space by private actors, a process that ultimately relies on privately funded security apparatuses.

This spatial ordering – a process within which the private sector is pivotal – was significantly consolidated under the CDA, where business organisations were expected to participate more fully in the funding, planning and delivery of crime control agendas via developing crime prevention partnerships and strategies. This spatial ordering strategy – involving the administration and distribution of crime control delivered via public–private sector partnerships – incorporates a range of phenomena: business watch schemes; pro-prosecution and exclusion policies to deal with small traders, shoplifters, beggars and protestors; CCTV and electronic surveillance systems coordinated across the city centre; security guard communication networks; and themed anti-crime campaigns.

For Garland, the growth of the commercial security industry and the rise of corporate anti-crime initiatives has led to a new 'private justice', where highly developed forms of surveillance and exclusion from commercial zones have become more and more routine; indeed, perhaps more routine than public forms of justice (Garland, 2000). Private justice is less concerned with deterrence or punishment than with practical prevention: the detection and removal of risky individuals (Shearing and Stenning, 1987). By and large, this is characterised as part of a shift from the moral to the instrumental regulation of those that obstruct the smooth running of arenas of production and consumption.

Now, there clearly is a sense in which businesses, like many individuals, have been responsibilised, consistent with former Home Office minister Paul Boateng's demand that '[i]t is vital that we work together to cut crime and disorder. It is no longer enough for individuals or as [sic] businesses to say that these are matters solely for the police' (Boateng, 1998, p 4). The emergence of government initiatives such as Business Crime Check and Communicate, which encourages businesses to participate in crime reduction partnerships and commit funding to partnership initiatives, can be conjured up as prime examples of responsibilisation. Also falling into this rubric is the incorporation of crime-averse designs into products and building plans, investment in high-visibility security measures, ensuring the prosecution of burglars, beggars and shoplifters, and so on (see Home Office, 1998a).

Responsibilisation demands resource commitments, fundamental changes to management systems and staff training, and involvement in a range of new collaborative arrangements on the part of businesses. In addition, commitments to assist in the prosecution of – and even the use of civil litigation against – those who commit offences in business premises are also expected. From this perspective, responsibilisation generates new costs of self-protection as well as exposing businesses to potential forfeits for failure to take the appropriate steps. Failure to fulfil responsibilities may jeopardise the right to state protection and provision. In this context, it makes sense that we are encouraged to see business organisations and corporations as the objects of responsibilisation just like everybody else.

But what is missing from much of the commentary on the corporatisation of crime prevention is that corporations have used CDRPs and coalitions – so concretised through the initiative of community safety – to enhance their *moral* authority, and at the same time to enhance their ability to shape public and social policy. This type of influence remains beyond the reach of other 'responsibilised' agents, while at the same time corporations have the means to escape many of the consequences of responsibilisation that are not available to individuals or other civil society groups. Private corporations are, by dint of their position as key institutions in capitalist social orders, able to use their structural power and influence to offset the deleterious or arduous burdens implied by the responsibilisation process. Their institutional position as dominant economic and social actors in the neo-liberal social order enables corporations to influence definitions of the legitimate targets of crime control, of the legitimate victim and of the crime problem itself. In turn, these redefinitions provide further layers of insulation against corporations themselves being viewed as offenders, that is, as threats to, rather than key actors in the provision of, community safety.

Legitimate and illegitimate targets of crime control

Numerous studies have shown that the targeting process formulated within entrepreneurialised crime control networks is aimed at the least powerful inhabitants of the city: potential shoplifters, unlicensed street traders, beggars, *Big Issue* sellers, football supporters, young people in general (Norris and Armstrong, 1999; Mitchell, 2003; Coleman, 2004) and those who might form a source of cultural opposition, such as graffiti artists (Ferrell, 2001). In other words, there is a re-emphasis on the control – and ultimately the removal – of those 'usual suspects' and street activities seen as forms of hindrance to entrepreneurial rule.

Urban regeneration strategies constitute a form of 'governing through crime', whereby images and discourses on 'the crime problem' sit at the centre of, and provide a rationale for, key aspects of the urban renaissance agenda. Legislation such as the CDA and the 2003 Anti-Social Behaviour Act provides illustrations of this shift in the governing process in linking 'quality of life' (including local economic, political and cultural development) with certain forms of behaviour and criminal activity. However, the absence of corporate crime from these initiatives underlines the importance of critically deconstructing the rationale behind entrepreneurial governing and to ask what kinds of crime cities and citizens are being governed through. Of equal significance is the need to unravel the problem of what kinds of crime, harm and risk fall *outside* of the entrepreneurial governing agenda, and how they fall outside of those agendas. At the moment, breaches of toxic waste regulations, defrauding of consumers and illegal killings in the workplace, for example, are nowhere to be found on the community safety agenda in the UK. The prime targets of crime control, especially in urban environments, are those that threaten to disrupt regimes of consumption. Increasingly being added to the list of usual suspects are those that protest against the activities of private corporations, or those that offer some form of political opposition or alternative to entrepreneurial rule. The key legal case here is *Appelby v UK* (Washington), where a group of protestors invoked Article 10 of the European Convention on Human Rights on freedom of expression. According to the court, however, the privatised town centre was deemed 'unique in as much as though it is the Town Centre, it is also privately owned' (Gerstenberg, 2004, p 61). According to the private company claiming ownership rights of the town, its 'stance on all political and religious issues is one of strict neutrality' and therefore they would not permit any political protest (Gerstenberg, 2004, p 61). In upholding the company's claim, the court gave precedence to property rights above the right to free speech, and thus opened the way for corporations claiming 'ownership' of formerly public spaces to use the law to control those that use the city centre for non-commercial, 'neutral' purposes.

Crucially, private capital is being given a greater role not only in the administration and control of these spaces, but also in the definition of the legitimate targets of control. This definitional role for businesses also applies in relation to the reconstitution of the 'victim' of crime. The key role that corporations now occupy in the shaping of crime control agendas also enables them to influence the dominant construction of the legitimate victims of *crime*, those most deserving of security protections. The corporatisation of crime prevention has thus facilitated the integration of the business community into a wider community of legitimate crime victims. Nationally and locally, business organisations and trade associations are involved in a concerted effort to reframe how the process of criminal victimisation is perceived by local publics. This is most obvious in local crime audits conducted by local CDRPs in England and Wales. Forty-three per cent of audits published in 2002 identify crimes against business as a priority for intervention, compared with 16% in 1999, the first year that the local audits were published. Crimes against business surveys have proliferated and paint a similar picture of the toll of business victimisation as more ubiquitous and economically damaging than offences committed against individuals (Hill, 2004). At a national level, the Home Office has been a key mover in developing a flourishing research area around crimes *against* business (Hopkins, 2002). This further legitimises businesses' own efforts to measure their victimised status.

The role of corporations in crime control creates new responsibilities for business and at the same time enhances their hegemonic ability to redraw the legitimate targets of crime control strategies, redefine victims and reshape the parameters of 'crime'. Elsewhere, we have presented evidence of a downturn in local crime control efforts, linked to the process of recreating entrepreneurial cities (Coleman et al, 2005). The local privileges for corporations that stem from capital's hegemonic role in the process of 'governing through crime' sit symbiotically with a more general valorisation of 'private' entrepreneurialism. As the legitimacy of business organisations has increased under conditions of neo-liberalism, so the legitimacy of their control has declined (Snider, 2000; Tombs, 2001). The historical difficulties of labelling the illegal activities of corporations as criminal have become exacerbated within the context of entrepreneurial urbanism, where the naked pursuit of profit is elevated to the status of moral exigency. This is having the effect of legitimating virtually any activity because businesses engage in it, exemplified by the valorisation and normalisation of business expertise in antisocial behaviour legislation, involvement in public CCTV and street warden schemes, and the funding and creation of 'public realms'. This valorisation, as reflected in various government documents (see Coleman, 2005), has the effect of delegitimating opposition and pro-regulatory forces for their 'anti-business' rhetoric and practice.

Conclusion: redefining 'community safety'?

The terrain of 'crime prevention' – within which community safety has assumed a central place – is one that is narrowly focused, as criminal justice systems (and criminologies) have almost always focused on the crimes and incivilities of the relatively powerless. But despite the arguments of this chapter, there remain some good reasons for thinking there may be more room for debate in the field of corporate crime control than is betrayed by current realities and trends. Certainly, as we indicated earlier in the chapter, despite the absence of corporate crime on crime prevention agendas, there is no ontological reason for this state of affairs; and the lens of community safety does provide an opportunity for criminal justice professionals to begin to develop such a corporate crime prevention strategy (Croall, 1998, 1999; Whyte, 2004b). Indeed, many of the legal and technical devices being used and developed to control conventional crime may also be appropriate for controlling corporate crime – the barriers to corporate crime prevention may be associated with a lack of political will, or our inability to re-imagine the legitimate targets of those agendas, rather than any inherent problems in the legal or criminal justice system. But again we must think as if these barriers *can* be overcome, and examine instances where this has happened.

Indeed, although issues of corporate crime are not recognised or even mentioned in mainstream local crime control agendas in the UK, corporate crime control has actually been subsumed into some crime control strategies, even if it is not recognised as 'corporate crime control'. Two examples illustrate this point. First, civilian police wardens in UK cities are expected to adopt zero-tolerance approaches to illegal advertising and trade-waste dumping in commercial areas, as well as the usual targeting of beggars and shoplifting suspects[2]. This example indicates that it is possible that the cleansing of commercial zones can involve an assault on the more visible aspects of – albeit low-level – corporate offending. Further, two recent cases, in June 2003 and March 2005, are of interest because they involve the use of antisocial behaviour legislation to deal with corporate activity. In the 2003 case, executives from the Sony and BMG corporations found themselves in the dock in an antisocial behaviour hearing. The court hearing followed a Camden Borough Council investigation that identified two Sony executives as being responsible for commissioning illegal fly-posting in the borough. The court did not grant an Anti-Social Behaviour Order (ASBO) in this case, after Sony and BMG gave an undertaking to desist from all fly-posting activities in the area. In the second case, also initiated by Camden, the court issued an ASBO against the chief executive of a company called Diabolical Liberties for organising fly-posting in Camden. The Camden cases thus opened up the possibilities for developing what have been referred to as 'corporate ASBOs'[3] (Whyte, 2004c).

Thus the regressive tendencies in the politics of community safety should not prevent us from considering the merits and contours of a reformed 'community safety' within a strategy of corporate crime prevention. And if we begin to think in these terms, we can formulate some modest proposals for the reform of crime prevention agendas. First, crime prevention partnerships should be reoriented to include regulatory agencies, workers' organisations, consumer groups and environmental pressure groups. In discursive terms, this is a relatively straightforward task. For example, the rhetoric behind the conducting of the post-1998 community safety audits clearly allowed the inclusion of corporate crimes within crime prevention agendas (Whyte, 2004b). What is required therefore is sustained political pressure, not least locally, on the key primary definers that oversee the design and conduct of such audits. Second, we should seek new, as well as redefine existing, forms of surveillance from below on the basis that workers, social movements and other organised, if marginalised, interests fit well with situational crime prevention's preoccupation with the guardians of places, victims and offenders. They are rarely, if ever, viewed as such, but there is no reason in principle why they cannot be. Third, it is crucial that all available data on corporate crime should be disseminated and publicised as widely as possible by local crime prevention agents as a means of raising awareness of the risks of victimisation, and as a means of responsibilising, and encouraging the vigilance of, the general public. Again, this would allow us to build on what is evidently significant, if latent, public support for the control of corporate crime (Braithwaite et al, 1987).

Here we should recall Sutherland's observation to the effect that a precondition of corporate crime being tackled with any degree of efficacy is the development of 'organised resentment' on the part of the wider public and key organised interests (Sutherland, 1983, p 60). Support for this is to be found in Snider's analyses of the dynamics of regulatory reform (Snider, 1991), and the arguments of others who have documented the claim that corporate crime can only be subject to critical state activity on the basis of an emerging 'social movement' (Kramer, 1989). Indeed, under certain political, social and economic conditions, corporate crime prevention can become a key state priority – as happened in Finland from the mid-1990s onwards (Alvesalo and Tombs, 2001). And so, if the brief, indicative proposals above seem the product of wild imagination, this is certainly no reason for not setting them out. For our imagination has been stunted rather than encouraged by the development of the idea of community safety, the dominant definitions of which have been too little challenged by criminologists themselves. This chapter has aimed to open up to debate potential fields of intervention that at the moment, certainly in the UK context, look distant. Yet this is no reason for paralysing pessimism; as Mathiesen (2000) reminds us, the major social upheavals of our age have remained almost unthinkable until they have actually happened. State agendas, no matter how immovable they may seem, can always be made more malleable by shifts in social mood, by the changing contours of social movements, or by unexpected events. As researchers and writers, it may not be in our power to predict those shifts. But it is in our power to imagine, to speculate and to raise questions, and in so doing to highlight where alternatives to existing social arrangements lie, and what form such alternatives may take.

Notes

[1] And others: see, for example, Crawford, 1998; Coleman, 2004; Coleman et al, 2006.

[2] We are grateful to Jonny Burnett for pointing out to us this phenomenon that he has encountered in the course of his own research fieldwork.

[3] The term corporate ASBOs, used by several news sources at the time of these cases, is a bit of a misnomer. Under the relevant legislation, only individuals can be the subjects of ASBOs. Legislative reform would be required to enable ASBOs to apply to corporations, although it would require a relatively uncomplicated legal reform.

References

Alvesalo, A. and Tombs, S. (2001) 'The emergence of a "war" on economic crime: the case of Finland', *Business & Politics*, vol 3, no 3, pp 239-67.

Alvesalo, A., Tombs, S., Virta, E. and Whyte, D. (2006) 'Re-imagining crime prevention: controlling corporate crime?', *Crime, Law and Social Change* [in press].

Boateng, P. (1998) 'Foreword', in Home Office, *Community Crime Reduction Partnerships: The Retail Contribution*, London: Home Office Communication Directorate, p 4.

Braithwaite, J., Grabosky, P. and Wilson, P. (1987) 'The myth of community tolerance toward white-collar crime', *Australia and New Zealand Journal of Criminology*, vol 20, no 2, pp 33-44.

Brown, P. (2001) 'Incinerator breaches go unpunished. Poisonous chemicals pumped into atmosphere, report reveals', *The Guardian*, 22 May (www.guardian.co.uk/uk_news/story/0,,494451,00.htm).

Coleman, R. (2004) *Reclaiming the Streets: Surveillance, Social Control and the City*, Cullompton: Willan Publishing.

Coleman, R. (2005) 'Surveillance in the city: primary definition and urban spatial order', *Crime, Media, Culture: An International Journal*, vol 1, no 2, pp 131-48.

Coleman, R., Sim, J. and Whyte, D. (2002) 'Power, politics and partnerships: the state of crime prevention on Merseyside', in G. Hughes and A. Edwards (eds) *Crime Control and Partnerships: The New Politics of Public Safety*, Cullompton: Willan Publishing.

Coleman, R., Tombs, S. and Whyte, D. (2005) 'Capital, crime control and statecraft in the entrepreneurial city', *Urban Studies*, vol 42, December, pp 1-20.

Crawford, A. (1998) *Crime Prevention and Community Safety: Politics, Policies and Practices*, London: Longman, pp 27-8.

Crawford, A. (1999) *The Local Governance of Crime: Appeals to Community and Partnerships*, Oxford: Oxford University Press.

Croall, H. (1998) 'Business, crime and the community', *International Journal of Risk, Security and Crime Prevention*, vol 3, no 4, pp 281-92.

Croall, H. (1999) 'Crime, business and community safety', *Scottish Journal of Criminal Justice Studies*, vol 5, no 2, pp 65-79.

Environment Agency (2003) 'Annual Report and Accounts 2002/03' (www.environment-agency.gov.uk/commondata/105385/ar0203complete_569081.pdf).

Ericson, R. and Haggerty, K. (1997) *Policing the Risk Society*, Oxford: Clarendon.

Ferrell, J. (2001) *Tearing Down the Streets: Adventures in Urban Anarchy*, New York, NY: Palgrave.

Garland, D. (2000) 'The culture of high crime societies: some preconditions of recent law and order policies', *British Journal of Criminology*, vol 40, no 3, pp 347-75.

Gerstenberg, O. (2004) 'What constitutions can do (but courts sometimes don't): property, speech, and the influence of constitutional norms on private law', *The Canadian Journal of Law and Jurisprudence*, vol 1, no 1, pp 61-81.

Hall, T. and Whyte, D. (2003) 'On the margins of provision: community safety, partnerships and the policing of domestic violence on Merseyside', *Policy & Politics*, vol 31, no 1, pp 3-18.

Hill, S. (2004) *Setting Business Free From Crime: A Crime Against Business Survey by the British Chamber of Commerce, April 2004*, London: British Chamber of Commerce.

Home Office (1998a) *Community Crime Reduction Partnerships: The Retail Contribution – Additional Reference Material*, London: Home Office.

Home Office (1998b) *Guidance on Statutory Crime and Disorder Partnerships: Crime and Disorder Act 1998*, London: Home Office.

Hopkins, M. (2002) 'Crimes against businesses: the way forward for future research', *British Journal of Criminology*, vol 42, no 4, pp 782-97.

Kramer, R. (1989) 'Criminologists and the social movement Against corporate crime', *Social Justice*, vol 16, pp 146-64.

Mathiesen, T. (2000) 'Towards the 21st century: abolition – an impossible dream', in W. West and R. Morris (eds), *The Case for Penal Abolition*, Ontario: Canadian Scholars' Press, pp 333-53.

Mitchell, D. (2003) *The Right to the City: Social Justice and the Fight for Public Space*, New York, NY: The Guilford Press.

Norris, C. and Armstrong, G. (1999) *The Maximum Surveillance Society: The Rise of CCTV*, Oxford: Berg.

O'Malley, P. (1996) 'Risk and responsibility', in A. Barry, T. Osborne and N. Rose (eds) *Foucault and Political Reason: Liberalism, Neo-liberalism and Rationalities of Government*, London: UCL Press, pp 189-207.

Pearce, F. (1990) *Second Islington Crime Survey: Commercial and Conventional Crime in Islington*, Middlesex: Middlesex Polytechnic.

Punch, M. (1996) *Dirty Business. Exploring Corporate Misconduct. Analysis and Cases*, London: Sage Publications.

Rebovich, D. and Lane, J. (2000) *National Survey on White Collar Crime*, Morgantown, WV: National White Collar Crime Centre.

Shearing, C. and Stenning, P. (eds) (1987) *Private Policing*, London: Sage Publications.

Slapper, G. and Tombs, S. (1999) *Corporate Crime*, London: Longman.

Snider, L. (1991) 'The regulatory dance: understanding reform processes in corporate crime', *International Journal of the Sociology of Law*, vol 19, pp 209-36.

Snider, L. (1993) *Bad Business. Corporate Crime in Canada*, Scarborough: Nelson Canada.

Snider, L. (2000) 'The sociology of corporate crime: an obituary (or: Whose knowledge claims have legs?)', *Theoretical Criminology*, vol 4, no 2, pp 169-206.

Sutherland, E. (1983) *White Collar Crime: The Uncut Version*, New Haven, CT: Yale University Press.

Tombs, S. (2001) 'Thinking about "white-collar" crime', in S-Å. Lindgren (ed) *White-Collar Crime Research. Old Views and Future Potentials. BRÅ-Rapport 2001: 1*, Stockholm: Brottsförebyggande rådet/Fritzes, pp 13-34.

Tombs, S. and Whyte, D. (eds) (2003) *Unmasking the Crimes of the Powerful: Scrutinising States and Corporations*, New York, NT: Peter Lang.

Whyte, D. (2004a) 'Regulation and corporate crime', in J. Muncie and D. Wilson (eds), *Student Handbook of Criminal Justice*, London: Cavendish, pp 133-52.

Whyte, D. (2004b) 'All that glitters isn't gold: environmental crimes and the production of local criminological knowledge', *Crime Prevention and Community Safety*, vol 6, no 1, pp 53-63.

Whyte, D. (2004c) 'Punishing anti-social business', *New Law Journal*, 3 September, vol 154, no 7142, p 1293.

ELEVEN

Community safety and victims: who is the victim of community safety?

Sandra Walklate

The first duty of government is to protect the lives and property of all citizens, and thus by definition, reduce the citizen's likelihood of becoming a victim of crime. (1999, 'Editorial', *Police*, vol 31, no 4)

Introduction

It is now commonplace to discuss the contemporary condition of social life by reference to the risk society thesis and, of course, much has been made already of the differential impact of the risk society on contemporary life in relation to crime. Young (1999, 2003), for example, talks of the move from the inclusive to the exclusive society and the concomitant rise in vindictiveness and Garland (2001) tells us about the embeddedness of risk-associated ideas in relation to criminal justice policy through the vehicle of the 'culture of control'. Both of these analyses (among others) take as given the importance of the crime victim, not just as a symbolic reference point for government policy, but also as a dominant one (Garland and Sparks, 2000). Moreover, in the context of the emergence of community safety in relation to crime prevention, the role of the victim, or more specifically, criminal victimisation, has come to occupy centre stage. Local authorities in England and Wales are required to conduct criminal victimisation surveys as a key element in informing their crime reduction strategy documents. Some limited initial optimism was expressed about the likely outcome of this community safety turn. For while Crawford (1998, pp 248-50) itemises the ways in which strategies of responsibilisation permeate the community safety approach to crime prevention (in which victimisation prevention [Karmen, 1990] is a key characteristic), he recognised that there remained the question of 'security differentials': put simply, who was likely to get access to what kind of protection? Nevertheless, the door was considered open for the problem of crime and its relationships with safety to be differently interpreted. In addition, Hughes and Edwards (2002) talk of the possibility such processes offered for what they called the 'rehumanisation' and 'resocialisation' of security and safety.

Arguably, however, as the community safety agenda has unfolded in the intervening period, analyses such as these do not delve deeply enough into the mechanisms underlying the processes associated with the rise of victimhood and its impact. The purpose of this chapter is to suggest such an analysis and to offer a critical understanding of the current imagining of the crime victim in the discourse of community safety. In order to do this, the chapter falls into four sections. The first will consider what it is that is meant by community in the context of community safety. The second will consider what is meant by safety in this same context. The third, as a consequence, will offer a perspective on the nature of the crime victim presumed by the community safety discourse by considering, fourth, the concept of protection (highlighted in the quote at the start of this chapter) in understanding who the victim of community safety might be. But first a few words on images of the community in relation to crime and safety.

Whose community?

Hope (1995) charts community-based crime prevention practices from the Chicago School's Chicago Area project established in the 1930s (working with an assumption of the disorganised community), through the input of community work up to the 1970s (the disadvantaged community) to the appeal to the community's surveillance of itself (the frightened community) that became fashionable in the 1970s in the US and during the 1980s in the UK (through initiatives like Neighbourhood Watch, for example). Despite the different political complexions of these crime prevention paradigms, Hope argues that all of these approaches share a common belief that:

> ... community structure itself shapes local rates of crime – that community crime rates may be the result of something more than the mere aggregation of individual propensities for criminality or victimisation. (Hope, 1995, p 129)

As a consequence, those active in the field of community crime prevention have looked to alter, strengthen or enlist existing community organisations and the activities of community members in order to reduce crime in residential neighbourhoods. The setting up of community-based projects for the unemployed and for young people, Neighbourhood Watch schemes and moving council offices out of town halls and into neighbourhoods have all been advocated at one time or another as methods of empowering communities or involving communities in improving their particular conditions. So, despite Walklate's (1991) suggestion that some of these moves could be interpreted as 'community blaming', there are some good grounds for the current emphasis on community not just as a source of rhetoric but also as a means of offering real change.

There is, however, a fourth way of thinking about community to add to Hope's (1995) analysis. This is found in the work of Young (2001) in which he presents a characterisation of community as de-territorialised and no longer rooted in face-to-face interaction, a concept of community that emphasises such a transient, mediated and differentiated view that a unitary and unified understanding of community safety is rendered highly problematic. While Young's analysis arguably captures some dimensions of community life found in large urban areas, even in this analysis the emotional appeal of community, its feel-good factor, is not completely lost. However, what underpins these appeals to community?

Some time ago, Willmott (1987) commented that community was a 'seductive word'. As with the concept of prevention, there is a presumption that communities are a 'good thing'. This is deeply embedded not only in popular consciousness but also in much sociological thinking. That thinking commonly assumes that traditional communities, together with extended family ties, neighbourliness, a sense of belonging, and a personal sense of place and identity, have been, or are being, destroyed by the processes of modernisation.

For example, in some rural communities, issues surrounding fox-hunting have become a symbol for their deeper insecurities about changing patterns of life. A number of more profound issues, for instance poor public transport, the impact of European regulations on farming life, the 2000 Countryside and Rights of Way Act, and housing, have had a far greater practical impact. Yet despite the continued use of the concept of community as a 'signifier and a referent around which complex and contradictory effects, meanings and definitional struggles coalesce' (Crawford, 1995, p 98), it remains relatively uncritically developed in relation to policy. New Labour's adoption of Etzioni's (1997) understanding of the need to reinvent communities of the past that spoke with one sense of morality and one sense of public interest, for example, marks a contemporary gloss on some traditional sociological questions. This is not the place to discuss the implication of this embrace of communitarianism for crime prevention policy in general (but see Hughes, 1998), but it does lead us to consider the question of what we understand by the concept of community above and beyond its feel-good value.

Willmott (1987) suggests that it is useful to distinguish between the 'territorial' community (those people who live in a particular area), the 'interest' community (those people who have something in common over and above the geographical area in which they live), and the 'attachment' community (people who have a sense of belonging to a place). Of course, the way in which we experience living in our communities may comprise any one or a mixture of these categorisations at any moment in time and may change over time. However, it must be remembered that viewing communities as people experience them is not necessarily the focus of either policy initiatives or political rhetoric, especially in the context of notions of community safety. Indeed, in the contemporary British context, there have clearly been some contradictory forces in play, as Zedner and Lacey observe. They state:

> Thus successive governments whose policies have taken away power
> and resources from local communities have encountered a particular

> *need* to appeal to the existence of 'community' in the face of
> increasingly unmanageable consequences of social policies which
> celebrate the individual and denigrate the social. (Zedner and Lacey,
> 2000, p 158)

Such a contradiction has an important relevance for policy, since embedded within it is a view of communities from above rather than below (that is, how communities should be rather than how people experience them). As a consequence, such a stance presumes that communities need to be empowered, enlisted and harnessed, rather than recognising them as having well-established and perhaps not so well-established mechanisms of sociability and social solidarity of their own. From this viewpoint, some communities may be far from disorganised and fearful of crime (that is, victimised in the conventional sense) but may be highly organised, with crime and the management of crime an integral part of the community's own survival strategies (see, for example, Walklate and Evans, 1999). In some areas, this might also require the recognition of the role that organised crime might play in a locality. Such a role might not only encompass intimidation, but might also provide an alternative job structure, for example, from (illegitimate) criminal gang activity to (legitimate) security work. Crime prevention informed by such a structured sense of well-being (Walklate, 2002) would, as a consequence, take people's 'lived realities' (Crawford et al, 1990) very seriously indeed.

If this kind of image of a community is taken seriously, then it would render problematic what kind of crime is defined as the problem and by whom, what is understood by crime prevention and by whom, and ultimately what is understood by community safety and by whom (see also Gilling, 1999). In other words, it would pose an image of community that would be at odds with that assumed by the mainstream community safety industry. In addition, if this line of thought is pursued in more detail, it might also mean that we need to ask a different question. That question (reflected in the quotation at the beginning of this chapter) might be, what do we understand by protection and who do we expect to protect us?

Suffice it to say at this juncture that the blanket adoption of the concept of community that has become embedded within the contemporary focus on community safety and its associated activities extends in an uncritical fashion a rather conventional sociological view of community and community life. However, before taking this viewpoint further, it is worth commenting on the second concept in play here: that of safety.

Whose safety?

By way of exploring the question of whose safety is embedded within the community safety industry, I would like to offer two examples, both of which attend to the issue of what kind of crime it is assumed that we need to be kept safe from. The first example is that of domestic violence.

It goes without saying that considerable energy and effort has been put into policy initiatives under the auspices of community safety among other arenas in relation to domestic violence over the past 15 years (see Chapter Four in this volume). Much of the contemporary policy focus on this issue began with Home Office circular 60/90, which was modelled on the North American policy response to domestic violence. Moreover, while the uniform validity and value of this model has been seriously challenged by criminological evidence in the US (see Sherman et al, 1991), it has proceeded apace in this country and has since been reinforced by Home Office circular 19/2000. This second circular extended the understanding of what might be considered as domestic violence and who might be considered a victim of it. It is now difficult to find a crime and disorder reduction strategy document (the policy side to debates on community safety) that does not list domestic violence as one of its reduction targets, if not a prioritised one. It might be a moot point as to the extent to which this reflects a serious embrace and/or concern about domestic violence per se or a desire to fulfil the requirements of the Public Service Agreements for 2003-05. However, such questions notwithstanding, as the joint report of Her Majesty's Inspectorate of Constabulary (HMIC) and Her Majesty's Inspectorate of Crown Prosecution Services (2004) indicated, 86% of such strategies had prioritised domestic violence, but only 7% had associated targets. Interestingly enough, the report also indicated that despite more than a decade of activity and resource allocation in this area, the agencies scrutinised for the inspection still did not work with a common definition of domestic violence and the attrition rate (on HMIC's figures) from 463 incidents to which the police were called, to 45 convictions for associated offences, was a cause for concern. The question to be considered is why should we expect any of this to be any different?

Part of the answer to this question would require an analysis of the way in which policies develop a 'life of their own' somewhat independent of their utility. However, in addition, part of the answer relates to which policies in this arena can reasonably be expected to succeed, given the tensions between the policies themselves and the nature of domestic violence, and the notion of community safety. It is important to remember that domestic violence occurs in the context of a *relationship*, and relationships do not lend themselves easily to incident-oriented policy responses. In the context of this chapter, this implies recognising that what women want, that is, what they want to be kept safe from (or for that matter what men want or want to be kept safe from) in the context of their relationships, may not be what the policy intervention has in mind. Kirkwood (1993) and Hoyle (1998, 2000) both document the tensions for the women in their samples in relation to this. As a policy priority, this raises much more philosophical questions, such as how much liberty should be traded for security or, rather more prosaically, whose community and whose safety is being prioritised here, and why (Hudson, 2003)?

The inclusion of domestic violence as a priority in many crime and disorder reduction strategy documents, as indicated above, raises other pertinent questions about policies in this arena. Who decided on the priorities? What kind of community consultation took place? What is the evidence that there was support for such prioritisation, or was this a case of the experts knowing best given the need to comply with service agreements? Similar questions might also be raised by the second example used here, which draws on some empirical work by Whyte (2004).

Whyte (2004) starts from the view that in a part of the country in which there were 'highly visible' and 'unambiguous' crimes of concern, why did they not feature in the community-based crime reduction strategy documents? He examined the targets of all crime reduction strategies in the North West of England for 2001 and found that these strategies reflected a remarkable commonality with the list of priorities made by the Home Office: 26 listed vehicle crime as a priority, 24 burglary, 15 drug-related crime, 15 violent crime, 12 antisocial behaviour, 12 youths causing a nuisance, 11 road safety/speeding, eight domestic violence, eight robbery, and seven the fear of crime. In some respects, this is a rather unremarkable list until it is considered that in that same region, as Whyte reports, 'there is one of the most heavily concentrated sites of chemical production in Western Europe where just 2 plants release about 40% of all the factory produced cancer causing chemicals in the UK into the air every year' (p 59). It is no great surprise, then, to note that Widnes, an area in close proximity to this industrial site, has one of the highest incidents of cancer per head of population in England and Wales. Yet as reported by Whyte, the Environment Agency initiated only 98 prosecutions in 2001/02 in the region: one for industrial process offences, two for radioactive substance offences, 62 for waste offences and 32 for water quality offences. He concludes that:

> To the extent that the CDA (Crime and Disorder Act) actually represented an opportunity for imagining new possibilities for crime control beyond its traditional preoccupations with relatively powerless groups of offenders, it appears on the evidence here to have failed.... The criminological industry, in the midst of this remarkable boom period, trundles on, all but ignoring some of the greatest threats to the safety of our communities. (Whyte, 2004, p 60)

A cursory glance through any of the iterations of the crime reduction strategies produced so far would confirm such a pessimistic conclusion. Moreover, it is hard to find any that have critically evaluated the success or otherwise of the rather conventional agendas they have set for themselves, let alone moved towards the challenge of what kinds of crimes communities need to be kept safe from.

So, the work by Whyte (2004) raises slightly different, though related, questions to those of domestic violence: who decided that these kinds of issues of safety were to be excluded or included from crime and disorder partnership agendas, whose interests are served by that exclusion or inclusion, who was consulted or not in that process, whose liberty has been prioritised here and which concept of justice does that reflect? These are contentious questions indeed, but the point of making them draws attention to the importance of understanding the structure of communities, and all its multilayered facets, and the relationship between that structure, the structure of community safety agendas and the image of the victim that is presumed in the policy responses that have been constructed under the guise of community safety. From one point of view, these questions again, as with the discussion above, suggest that it may be more illuminating to ask whom we expect to protect us and what we expect them to protect us from.

To summarise, the discussion so far has intimated that the community safety perspective in policy responses to crime has operated with very conventional images of both the nature and structure of communities and notions of what it is that communities need to be kept safe from in relation to crime. Those images reflect multifaceted assumptions about victimhood, from the nature of communities that need intervention to the kinds of crimes that worry people. The question remains: are these assumptions legitimate or is there another vision of victimhood that helps make better sense of why the community safety agenda takes the shape that it does? This will be considered by asking the question: whose protection?

Whose protection?

The question of protection is a multifaceted and multilayered affair (see Walklate, 2004). At an individual level, there is much that people do, and are exalted to do, to keep themselves safe in the face of the fear of criminal victimisation (Garland, 1996). Such exaltations can result in some individuals protecting themselves so effectively that they become locked in their own homes or their own safety routines regardless of their actual risk from criminal victimisation. For example, the actuarial expectations of the insurance industry now require individuals to protect their homes against burglary in approved ways or to fit steering wheel locks to their cars and alarms or immobilisers to their motorcycles. As Stanko (1990) has observed, such 'victimisation prevention' advice has also extended itself to questions relating to women's safety in a range of public arenas, sometimes without paying too much attention to the fact that women (and children) are much more vulnerable in relation to their well-being in the private than the public domain.

The interpersonal level of protection might loosely refer to what we might expect from people close to us, whether as intimates, friends or neighbours. These are the people we think we know or we have learned to trust about different things and in different ways. However, while it might be that this level produces strong feelings for and actions in respect of protection (a friend responding on behalf of another in a street fight, for example), it is also the level that produces the most likely betrayal of that protection. It is not necessary to cite the statistics on 'domestic' violence here, or the cross-national evidence that women are most likely to be murdered by an intimate or a former intimate, and men by an acquaintance (see Wilson and Daly, 1998). Such 'facts' are well known. However, knowing 'your offender' is a pattern that cuts across all kinds of criminal behaviour, as some parts of this discussion have intimated.

The familial level of protection encourages us to think about a range of other relationships that are also interpersonal but about which we have little choice. In this context, issues of child protection and protection of the elderly come to the fore: what is it acceptable for parents (and other family members) to do with and for their children (as in the case of child abuse), or conversely, what is it appropriate for children (and other family members) to do with and for their parents as in the case of elder abuse? In each of these examples, different societies draw different boundaries around what is acceptable and unacceptable and the points at which it is appropriate for the state to intervene.

The preceding discussion has already illustrated the way in which, at the level of community, people may or may not feel protected, and may or may not expect protection. Some of these mechanisms may be quite formal and formalised insofar as they derive from agency-led interventions and others will be led by alternative mechanisms of control (see, for example, Evans et al, 1996; McEvoy and Newburn, 2002). At the institutional level, it is possible to situate a wide variety of behaviours and expectations, ranging from the requirements of health and safety legislation through codes of practice relating to racial and sexual harassment to the '*in loco parentis*' role of the school, within a framework of protection. All of these examples convey different messages about who is responsible for what. At this level, much has been directed at the police in particular, and the criminal justice system in general, as institutions, from whom we should be able to expect protection from crime and criminal victimisation. Stanko (1998) has commented on the contradictions this poses in relation to expecting the police to provide protection from 'domestic' violence, for example (see also above). Indeed, Garland's (2001) analysis points to the way in which the criminal justice systems in the UK and the US have adapted to their own failure to provide this.

However, analyses of the role of the state in delivering protection in the context of debates around community safety have been somewhat thin on the ground. Arguably, even Garland's (2001) elegant analysis of the 'culture of control' has rather underplayed the importance of the state, and the perpetuation of state interests, in the manifestation of this culture. Yet there is something to be explored here. Tilly (1985) once described the role of the state as a protection racket whose legitimacy in this capacity has been sustained by its ability to coerce order as well as having access to the means of maintaining order. Much of this has been historically directed to those dangerous classes in dangerous places, but as Chevigny (2003, p 91) has observed, 'even more basic to that work seems to have been a promise of safety, to the poor as much as to everyone else'. This line of argument is developed by Loader and Walker (2001, p 28) in calling for a reconstitution of the connections between policing and the state, since, as they rightly assert (in my view), 'the sense of belonging to and having a stake in a political community assists both directly and reciprocally in the production of the public goods of ontological security and stable cultural identity with which the public police are also concerned'. However, the importance of the role of the state in providing such a public good of protection goes above and beyond the connections between the public police and the state. It is within a deeper analysis of the role of the state that the relationship between victimhood and community safety can be found.

Conclusion: the state, victimhood and community safety

Much of the preceding discussion has taken as given the contemporary importance of the victim as a symbolic reference point in the formation of criminal justice policy, including policies and debates around community safety. What that discussion has also endeavoured to demonstrate is that within that discourse it is possible to identify very conventional understandings of communities and what it is that they need to be kept safe from; conventional understandings that from one point of view lend weight to the argument developed by Furedi (1997) on the culture of fear ('I am a victim, therefore I am') and commented on earlier by Young and Rush (1994) as the increasing elision between citizenship and victimhood. In both of these analyses, we are all the victims of community safety, both as subjects and as objects of such policies. However, our understanding of the nature of community safety and its reproduction of this status needs to go a little deeper. We need to reconsider Tilly's (1985) observation on the role of the state as a protection racket.

Jessop (2002) defines the state as:

> a relatively unified ensemble of socially embedded, socially regularised, and strategically selective institutions and organisations, social forces and activities organised around (or at least involved in) making collective binding decisions for an imagined political community. (Jessop, 2002, p 40)

He goes on to add:

> The hegemonic projects that seek to reconcile the particular and the universal by linking the nature and purposes of the state into a broader – but always selective – political, intellectual, and moral vision of the public interest, the good society, the commonweal, or some analogous principle of societalisation. (Jessop, 2002, p 42)

There are two important clues in these quotes connecting Jessop's analysis of the current form of the capitalist state to contemporary criminal justice policy in general and community safety in particular. These are the imagined political community, and the moral vision of the good society. In the foregoing discussion, it is possible to see that both of these practices are manifest in community safety discourse and praxis, from the symbolism of the victim, through the imaginings of consensus around what it is that communities need to be kept safe from, to the moral vision assumed in the concept of community deployed in community safety rhetoric. These practices serve to maintain the state, albeit as Jessop (2002) would argue, a state that is contemporarily quite a complex, hegemonic entity, but one that nevertheless retains its deep structural form while on the surface giving free rein to the culture of control (Garland, 2001), vindictiveness (Young, 2003) and the rise of the community safety officer (Hughes and Gilling, 2004).

In this deep structural sense, the notions of 'victimhood' as embedded within criminal justice policy in general and community safety in particular have become a key strategy for the continued maintenance of the (capitalist) hegemonic state. Its practices appeal to an 'imagined political community' (the victim as citizen) yet simultaneously offer a vehicle for envisaging a 'good society' in which we are all safe. In retrospect, the strategies of responsibilisation listed by Crawford (1998) have served to protect the state as well and the question remains as to whether or not this provides the space for the construction of community safety as a social good. The prospects to date do not look good, since in the vision of the state implied here, not only are we all the subjects and objects of community safety (that is, the victims), but the real needs of both individuals and communities who may have a just call on resources to make their lives better have become subsumed or lost in the state's generalised project to render us all as citizen-victims. This is the state's protection racket.

References

Chevigny, P. (2003) 'The populism of fear; politics of crime in the Americas', *Punishment and Society*, vol 5, no 1, pp 77-96.

Crawford, A. (1995) 'Appeals to community and crime prevention', *Crime, Law and Social Change*, vol 22, pp 97-126.

Crawford, A. (1998) *Crime Prevention and Community Safety*, London: Longmans.

Crawford, A., Jones, T., Woodhouse, T. and Young, J. (1990) *The Second Islington Crime Survey*, London: Centre for Criminology, Middlesex University.

Etzioni, A. (1997) *The New Golden Rule*, London: Profile Books.

Evans, K., Fraser, P. and Walklate, S. (1996) 'Whom do you trust? The politics of grassing on an inner city housing estate', *Sociological Review*, vol 44, no 3, pp 361-80.

Furedi, F. (1997) *The Culture of Fear*, London: Frank Cass.

Garland, D. (1996) 'The limits of the sovereign state', *British Journal of Criminology*, vol 36, no 4, pp 445-71.

Garland, D. (2001) *The Culture of Control*, Oxford: Oxford University Press.

Garland, D. and Sparks, R. (2000) 'Criminology, social theory and the challenge of our times', *British Journal of Criminology*, vol 40, no 2, pp 189-204.

Gilling, D. (1999) 'Community safety: a critique', in M. Brogden (ed) *British Criminology Conference Selected Proceedings,* Volume 2 (www.britsoccrim.org/v2.htm).

HMIC (Her Majesty's Inspectorate of Constabulary) and HMICPS (Her Majesty's Inspectorate of Crown Prosecution Services) (2004) *Violence at Home: A Joint Thematic Inspection of the Investigation and Prosecution of Cases Involving Domestic Violence,* London: HMIC.

Hope, T. (1995) 'Community crime prevention', in M. Tonry and D. Farrington (eds) *Building a Safer Society. Crime and Justice,* vol 19, Chicago, IL: University of Chicago Press, pp 21-90.

Hoyle, C. (1998) *Negotiating Domestic Violence,* Oxford: Oxford University Press.

Hoyle, C. (2000) '"Being a nosy bloody cow"; ethical and methodological dilemmas in researching domestic violence', in R. King and E. Wincup (eds) *Doing Research on Crime and Justice,* Oxford: Oxford University Press, pp 395-406.

Hudson, B. (2003) *Justice in a Risk Society,* London: Sage Publications.

Hughes, G. (1998) *Understanding Crime Prevention,* Buckingham: Open University Press.

Hughes, G. and Edwards, A. (eds) (2002) *Crime Control and Community: The New Politics of Community Safety,* Cullompton: Willan Publishing.

Hughes, G. and Gilling, D. (2004) 'Mission impossible? The habitus of the community safety manager and the new expertise in the local partnership governance of crime and safety', *Criminal Justice,* vol 4, no 2, pp 129-49.

Jessop, B. (2002) *The Future of the Capitalist State,* Cambridge: Polity Press.

Karmen, A. (1990) *Crime Victims: An Introduction to Victimology,* Belmont, CA: Wadsworth Publishers.

Kirkwood, C. (1993) *Leaving Abusive Partners,* London: Sage Publications.

Loader, I. and Walker, N. (2001) 'Policing as a public good: reconstituting the connections between policing and the state', *Theoretical Criminology,* vol 5, no 1, pp 9-35.

McEvoy, K. and Newburn, T. (eds) (2002) *Criminology and Conflict Resolution,* London: Palgrave.

Sherman, L.W., Schmidt, J.D., Rogan, D.P., Gartin, P.R., Cohn, E.G., Collins, D.J. and Bacich, A.R. (1991) 'From initial deterrence to long term escalation: short arrest for ghetto poverty violence', *Criminology,* vol 9, no 4, pp 821-49.

Stanko, B. (1990) 'When precaution is normal: a feminist critique of crime prevention', in L. Gelsthorpe and A. Morris (eds) *Feminist Perspectives in Criminology,* Milton Keynes: Open University Press, pp 173-83.

Stanko, B. (1998) 'Desperately seeking safety: problematising policing and protection', in J. Vagg and T. Newburn (eds) *British Criminology Conference Selected Proceedings Vol 1 Emerging Themes in Criminology,* Loughborough: BCC.

Tilly, C. (1985) 'War making and state making as organised crime', in D. Rueschmeyer, P.B. Evans and T. Skocpol (eds) *Bringing the State Back,* Cambridge: Cambridge University Press, pp 169-91.

Walklate, S. (1991) 'Victims, crime prevention and social control', in R. Reiner and M. Cross (eds) *Beyond Law and Order*, London: Macmillan, pp 204-22.

Walklate, S. (2002) 'Gendering crime prevention', in G. Hughes, E. McLaughlin and J. Muncie (eds) *Crime Prevention and Community Safety*, London: Sage Publications, pp 58-76.

Walklate, S. (2004) 'The protective society? Seeking safety in an insecure world', *Community Safety Journal*, vol 3, no 1.

Walklate, S. and Evans, K. (1999) *Zero Tolerance or Community Tolerance? Managing Crime in High Crime Areas*, Aldershot: Ashgate.

Whyte, D. (2004) 'All that glitters isn't gold: environmental crimes and the production of local criminological knowledge', *Crime Prevention and Community Safety: An International Journal*, vol 6, no 1, pp 53-63.

Willmott, P. (1987) 'Introduction', in P. Willmott (ed) *Policing and the Community*, London: Policy Studies Institute, pp 1-6.

Wilson, M. and Daly, M. (1998) 'Sexual rivalry and sexual conflict: recurring themes in fatal conflicts', *Theoretical Criminology*, vol 2, no 3, pp 291-310.

Young, A. and Rush, P. (1994) 'The law of victimage in urbane realism: thinking through inscriptions of violence', in D. Nelken (ed) *The Futures of Criminology*, London: Sage Publications, pp 154-72.

Young, J. (1999) *The Exclusive Society*, London: Sage Publications.

Young, J. (2001) 'Identity, community and social exclusion', in R. Matthews and J. Pitts (eds) *Crime, Disorder and Community Safety*, London: Routledge, pp 26-53.

Young, J. (2003) 'Merton with energy Katz with structure: the sociology of vindictiveness and the criminology of transgression', *Theoretical Criminology*, vol 7, no 3, pp 389-414.

Zedner, L. and Lacey, N. (2000) 'Community and governance: a cultural comparison', in S. Karstedt and K.D. Bussmann (eds) *Social Dynamics of Crime Control*, Oxford: Hart Publishing, pp 159-72.

TWELVE

Young women, community safety and informal cultures

Lynda Measor

Introduction

Community safety policy is one of a number of initiatives governments have developed to address crime and related problems of disorder and insecurity. Community safety policy has grown slowly in importance and significance since the 1980s and now stands as the essential core of a collection of strategies (Tilley, 1994; Crawford, 1997; Gilling, 1997; Hughes, 1997; Stenson, 1998). Various critiques of community safety approaches have developed within criminology (Crawford, 1997; Hughes, 1998; Stenson, 1998; Garland, 2000; Coleman et al, 2002). Little attention has been paid, however, to the implications that community safety approaches may have for women in communities – as opposed to men or children.

This chapter explores the implications that community safety policies have for young women. It does not aim to offer a broad analysis of all the gender implications of the shift to community safety approaches. It is based on one research study of young women who live in a particularly deprived area, where they perceive the risks to their safety and their well-being to be high. The chapter focuses on data that indicate the strategies adopted by some of them.

Background and methodology

The evidence in this chapter is not drawn from direct research into criminology or fear of crime. Rather it emerged in a project that studied teenage pregnancy funded by the Department of Health (Bell et al, 2004). The study was qualitative and sought to understand more about the factors that influence young women who become pregnant in the UK. The research project was based in three separate sites throughout the UK, but the data in this chapter are all drawn from one site, a seaside town in the South East of England that had higher than average rates of teenage pregnancy.

The argument developed here is that these data offer insights that can be applied to understanding some of the barriers to the development of effective community safety strategies. There are methodological difficulties that must be acknowledged. The research was a small-scale study and we must be cautious of drawing generalisations from it. The data are reported by and derived from individuals who discuss the actions and motivations of others. Nevertheless, the data were gathered from information given to us by a number of young people, interviewed separately on different occasions. The results surprised us and we have not seen anything else like it written about extensively elsewhere. The issues were first introduced by some of our key informants. The researchers then routinely discussed them with other young people who recognised and confirmed the developing analysis (Burgess, 1984)[1].

Community safety

The term community safety is 'notoriously slippery, resisting definition partly because it is used and applied at local levels in a variety of ways' (Stenson, 2002, p 112). The starting point of the definition used in this chapter is a Home Office circular that argued that crime prevention could not be left to the police alone but was a task for the whole community (Home Office, 1994). The 'whole community' implies a role for local citizen involvement and the full array of both statutory and voluntary agencies, including, of course, the police. Yet it is important to recognise that community safety also involves the development, deployment and use of new forms of knowledge and expertise. These theoretical developments have significant implications for policy and practice.

Women's strategies

The data presented in this chapter indicate that the young women and their families living on the two very deprived estates we studied had a high sense of risk and fear. They fear actual crime – the loss of material possessions to robbery or burglary, or the loss of physical safety through violent attack. They also fear the lower-level risks of deprived communities, the humiliation, harassment and degradation they say characterises their estate contexts. Such data are depressingly familiar in a number of research studies (Lea and Young, 1984; Coleman et al, 2002). The data in this chapter alert us to some of the ways that young women respond to their situation. The strategies adopted are individual ones that seek to protect the individual woman, her children and also her family of origin from the risks they feel they face.

The 'names'

The starting point for respondents was their account of the insecurities and risks on the estate derived from fear of the families who have great power and influence there. These were 'the names', that is, families who had a 'reputation' and even dominance in such areas. We were told of how young women sought liaisons and sexual relationships with the men of such families. They also sought to have their children, even if they had little firm relationship or formal commitment from the men involved. Such liaisons were seen to bring safety and security from the risks permeating the estates because of the influence the 'names' carried.

We were given numerous descriptions of the 'names', people who had a 'reputation' in the estates we studied. A 'reputation' begins to be earned at school, when a boy is categorised as 'popular'. The following data were generated in a focus group with 15-year-old girls in the school on the Valley estate. It suggests the significance of physical characteristics and the importance of fighting, which demonstrates 'being hard', a key element in growing a 'reputation':

> Julie: They are good at something. Some popular people are big, good at fighting and stuff like that.

Connell and Segal have alerted us to the way that patterns of defining and 'doing' masculinities leads to such rivalries among groups of young males in school and informal cultures from a young age (Connell, 1987; Segal, 1997). But something more than those struggles appears to be at stake in this context. Individual attributes are important, but 'reputation' is also associated in these cases with where you live:

> Anna: Like, if you're from Hillsdown, Hillsdown people, people from Hillsdown estate, girls and boys. Hillsdown, also Valley estate and even Ashingdean estate, they think they are really hard. But it is especially Hillsdown, if they come from Hillsdown, you don't want to mess with them because reputation is a big part, so they are scary, and respected because they scare people, because they can do this, and they can do what they want.

We have a picture of the fear and domination that those with 'reputation' inspire and exercise on the estates we studied. Young people grow up in this atmosphere and become aware quite early on of the power that such people can deploy. They learn 'respect' for such individuals and they learn 'not to mess' with them. Young people grow up with a map in their heads of the power and influence that operates on their estates and throughout the other areas of the town seen to be peopled by those who are 'hard'.

From their early years at secondary school, those who are 'popular' and have a 'reputation' draw other young people to them in complicated patterns of relationships. A key element is that they offer some security:

> Julie: And the reason why they are popular then is 'cos people want to get in the same crowd as them ...

> Amy: So that they won't get beaten up.

Julie: Yes, so that they are protected.

'Being in the same crowd' is seen to offer some protection, some security to those who do not feel they have the personal attributes to develop a 'reputation' on their own. They are not 'big', they are not seen as 'hard' and have little ability to fight. The strategy they employ is to form an alliance with those who are 'hard' to establish a place in the 'same crowd'. The hope is then that they will be less at risk of violence from those who are the fighters in their own crowd, but also that being a part of the circle of someone with a 'reputation' can offer protection from other groups in the estates identified as being risky. From an early age in adolescence and perhaps earlier, young people on these estates learn strategies of alliance and liaison for their security.

'Reputation' is founded on individual attributes and reinforced by the place the 'hard' individual comes from. It is, however, family connections that confirm a *big* reputation for a young man:

> Jan: Yeah, so say like your dad has been inside for so many years and you will sort of … everyone will look at you to have the same responsibility, to go inside for so many years, you come out and you will be a hero to everyone sort of thing, you would be respected because you were…

> Interviewer: So that would … so the son of one of those blokes who have been inside for a long time would be one of the popular boys?

> Group (several voices): Yeah! (in agreement)

> Interviewer: Automatically?

> Julie: Yeah, automatically for the name, if he was a tramp he would still be a popular boy because of the name.

> Group (several voices): Yeah! (in agreement)

> Teaching Assistant: One lad has just left now who was very popular purely because of his brothers. Now the lad himself was quite a wuss, he wasn't a particularly strong character and yet no one would have dreamt of picking on him purely because of his surname.

It is clear from this that the young people involved have a clear picture of the place and the significance of individual young men and their family connections in the estates on which they live. 'Reputations' develop on the basis of 'being hard' and being able to fight but reach special status when the individual young man has a connection through the family to criminal activity. By the time they have reached adolescence, these young people have a clear 'chart' of the risk that such individuals pose and the workings of the power such families operate on their estates. They have also evolved strategies that aim to garner protection.

Data gathered from other groups of young people reinforced the same picture. In a focus group held in a centre for young people who were excluded from school, but who lived on the same estates, the following account emerged:

Sharon: I know plenty of people who use their name as popularity.

Marie: Yeah, so do I.

Martin: Where do we begin?

Sharon: You have got the Wenlocks, everyone has heard of the Wenlocks family.

Martin: You have got the Wenlocks, who are notorious round here. They live in Valley estate and in Hillsdown estate.

From this independent source, we gain the same picture as the girls in school gave, of estates that have clearly identified families who are 'names' on them. Individuals within these families use their names to gain 'popularity', give themselves a dominant status and also to keep themselves safe:

Sharon: They go round starting trouble and if you do anything back, they go don't start on me I am a Wenlock.

Marie: They have got a hell of a lot of family to back them up, you touch one hair on any of their heads, you may as well leave this town but that's not the point.

Martin: You may as well leave England!

The account these young people give supports the analysis made above. Those involved in giving this narrative reveal fear of the families they are describing and recognise the power they can manipulate, in exactly the same way the girls in the school did. They go on to describe the extensive networks of connected families throughout the estates:

Martin: They have got a lot of friends everywhere, the Towneys, the O'Donnells. Ooh, I've said the names!

Interviewer: Don't worry, I will never use their names, you know I will keep their names confidential.

Martin: It doesn't matter, the police know about them anyway.

The families are recognised to have criminal connections. Again, the accounts given in the secondary school are supported:

Interviewer: The police know about them?

Marie: Oh yeah!

Interviewer: Are these families where the *men* in the family have been in prison?

Sharon: Both, the men and the women.

Marie: I think for one of the families they were all done for drugs.

Sharon: The Towney brothers were done for drugs and murder.

The criminal activities described are serious and the families involved in such activities have a notoriety that is one element in what gives them their 'names'. The empirical work undertaken here reveals young people from two estates, Valley and Hillsdown, who have a clear sense of themselves as belonging to a particular area. Those living on the estates see themselves as sharing a particular geographical location with specific boundaries that give the area a distinctive identity. The young people describe estates riven by tensions, enmities and competition for status. Later in this chapter we consider what impact these issues have on policies based on notions of 'community'. So far the data we have considered have equal application to both young men and young women. If you are not a member of one of the 'names' families, then you are faced with some decisions about how you relate to them. Individual young people will, of course, make individual decisions – and they begin to make them at quite a young age. It is to the decisions that young *women* make in relation to the 'map' of the families of influence around them that we now turn.

Young women and the 'names'

Young women grow up knowing about the 'names' and recognising the power that such families wield. We generated other data that suggested they seek new kinds of alliances with these sources of localised power and respect as they mature. Some young women seek sexual relationships with the men of such families, and seek to have children with them. Such alliances follow the same pattern and motivations as the ones we identified in the data from the school and the Pupil Referral Unit. The liaisons offer status in the community and can bring some esteem. But most of all they offer protection; an alliance with a 'name' means that other people will recognise the risks in 'messing with you'. One teenage mother aged 14 was well aware of the respect and the reputation for 'hardness' – for being someone who should be treated with care – that such a liaison carried:

> Tracey: They think that they're hard and that – and have their baby and that, they think like say if they've got a baby with one of the most looked up to persons in Valley, they think they're 'that'.

The baby's father, who was 17, agreed:

> Mark: They think they're something.

In a situation of deprivation, esteem is an important good (Young, 2001), but it may be in this situation that having a baby with a 'looked up to person' in Valley estate offers other more concrete resources than that.

The focus group of excluded young people generated the following account:

> Martin: Some women do it with those names, those people, so that they think ...

> Sharon (interrupts): ... so that they will be protected and that they will be one of those people who won't be messed with.

> Marie: That's right!

> Martin: It doesn't always work though.

The focus group identified the need for protection that ordinary families want and feel they need. Sexual liaisons with the 'names' are seen to offer a way out of the indignities, vulnerabilities and criminality that characterise the estates studied:

> Interviewer: So you think that there might be some girls who would like to get pregnant by boys from one of these families?

> Sharon: Yes!

> Marie and Martin (talking at same time): Yes!

> Interviewer: Say that again, 'cos you were both talking at once and I missed what you said.

> Sharon: I know plenty of people who said they want Gary Wenlock in their bed. Yeah any girl that sleeps with Gary Wenlock is like, 'I had sex with Gary Wenlock, I had sex with Gary'.
>
> Interviewer: Right, is that, that they want sex with him or is that actually they want to be pregnant?
>
> Sharon: Both, I think.
>
> Interviewer: Can you tell me why?
>
> Sharon: 'Cos it's well known – the fact that Gary won't wear condoms.

This shows the gloss that being a 'name' extends to young men in those families, and indicates that young women who choose to fly close to that flame do so on very unequal terms. Some young women want to be associated with the 'names' and with the notoriety and perhaps even glamour that goes along with them.

A later interview reinforces these insights and allows us to extend and develop the analysis outlined so far. The interview was with a young woman from a travellers' family who had lived most of her life in caravans in the area around the seaside town. She too recognised the picture of the named criminal families, and discussed the way some young women related to them:

> Katy: Mmm. It's true, you'll get a few families that are known to be really tough…. Right … and really successful criminals. That's true, yeah. Right, yeah, yeah, I get it, I'm with you. I know some of these families myself. On the estates, they're like celebrities almost. Mmm. They're like, er, you know, like the names. There's like … a girl, even a 15-year-old, will say 'Oh, I've got, you know, so and so's kid, that's like, it brings more, like, reputation to their family and so on, you know.

Having a connection with one of the 'names', then, is seen to bring esteem to a family that may have very little of its own. The 'celebrity' of the 'names' rubs off onto the other family. Esteem, as we have already seen, however, is not the only issue:

> Katy: But actually if you have a kid with one of these families it brings protection to your family. That's true also.
>
> Interviewer: Is it?
>
> Katy: Yeah, it is, yeah. It's, um, it used to work that way in the old, in the old, old traveller society.

Interviewer: Did it?

Katy: Yeah. It's like a common thread. It, it does happen on council estates. I know it does. 'Cos I know girls who've done it. There used to be like, for the people who, er, you know, the most successful workers, the most successful criminals, who had the most money, you know would prey on the other families who didn't have so much, you know, and if a girl from that family had a kid with a boy from that family, they, they were kind of alright, you know. It does bring you some kind of security.

The traveller girl, who is both of and outside the society being study here, identifies the important factors of protection and security that can be obtained from association with the 'names'. One of the ways of securing such an alliance is through a child. A Teaching Assistant who both lived on Valley estate and worked in the school that served it agreed with the analysis:

Teaching Assistant: You see, there is on the estate a certain amount of prestige, let's say a very popular lad got two, maybe three, girls pregnant they would be respected 'cause they have got his child.

A number of pupils who heard her comments were in agreement with them:

Interviewer: Is that true?

Anna and Julie: Yeah!

Anna: Basically, if there are two families and he, boy, and a girl sleep together, then it sort of brings those families together to be one giant, just because of those two sleeping together. It's like a big reputation for both families because they can sort of rely on each other and I mean if they keep going steady it sort of comes together.

Alliances between families are brokered and fostered by the activities of their young people in the accounts of the respondents in this study, who all had close connections to the estates they were discussing. We have a description of a culture in which individuals recognise, and, of course, at a theoretical level continue to construct, the map of power, influence and resources in their community. Young women choose to deploy sexuality and sexual attractiveness to gain access to some of it. Young women use sexuality and, importantly, fertility as a resource in order to secure protection by mobilising influence on the 'names' of those who already have it on the estates. Establishing an effective liaison with one of the 'names' may also have economic implications if the criminal family is a successful one, but we did not collect data on this issue. It was the issues of protection and security that were emphasised by our respondents.

It is important to recognise that protection and security is not guaranteed by a simple sexual encounter. The girl involved needs to have some level of connection with the family with one of the 'names'. The son involved needs to acknowledge some level of connection with the girl involved before he will take on the responsibility for the girl and for the baby.

The young women who take this course of action and seek to make alliances with the 'names' may not, of course, be making entirely rational or even effective decisions or decisions that fully consider the long-term consequences of their actions. Their actions nevertheless have a rationale that displays an accurate grasp of the patterns of power, conflict and risk of the places where they live. It is not being claimed that this is the only strategy that women choose in such situations; there is not one strategy, there are many. Nor are we suggesting that the motivation for security is the only factor in determining high teenage pregnancy rates in areas with high rates of deprivation and social exclusion.

Community safety and the estates

We need now to make an assessment of the implications of these data for community safety approaches. It is important to question what such data tell us about strategies that have at their core an aim to work with and for the 'whole community' in partnership with relevant agencies seeking to reduce crime and improve 'safety'. In these data, young people identify the risks that they perceive exist on their estates deriving from the 'names'. The young people seem to consider that an effective source of real protection comes from alliance with the men of the powerful and criminally aligned families on the estate. One way for young women to cement such an alliance of two families and gain the protection of the powerful one is to have the child of one of the men. This offers in their view a real measure of security. It means no one will dare 'mess with you'. Young men may develop a whole series of other approaches that probably rely on friendship networks and on shared criminal risk-taking activities but they are not the focus of this chapter, although the data we have indicate that their activities display the same aims of negotiating with the 'names'.

Community safety agencies and activities play no part in the accounts given by respondents of the sources of security available in the estates. It is noticeable that the young women involved seem to have little or no confidence in the ability of any statutory agencies to offer them levels of protection equal to those of the 'names'. The police are not seen to be able to offer security against the risks of 'being messed with'. The other agencies represented in the 'bewildering range of partnerships' (Stenson and Edwards, 2001, p 111) involved in community safety do not appear in the data as alternative sources of 'protection'. Instead, residents of such estates turn to their own resources.

Coleman et al have argued that we need to challenge the 'official discourses of empowerment' that surround a number of community safety initiatives (2002). These data from my study, presented in this chapter, offer an example that indicates that what is done has little impact on the perspectives residents have about their lack of safety and security. CCTV schemes, lighting, hedging, or the provision of diversionary activities for young people, for example, have not resulted in this situation in local families feeling safer and more secure. They do not feel empowered by what is put in place. In their accounts, the state and the local statutory agencies are largely absent; the 'official' discourse is silenced by the paradoxical strengths and weaknesses of the community. These weaknesses contribute directly to the risks of both crime and harassment that members of the community have to endure and the strengths concern the (extended) families of power, influence and reputation who run the estates.

Community safety strategies are distinguished partly through their commitment to delivering services, welfare and security in the 'Third Way' for reasons that are widely discussed (Stenson, 1998; Hughes and Edwards, 2002). They place responsibility for crime prevention on a number of agencies and individuals and shift responsibility away from either the police or more widely the state. There is no evidence here that the 'mixed economy' model of public, private and voluntary organisations deployed by community safety strategies has been any more successful in reducing and controlling crime and increasing residents' sense of security than crime prevention run by statutory agencies. The data in this chapter suggest some of the deficits that such approaches, which have undercut 'welfare' provision, entail and the areas of crime and disorder that they leave untouched.

Community safety initiatives grew out of and reflected a decreasing confidence in the central state's willingness, if not ability, to deliver effective security and safety for citizens (Jordan, 1998; Stenson and Edwards, 2001). They developed in part from the despondent sense that 'nothing works'. This led to the mixed economy of provision discussed above, but a further implication of the community safety discourses is that citizens are encouraged and exhorted to take greater responsibility for their own security and well-being (Garland, 2001; Young, 2001). We can see young people in these data acting in ways they consider reduce the risk to them. They take responsibility for their own security and take action to ensure some protection. This may not be the kind of action government had in mind; they do not seek resources from their 'whole community' nor from multi-agency partnerships. They act rather in some time-honoured way to seek protection within their 'manor'. What we see in these accounts is a scurry for individual protection that the state cannot offer. It is this issue of individualism that we turn to next.

Individualism

Hughes has been critical of community safety approaches that offer little but 'pious words of encouragement to poor communities to help themselves through their own endeavours in the spirit of voluntarism' (Hughes, 2002, p 277). In fact, the data drawn from the research in this chapter indicate that helping themselves was precisely what the young women and their families did. They acted in ways they thought were likely to enhance their safety and their security. They did this through building a tie of flesh, and sealing it permanently with a blood connection. Metaphor apart, what is important is that such families took an individual solution and an individualistic solution. There is in their actions no concern for solidarity or collaborative action on risk of all kinds, there is no concern to enhance security for the 'whole community'. These women 'make shift' for themselves, using the resources they have. The data equally undermine the analysis that underclass theorists such as Murray have made (1990). He argues that the key characteristic of an underclass is its apathy and its inability to take active steps to improve its own conditions. This research, however, indicates young women attempting to secure themselves – and for those involved, it makes sense. The data do, however, raise some difficult questions about the reliance placed on community and on ideas about communities working together that underpin community safety approaches, and it is to these we now turn.

The 'whole community'

New Labour has promoted ideas of developing safety through working with, and for, the 'whole community' (Blair, 1993):

> Community is a robust and powerful idea. It means teamwork to get things done. It means mutuality – rights and responsibilities. It means justice. (Mandelson and Liddle, 1996, p 19)

The data presented in this chapter, however, reveal communities that are fractured and divided in ways that make such an approach seem hopelessly idealistic. Many community safety schemes promote models of communities of active citizens that work in partnership with the police against 'outsider' crime (Jordan, 1998). There are well-known problems of creating 'outsiders' and others by such a policy (Crawford, 1998; Koch, 1998). If the analysis here has merit, however, it indicates that the major problem a deprived area experiences is not with 'outsider' crime but with crime that originates from within the community (Lea and Young, 1984). The data cited here indicate that risk is perceived to come from within the community; it originates from those who live next door or across the road and it is a serious and substantial risk.

Community safety approaches fail to recognise the competition for resources within deprived areas. They work instead with a discourse that relies on 'the interests of the city as a whole', for example (Coleman et al, 2002, p 100). Critiques of community safety policy emphasise, by contrast, how severe such conflict can be and identify the 'corruscating divisions that dominate the local and national landscape of the UK' (Coleman et al, 2002, p 105). There may be little hope of developing collaborative cooperative strategies similar to those argued for by Etzioni (1995).

Some theorists have seen community governance as offering genuine options for associative, participatory and democratic ways forward (Held, 1995; Hirst, 2000). Critical pluralist thinking on community governance advocates the cultivation of 'self-governing' communities allowed to regulate the affairs of their own members according to the values shared by those members. The data in this chapter shed a pessimistic light on such thinking because they alerts us to patterns of division and norms of competitive individualism that regulate the community and might obstruct any such development.

Social democratic approaches to crime prevention in the 1980s called for a role for community-based initiatives. Other more radical voices at the same time argued that policies geared to community empowerment could play an important role in regeneration and the fight against crime and victimisation (Lea and Young, 1984; Hope and Shaw, 1988). The data presented here offer a critical assessment of how much has been achieved. A radical analysis would argue that this is not surprising, given the economic divisions and inequalities that characterise our society. Crime control measures – like those involved in community safety – seek to regulate crime and the wider society in a number of ways, all of which work to support dominant coalitions of economic interest (Hay, 1996). In this perspective, community safety is yet one more strategy to try to contain the casualties and the fallout that are an inevitable result of the competitive stakes. Neo-liberal policies have made the position of those at the bottom of the competition even more difficult as the various securities provided by social policy initiatives are now gone. Punitive regimes remain, and so do strategies like community safety that do not address the inequality of which Coleman et al speak but rather contain and control it (Coleman et al, 2002).

In such a context, community safety partnerships that advocate multi-agency work, joined-up thinking and voluntaristic regeneration and collaboration are unlikely to enjoy significant success. As Scheurich pointed out in his work on the 'archaeology' of social policy:

> Does it not seem highly questionable that a large social problem ... requires something as simple as linking existing governmental and professional arrangements. If present services have to date been unable to 'solve' this largely social problem it is difficult to believe that linking them together would seriously impact on a problem as sizeable as this. It would surely call for a major restructuring of services. Or even the social order itself. (Scheurich, 1977, p 110)

The nature of community and the nature of family

One of the key assumptions about high crime communities is that they are defeated, lacking in cohesion and highly disorganised (Foster, 2002, p 175). Etzioni's core message is that communities have broken down, leading to a crisis of values and a loss of virtue. Foster argues that this is not necessarily an accurate picture and points to the existence of quite well-structured and well-understood criminal hierarchies and organised crime networks within established communities (Walklate, 1998; Foster, 2002, p 175). Taylor argues that in areas of long-term disadvantage and decline 'new organised crime syndicates develop' (1999, p 168). It is to these realities of power, prestige and resources within their communities that the young women orient themselves. The evidence in this chapter indicates not a community that has broken down but one that works quite effectively (although not necessarily to everyone's benefit – like any community).

Etzioni also discussed the importance of the family as an engine of moral growth, capable of developing responsible citizens committed to community and society, an idea that has been adopted by New Labour (Utting et al, 1993; Labour Party, 1996). A breakdown in the family is defined as one of the factors that leads to disorganisation of community and society. The data presented in this chapter, however, indicate the existence of strong families in the 'tribal' units of the criminal families. They also reveal families that benefit from the actions and alliances that their daughters achieve with the 'names'. There is no evidence of wholesale disorganisation in families; rather, there is evidence of strong family relationships – but they work for different ends and with different means than government might want, and with strategies that marginalise and leave statutory agencies silent.

The data presented in this chapter indicate that we may need a more complex model of understanding the relationships that women have to crime. We know women have greater fear of crime than men (Chambers and Tombs, 1984; Hough, 1995; Ditton and Farrall, 2000) and have some insights into what might underpin some of that fear (Hollway and Jefferson, 2000). We know women commit less crime and that it is of a less serious nature than that committed by men. Campbell described estates where 'angry young men admired and serviced a criminalised brotherhood', with women by contrast 'working to create networks that could generate self-help and social capital' (1993, p 244). There was evidence of women engaged in just such activities on the estates in this research, but the data presented here suggest also that some women are willing to ally with, and profit from, criminal activities and circles of influence. While we have journalistic and literary accounts of the lives and values and reactions of gangsters' molls and the mothers and aunts of figures like the notorious East End criminals, the Kray twins, there is little real criminological research.

Conclusion

The data presented here assert that we need to analyse what community and safety mean more systematically and understand more about the perspectives of those who live in areas where fears and perceptions of risk are high. The chapter also asks for a greater appreciation to be given to inequalities that underpin the bitter rivalries of those areas, and for policies that recognise and do not underestimate their importance in the development of community safety initiatives. At the moment, social problems are studied in independent silos; those studying teenage pregnancy do not normally communicate in any detail with those studying tooth decay, heart illness, substance misuse or crime. Yet it is the same groups of people who are at risk in all of these areas. Academics may need to move out of their personal and academic silos in order to make advances in understanding how crime and disorder are experienced by those who are most often its victims. If we want to understand the limitations of the policies adopted under the rubric of community safety, then the discipline of criminology may need to be prepared to look at wider issues and in different ways than it has done so traditionally.

Note

[1] All names and locations have been changed or otherwise anonymised.

References

Bell, J., Craig, G., Clisby, S., Measor, L., Petrie, S. and Stanley, N. (2004) *Living on the Edge: Teenage Pregnancy in Seaside Towns*, London: Department of Health.

Blair, T, (1993) 'Why crime is a social issue', *New Statesman and Society*, 29 January, pp 27-8.

Burgess, R. (1984) 'In the company of teachers: key informants and the study of a comprehensive school', in R. Burgess (ed) *Strategies of Educational Research*, Barcombe: Falmer Press, pp 79-101.

Campbell, B. (1993) *Goliath: Britain's Dangerous Places*, London: Methuen.

Chambers, G. and Tombs, J. (1984) *British Crime Survey*, Scotland/London: HMSO.

Coleman, R., Sim, J. and Whyte, D. (2002) 'Power, politics and partnerships: the state of crime prevention on Merseyside', in G. Hughes and A. Edwards (eds) *Crime Control and Community: The New Politics of Public Safety*, Cullompton: Willan Publishing, pp 86-109.

Connell, R. (1987) *Gender and Power*, Cambridge: Polity Press.

Crawford, A. (1997) *The Local Governance of Crime*, Oxford: Oxford University Press.

Crawford, A. (1998) 'Community safety and the quest for security: holding back the dynamics of social exclusion', *Policy Studies*, vol 19, no 3/4, pp 237-53.

Ditton, J. and Farrall, S. (2000) '"Fear" of burglary: refining national survey questions for use at the local level', *International Journal of Police Science and Management*, vol 3, no 10, pp 9-18.

Etzioni, A. (1995) *The Spirit of Community: Rights, Responsibilities and the Communitarian Agenda*, London: Fontana Press.

Foster, J. (2002) '"People pieces": the neglected but essential elements of community crime prevention', in G. Hughes and A. Edwards (eds) *Crime Control and Community:The New Politics of Public Safety*, Cullompton:Willan Publishing, pp 167-97.

Garland, D. (2001) *The Culture of Control, Crime and Social Order in Contemporary Society*, Oxford: Oxford University Press.

Gilling, D. (1997) *Crime Prevention*, London: UCL Press.

Hay, C. (1996) *Re-stating Social and Political Change*, Buckingham: Open University Press.

Held, D. (1995) *Democracy and the Global Order: From the Modern State to Cosmopolitan Governance*, Stanford, CA: Stanford University Press.

Hirst, P. (2000) 'Statism, pluralism and social control', in D. Garland and R. Sparks (eds) *Criminology and Social Theory*, Oxford: Oxford University Press, pp 127-49.

Hollway, W. and Jefferson, T. (2000) *Doing Qualitative Research Differently*, London: Sage Publications.

Home Office (1994) *Crime Prevention*, Circular 8/94, London: Home Office.

Hope, T. and Shaw, M. (eds) (1988) *Communities and Crime Reduction*, London: HMSO.

Hough, M. (1995) *Anxiety about Crime: Findings from the 1994 British Crime Survey*, Home Office Research Study No 147, London: Home Office.

Hughes, G. (1997) 'Policing late modernity: crime management in contemporary Britain', in N. Jewson and S. MacGregor (eds) *Transforming Cities: Contested Governance and New Spatial Divisions*, London: Routledge, pp 28-41.

Hughes, G. (1998) *Understanding Crime Prevention: Social Control, Risk and Late Modernity*, Buckingham: Open University Press.

Hughes, G. (2002) 'Plotting the rise of community safety: critical reflections on research, theory and politics', in G. Hughes and A. Edwards (eds) *Crime Control and Community:The New Politics of Public Safety*, Cullompton:Willan Publishing, pp 20-46.

Hughes, G. and Edwards, A. (eds) (2002) *Crime Control and Community:The New Politics of Public Safety*, Cullompton:Willan Publishing.

Jordan, B. (1998) *The New Politics of Welfare*, London: Sage Publications.

Koch, B. (1998) *The Politics of Crime Prevention*, Aldershot: Ashgate.

Labour Party (1996) *Parenting*, London: Labour Party.

Lea, J. and Young, J. (1984) *What Is to Be Done about Law and Order?*, Harmondsworth: Penguin.

Mandelson, P. and Liddle, R. (1996) *The Blair Revolution: Can New Labour Deliver?*, London: Faber.

Murray, C. (1990) *The Emerging British Underclass*, London: Institute of Economic Affairs.

Scheurich, J.J. (1997) *Research Methods in the Postmodern*, Barcombe: Falmer Press.

Segal, L. (1997) 'Feminist sexual politics and the heterosexual predicament', in L. Segal (ed) *New Sexual Agendas*, London: Macmillan.

Stenson, K. (1998) 'Displacing social policy through crime control', in S. Hanninen (ed) *Displacement of Social Policies*, SoPhi: University of Jyvaskyla.

Stenson, K. (2002) 'Community safety in Middle England – the local politics of crime control', in G. Hughes and A. Edwards (eds) *Crime Control and Community*, Cullompton, Willan Publishing.

Stenson, K. and Edwards, A. (2001) 'Rethinking crime control in advanced liberal government: the "Third Way" and the return of the local', in K. Stenson and R. Sullivan (eds) *Crime, Risk and Justice: The Politics of Crime Control in Liberal Democracies*, Cullompton: Willan Publishing, pp 1-19.

Taylor, I. (1999) *Crime in Context: A Critical Criminology of Market Societies*, Cambridge: Polity Press.

Tilley, N. (1994) 'Crime prevention and the Safer Cities story', *The Howard Journal of Criminology*, vol 32, no 1, pp 40-57.

Utting, D., Bright, J. and Henricson, C. (1993) *Crime and the Family: Improving Child-rearing and Preventing Delinquency*, London: Family Policy Studies Centre.

Walklate, S. (1998) 'Excavating the fear of crime: fear, anxiety or trust', *Theoretical Criminology*, vol 2, no 4, pp 403-18.

Young, J. (2001) 'Identity, community and social exclusion', in R. Matthews and J. Pitt (eds) *Crime, Disorder and Community Safety*, London: Routledge, pp 1-5.

Section four
Community safety: overrun by enforcement?

THIRTEEN

Community safety and social exclusion

Lynn Hancock

The links between the risk of criminal victimisation and urban social divisions have been clearly demonstrated using British Crime Survey (BCS) data (Hope, 1996, 1997, 1998, 2001a, 2001b) and other analyses integrating a range of population data with recorded crime statistics, as well as spatially referenced data sources over recent years (Hirschfield et al, 1995). While the relations between disadvantage and victimisation are neither simple nor mechanical, and these data have their limitations, the finding that the most disadvantaged groups are also the most likely to suffer higher levels of property and personal crimes has been firmly established. That more affluent groups in some urban areas (Hope, 2000, 2001b), particularly in inner-city, gentrifying areas (Hirschfield and Bowers, 1995, 1997), also face greater risk than the general population means that New Labour's emphasis on 'community safety' and being 'tough on crime' and its 'causes' resonates with the *experience* of victimisation for more affluent as well as disadvantaged social groups, alongside the fears of those who face considerably less risk.

The 'promise' of 'community safety' was attractive to the electorate and many critical commentators. For them, the possibility of addressing a range of harms experienced disproportionately by the less well-off was opened up. However, worries about the narrow, managerial, 'what works' agenda, with its focus on 'crime and disorder reduction' at the expense of more progressive ideas that align, potentially at least, with 'community safety' (Hughes, 2002), emerged with the Crime and Disorder Bill. Nevertheless, the promise of 'joined-up' government and the emergence of strategies to address the range of problems faced by disadvantaged communities in the government's commitment to tackle 'social exclusion', crystallised in its National Strategy for Neighbourhood Renewal, offered the opportunity to address a range of urban social problems, including crime, 'holistically'. Some commentators, however, had already expressed concerns about the 'criminalisation of social policy' (Squires, 1990; Carlen, 1996), which flowed from the way welfare agencies were increasingly involved in community safety under earlier urban policy frameworks. They observed that, in these circumstances, social exclusion and disadvantage were becoming less important issues in themselves. More and more they were the focus of intervention because of their implications for social disorder and crime (Crawford, 1997; Gilling and Barton, 1997). Others felt that crime-centred policies alone would not address the 'root causes' of crime and a focus on the range of urban social problems was, potentially at least, regarded as a gain maker and a step towards 'social justice' (Hope, 2001a, pp 435-6).

It is timely to review the direction 'community safety' and 'social inclusion' has taken since the 1998 Crime and Disorder Act and the Social Exclusion Unit's recommendation that a National Strategy for Neighbourhood Renewal be developed the same year. This chapter considers the assumptions underpinning, and the tensions and contradictions that have emerged between, 'community safety' and 'social inclusion' strategies and approaches. The argument, put briefly, is that we are witnessing a reconfiguration of inequalities in cities, which has profound implications for victimisation, criminalisation and criminality. The most marginal sections of working-class communities are bearing the brunt of these changes.

Urban divisions and victimisation

Accepting the limitations of the BCS, analysis of the findings for 2003/04 suggests that those who lack security measures on their homes are the most likely to suffer burglaries. While we can reasonably deduce that the more affluent are more likely to afford protection through the private market, the survey also reveals that young people aged 16-24, single parents, people living in affluent urban areas, the economically inactive, private renters, those in inner-city localities, and people on low incomes and in flats or maisonettes are among those most at risk from burglaries (Dodd et al, 2004). For 'criminal damage', people in 'urban areas and low income areas', younger respondents (16-24 years) and those occupying terraced houses or maisonettes face the greatest risks (Dodd et al, 2004, p 56). For violent crimes measured in the survey, young men, unemployed people, the single people (especially single parents), private renters, and young women, followed by those living in flats or maisonettes as well as more prosperous urban professionals were among those most at risk (in order of magnitude).

Among the most obvious methodological limitations of these findings are that neither young people below the age of 16 nor those living in institutional arrangements are included. Likewise, a number of crimes and harms are excluded. Were these to be incorporated into the analysis, particularly as far as young people are concerned, the pattern of compounded disadvantage would be considerably reinforced. What is also obvious is that the more economically marginal groups can occupy several of these categories at once, which increases their risk (Hope, 1998). Nevertheless, the overriding picture from the BCS is one where the least well-off and some more affluent groups in urban areas face greater crime risks than the population as a whole.

Most of these findings are not new. Tim Hope has written on the relative risks from property crimes in a number of articles (see Hope, 2001a, 2001b). Analyses of the BCS in 1992, for example, suggested that the highest crime communities were characterised by:

- residents lacking economic resources;
- predominance of rental housing tenure; and
- high proportions of young people (under 25), lone-parent households and single-person households.

Furthermore, where individuals possessed these characteristics and they were more prevalent in the local area, they were likely to face additional risks of victimisation. Hope concluded that 'crime victimisation may be concentrating in residential areas alongside the concentration of poverty and disadvantage' (Hope, 1998, cited in Hancock, 2001, pp 8-9).

One of the key factors that prompted Hope's observations at the time concerned the ways in which the urban housing market had changed, especially from the 1980s. Put briefly, the 'marketisation' project stressed private home ownership, or, failing that, renting in the private sector, or, lastly, renting through registered social landlords; local authority accommodation was in a process of 'residualisation'. The most economically disadvantaged groups were increasingly concentrated in particular areas of cities. Of course, the factors shaping patterns of victimisation and disadvantage are more complex; they are related to wider social, economic and political shifts. Nevertheless, changes in housing tenure meant that those bearing the brunt of these developments increasingly lived in close proximity (Hope, 1998, cited in Hancock, 2001, p 9).

In the contemporary city, some of these processes and particularly the 'marketisation' project have continued apace and have been discussed elsewhere (Hancock, 2001, 2003). Some forms of urban regeneration, notably but not limited to housing regeneration, have had implications for the social and spatial divisions that emerged in one of the study sites in particular (Merseyside). In the late 1990s, the 'gentrification process' gathered speed. There is a need for further research in the current setting, but what was significant then was the way that emerging social and spatial divisions were reshaping patterns of victimisation. The experience of victimisation was closely connected to the fortunes of the various sub-sections of the neighbourhood referred to as 'Earleschurch', which had hosted a range of regeneration initiatives. In this locality, the most economically marginal bore the brunt of the problems, although they were less likely to report them. The more affluent reported more crime and disorder to the police. On the whole they were less likely to experience incidents, but there was some evidence to suggest that their experience of victimisation was growing. In part, at least, reporting dispositions were related to affluent residents' capacity to afford relatively expensive home contents insurance policies and the 'excess' costs of making claims.

As the above discussion has demonstrated, some of the variables relating to victimisation have a strong socio-spatial dimension. However, and perhaps evidenced in the more recent BCS data, the patterns in the contemporary city appear to be less straightforward and more uncertain. Data aggregated at a local authority, postcode or even ward level would reveal a similar picture. A key question emerges: to what extent are current efforts to 'socially include' economically disadvantaged groups reshaping social relations in cities and to what extent are these influencing patterns of victimisation (if at all)? As a step towards addressing this question, the next section shows how 'inclusion' strategies in the modern period are reshaping inequalities that are becoming more manifest and proximate on the one hand, and on the other, paradoxically, increasingly obscured from view. The consequences for crime and criminalisation are then outlined.

Social inclusion, urban regeneration and its exclusionary effects

The stated aim of *A New Commitment to Neighbourhood Renewal: A National Strategy Action Plan* was to close the gap between the poorest neighbourhoods and the rest of the country over 10 to 20 years (SEU, 2001). Participation in the labour market is envisaged as the primary route to 'social inclusion' (SEU, 2001; Young, 2001). Old 'Thatcherite' notions that economically disadvantaged groups will benefit from the 'trickle-down effect' of urban regeneration remain pervasive in the government's thinking. The reform of welfare benefits, tax policies (tax credits, for example) and greater access to childcare (via Sure Start and the New Deal for Lone Parents, for example) aim to 'facilitate' access to paid work. The idea that developing 'social capital', 'community involvement' and 'participation' will help to secure benefits (including employment) for disadvantaged groups has also been promoted under the influence of the government's Etzioni-style communitarianism (Etzioni, 1993, 1997; Hancock and Matthews, 2001) as a core part of the strategy to regenerate urban communities.

Currently, urban regeneration is characterised by a market-driven enterprise, 'facilitated' by local authorities and their 'strategic' partners whose efforts centre on competing with each other to attract inward investors. In this context, places are 'rebranded' and space 'reconstructed' in efforts to attract wealthy visitors, tourists and shoppers (Raco, 2003; Coleman, 2004); consumption-based and 'culture-led' projects lie at the heart of regeneration partners' efforts (Jones and Wilks-Heeg, 2004; Mooney, 2004). That said, as Lees (2003) has argued, much of what is advocated as 'urban renaissance' is, in fact, a thinly veiled attempt to gentrify urban areas. What, then, are the consequences for 'community safety' and 'social inclusion'?

First, the government's communitarian vision, which underpins its 'social inclusion' policies and community safety/crime and disorder reduction legislation, comes under question in this context. As Skogan (1988) argued, 'in gentrifying areas there may be divisions that preclude community-wide support as new residents and property developers' interests (exchange values) may not coincide with those of long-term residents. Their influence may result in actions against undesirable people and land uses' (Skogan, 1988, cited in Hancock, 2001, p 153). On the one hand, this may result in campaigns on behalf of property developers and residents to exclude less affluent groups in a 'preservationist' manner (Skogan, 1988). But perhaps it is more likely that affluent groups seek protection via the market in security (Hope, 1999, 2001a), something to which we return below. Second, although it has always been the case that the more affluent have been able to exercise choice about where to live and to avoid high crime areas if they so wish (Lea and Young, 1993), those options are restricted for low-income groups and those of 'moderate means' as prices in inner areas have inflated[1]. The result of these processes is a reconfiguring and strengthening of the 'boundaries' of securitised enclaves (see also Hope, 1999).

Social exclusion and injustice

Welfare and tax reforms aimed at 'getting people into work' sustain rather than challenge the inequalities that accompany urban economic restructuring. We have seen, for example, how (at the national level) the Census (2001) revealed a polarisation in income inequality between 'wealthy achievers' (who grew from 19% to 25% of the population) and those of 'moderate means' and the 'hard-pressed' (whose combined percentage grew to 37%: 15% and 22%, respectively) following the Census in 1991 (Doward et al, 2003, p 7). The National Minimum Wage and tax credits may relieve absolute deprivation for many,[2] but relative deprivation is exacerbated in this context. While there is no simple geographic distribution pattern as far as income inequality is concerned, the large concentrations of poverty in the post-industrial towns of Glasgow, Liverpool and Middlesbrough and the like are thoroughly documented and need not be rehearsed here. Improvement on some indicators has been observed. Following regenerative efforts since the 1990s in Liverpool, for example, private sector investment in retail, hotels, offices, call centres and tourism has increased the number of employment opportunities in these sectors; by the same token (better) jobs have been lost, especially in manufacturing. There has, indeed, been a marked increase in affluence in some postcode areas, but entrenched poverty remains (Jones and Wilks-Heeg, 2004). Not surprisingly, therefore, analysis of Index of Deprivation data (despite some methodological problems associated with comparison over time) shows that 'by and large Merseyside's position was unchanged' between 2000 and 2004; some areas experienced improvement and others deterioration (Mersey Partnership, 2005, p 13).

There is a clear contradiction between trying to 'narrow the gap' between the most disadvantaged areas and 'the rest of the country' and local regeneration partnerships utilising the 'comparative advantage' of low pay in specific sectors in their efforts to attract increasingly mobile inward investment:

> Within specific sectors, Merseyside has a clear advantage – for example, starting salaries in call centres are generally lower on Merseyside than in the North East, South West, Wales and Scotland. (Mersey Partnership, 2004, p 48)

However, it is not just material inequalities that are reproduced in this context. The discourses around social exclusion itself 'reproduce, rather than successfully address, cultural aspects of injustice' (Morrison, 2003, p 139; see also Young, 1999; Haylett, 2001, 2003), which make crime and criminalisation more likely (Young, 2001). Drawing on the work of Nancy Fraser, where 'respect' and 'recognition' are centred in her discussion of cultural subordination and domination, Morrison (2003) demonstrates how the 'socially excluded' are constructed as 'the problem to be fixed' or corrected. The nature of economically disadvantaged communities, families, people's abilities and bodies and so on are devalued; they are contrasted with the 'included' – the 'we' in the policy documents. 'They' are 'misrecognised'.[3] Using the case study of Blackbird Leys, Morrison shows how a locality that had been stigmatised in local and national discourses, especially following the well-publicised urban disorders in 1990, witnessed the same stereotypes being replicated locally as part of the bidding process for a Single Regeneration Budget (SRB)-funded initiative in the area. As elsewhere, securing the funding relied on demonstrating that the area was among the 'worst off' on a range of indicators. 'Communities' in this context are portrayed as being both victimised and problematic on a range of indicators. People are described by their deficiencies and young people portrayed as 'threatening and potentially dangerous' (Morrison, 2003, p 152). The danger here, as Young has argued, is that these kinds of essentialising processes effectively locate deviance within the individual or group – and *not* in the included majority; simultaneously, they 'reaffirm the normality' of the included and in this way 'allow, in a Durkheimian fashion (see Ericson, 1966) the boundaries of normality to be drawn more definitely and distinctly' (Young, 1999, p 113).

As Young (1999) reminds us in his discussion of the criminogenic consequences of 'relative deprivation', it is not with the wealthiest that people compare themselves. This is most clearly revealed in recent popular talk about 'chavs', 'scallies' and 'neds'. These groups, we are informed, are defined by a disposition to criminality, antisocial behaviour, welfare dependency and particular behaviour as consumers of cheap or illicit goods and in the display of hyper-feminine and masculine identities. The object of the humour attendant in the discourses around 'chavs' is to point out the difference between an imagined 'them' and 'us' (see www.chavscum.co.uk); lifestyles, consumption practices and cultures shaped by structural location (class) are denigrated. Young people labelled in this way, like other members of the poor white working class, are accorded no positive meaning to their existence (Haylett, 2001).

In the 'new urban renaissance', the view of 'normality' is emphatically a middle-class one (Lees, 2003; Jones and Wilks-Heeg, 2004; Mooney, 2004). The target residents for repopulating city centres and inner-urban enclaves are the professional classes whose disposable incomes will boost the consumer city. As Lees (2003, p 71) notes, the apartments are 'expensive and for the most part, because of limited space, high cost and lack of facilities for children, are only attractive to wealthy professional singles and couples without children'. Moreover, because the kind of accommodation being designed (or redesigned) is associated not only with a particular lifestyle but with a specific stage in the life-cycle (people move out to accommodate their children and to send them to better schools), there are predictable consequences for long-term commitment to and the stability of these localities (Lees, 2003). They do not attract, nor do developers wish to accommodate, lower-income groups. At the same time, inflated property prices in areas that are attractive to middle-class repopulation mean that established local residents and their children who are committed to the area find it difficult to buy into the local property market, even if they earn comparatively good local incomes (Coligan, 2005). Furthermore, despite the widely welcomed *mixed-tenure* developments[4], there is evidence to suggest that 'mixed tenure schemes secured through planning conditions and developed by private sector house builders often fail to *integrate* the affordable housing units sufficiently. Often physical barriers exist (dividing walls and roads) between the tenures'[5]. And, of course, developers' design remits include 'security', an integral feature of the new city centre and emergent inner-urban, middle-class enclaves and warehouse conversions, alongside the reshaping of crime control practices in city centre public spaces (Coleman and Sim, 2005).

In contrast to the mediated image of the working-class community (see Johnstone and Mooney, 2005), and, perhaps too, the middle-class suburb, the gentrification process and the professional city dweller are presented as 'forward-looking' in a way that satisfies, on the surface at least, an appeal to 'diversity', 'difference' and the desire for 'cosmopolitan' living (Haylett, 2001). However, not surprisingly in the light of this discussion, there is evidence to suggest that social interaction in gentrified areas occurs largely *within* rather than *between* social groups (Butler and Robson, 2001, cited in Lees, 2003, p 78, emphasis added).

'Social Inclusion', criminalisation, crime and disorder

The National Strategy for Neighbourhood Renewal and supporting documentation from Policy Action Team reports recognise that factors other than crime and disorder, external to neighbourhoods and related to the restructuring of local and national economies (as well as local and national government policies), to a greater or lesser degree explain the spiral of neighbourhood decline in urban neighbourhoods (Hastings, 2003). Nevertheless, regenerative efforts by and large remain focused on the deficiencies of working-class families and 'communities'. As far as the link with crime and antisocial behaviour is concerned, local and national government strategies rely on an uncritical acceptance of 'broken windows' (Wilson and Kelling, 1982), and the rather flawed direction of causality (disorder leads to neighbourhood decline) implied in the thesis (see Matthews, 1992, 2003; Hancock, 2001). The *range* of conditions that cause distress in neighbourhoods or promote outward migration are ignored or downplayed.

Addressing 'antisocial behaviour' is regarded as being fundamental if social exclusion is to be addressed:

> At the heart of this Government's determination to tackle social exclusion is the National Strategy for Neighbourhood Renewal. That strategy must tackle and reduce the incidence and perception of anti-social behaviour if the Government is to achieve its aims of revitalising the most deprived communities. Communities drive this agenda. It is Government's role to empower them to succeed. (Home Office, 2003a, para 4.53)

The ambiguity and confusion surrounding working-class communities is, we might observe, neatly reflected in this quotation; 'communities' 'drive' these efforts, despite being 'blighted', and at the same time they need 'empowering'. They are the 'object of policy' and 'policy instrument' (Imrie and Raco, 2003, p 6). This elision arises because the government 'operate[s] with a simplistic communitarian vision' (Matthews, 2003, p 7). That said, more important for our present purposes is the way statements such as this assume and seek to create a community of interest around the objectives of current disorder reduction policies and the means of bringing them to fruition. The Number 10 Downing Street website, for example, informs us that:

> It [Antisocial behaviour] can hold back the regeneration of our most disadvantaged areas, creating the environment in which crime can take hold. It damages the quality of life for too many people – one in three people say it is a problem in their area.[6]

The 'problem' of 'young people hanging around' receives copious commentary in the official documents of national and local governments and will serve as a useful reference point in this discussion; its examination reveals some of the competing interests at play. There are, of course, problems associated with 'antisocial behaviour'; young people are more likely to be the victims of actions or conditions that cause 'alarm, distress and intimidation' in a variety of contexts. The 'evidence base' frequently utilised by government – the BCS – of course excludes young people. What it does show, however, is that 'teenagers hanging around' comes *behind* vandalism and graffiti, misuse of fireworks, problems associated with rubbish and litter, and illegal or inconveniently parked vehicles as 'very' or 'fairly' big problems for those included in the BCS (Wood, 2004). Indeed, the most important cause for concern is 'speeding traffic', which was also considered the 'biggest problem'. Importantly, a significant proportion of 'incidents' in the 'teenagers hanging around' category involved young people 'just being a general nuisance' (43%) or 'not doing anything in particular' (6%), especially in more affluent areas. Moreover, '[i]n over a third of incidents (36%), those perceiving problems acknowledged that the young people were not being deliberately anti-social'

(Wood, 2004, p 25; see also Squires and Stephen, 2005). The survey showed also that in these instances, for the most part, those involved did not know the young people involved in the 'incidents' they commented on in the survey.

The relationship between those who observe or report antisocial behaviour and those who are regarded as perpetrators is critical. Where young people causing 'annoyance' are regarded as 'part of the community', there is evidence to suggest that residents are more likely to be more sympathetic to the plight of young people (Hancock, 2001). This is not to say they 'tolerate'[7] 'antisocial behaviour'. (However, the reporting of particular behaviours in surveys or to the police does not automatically mean that a punitive response is desired; most will simply want the annoying behaviour to cease.) People may exercise toleration precisely because the impact of a criminal justice response is seen to be more damaging for the alleged 'perpetrator' than the 'annoying' behaviour people witness or experience. This may be especially the case where the relationship between the 'community' and key agencies such as the police has, historically, been one of antagonism (see Hancock, 2001, chapter 6).

In localities where regeneration/gentrification is promoted, a more 'punitive' response may emerge because the nature of 'social solidarity', the definition of 'out-groups' and 'local theories about the causes of crime', which flow from and in turn are influenced by the local 'social-cultural context' (Podolefsky and Dubow, 1981, p 15), are reshaped. At least as far as collective actions around crime and disorder are concerned, there is evidence to suggest that these contextual factors are *far* more important than 'crime' itself for understanding community action around crime and disorder[8]. There is a need to carry out further research on community responses to crime and disorder in the current context, since the myriad opinion polls, 'consultative' arrangements and surveys on this topic have notable limitations, as we have seen (see also Hancock, 2004). However, the kind of 'social mix' being promoted in the consumption-led, regenerating city, and the fragmentation of community life that has accompanied neo-liberalism (Currie, 2003), seem to point towards particular kinds of anti-crime (and disorder) activities. Podolefsky and Dubow (1981, pp 140-1) put it thus:

> Generally speaking, people in more socially integrated communities tend to think about the neighbourhood as 'our community' and the young in it as 'our kids' and therefore the problems as 'our problems'. In South Philadelphia, for example, where 40% of the residents report knowing the names of all the kids in the neighbourhood, the median length of residents (for adults) is over seventeen years, and young people tend to stay in or return to the community, 40 percent of all anti-crime activities mentioned on the survey involved positive youth oriented programmes such as recreation or employment.
>
> In locales which are characterised by a high degree of urbanism, in contrast, people are less socially integrated, less likely to think of the neighbourhood as 'our community' and less likely to view the youth

as 'our kids'. People who are concerned with the upkeep of the community may frequently be concerned with their financial investments as much as the social effects of a criminogenic environment on neighbourhood youth.

These authors pointed to the much greater likelihood of community groups emphasising 'victimisation prevention' in the latter instance. What is more, 'local theories' about the 'causes' of and 'solutions' to crime and disorder will be conditioned to a greater or lesser degree by dominant discourses around the 'what works' paradigm in community safety in the contemporary setting. We can also expect these discourses to influence people's responses (through the 'local social cultural context' in Podolefsky and Dubow's terms) in a way that promotes strategies that *appear* to be possible, effective or funded (they open up the 'structure of opportunity'), not least because of the potential alliances that can be made with 'primary definers' in the city (Coleman and Sim, 2005) or vice versa[9].

'Inclusion' policies and communitarian discourses obscure class divisions and hide from view the way power relations are defended. Instead, the problems of crime and disorder are *shared* by the 'community' as a whole, and it is the community as a whole that is assumed to benefit from crime and disorder reduction policies. The benefits to be gleaned from claiming moral and cultural superiority over others, attendant in the discourses around antisocial behaviour, for example, are downplayed (Haylett, 2001). And, as Young (2001, pp 30-1) has argued, in the late modern world where ontological insecurity is commonplace, 'essentialisms' have a positive function in the creation of a 'sense of self' and a major way of achieving this is through the denigration of others.

In Young's (1999, p 118) analysis, the processes apply as much to groups deemed to be 'included' as the 'socially excluded', but social exclusion chips away at one's sense of identity and facilitates the embracing of essentialised statuses which, in turn, can become self-fulfilling. The increasingly intensive strategies of control have unintended effects in this context (Hayward, 2002).

What is important, as Young's criminology informs us, is that the 'socially excluded' are often deeply included culturally. Rather than lacking culture or possessing an 'alternative' culture, Young, drawing on Merton (1938), emphasises the significance of 'inclusion' in the dominant culture, which centres around individualism, consumerism, competition and success, coupled with structural exclusion for understanding of discontent and crime in the late modern period. In this view, 'cultural inclusion' coupled with 'structural exclusion' is crucial for our understanding of discontent and crime. Furthermore, as we have seen, 'relative deprivation' is not only persisting but inequalities are becoming more apparent in the contemporary setting. For Young, relative deprivation creates sources of discontent that are liable to generate high crime rates, but relative deprivation needs also to be understood alongside 'misrecognition', which causes disaffection;

both concepts are crucial for understanding crime *and* punishment (see Young, 1999, 2001).

Whose safety?

Coleman and Sim (2005) discuss the development of control mechanisms and key responsibilisation strategies in the consumption-led regenerating city centre under contemporary crime control frameworks. They point towards the ways in which the 'rehabilitation of public space' emphasises the public rather than private sphere and also how this focus obscures the victimisation of the range of social groups that occupy 'the street'. Those seen to cause 'nuisance' are regarded as 'in' but not 'of' the desired or imagined 'community'; their misrecognition is reinforced. The Home Office's guidance on dealing with youthful antisocial behaviour neatly reflects this viewpoint:

> Where young people are gathering – of any age group – that may be threatening and/or intimidating for local people, it is important that the police and/or local authority talk directly to them about the impact they have.
>
> Visits, ABCs [Acceptable Behaviour Contracts]/ABAs [Acceptable Behaviour Agreements] are successful in many cases – they must have credibility though. If not adhered to then further sanctions must be sought. Also use individual Support Orders and Parenting Orders with ASBOs [Anti-Social Behaviour Orders] to help the young person and their family deal with their problems.
>
> Prevention and enforcement go hand in hand to successfully address youth nuisance. Make sure there are alternative activities available for those causing problems. If such opportunities are not taken advantage of, and if problems persist, then enforcement action must be used to protect the community. (Home Office, 2003b, pp 10-11)

A policy informed by a more critical understanding of 'community safety' and 'social exclusion' (and, indeed, more liberal variants of communitarianism) would suggest a more critical focus on the perceptions many adults hold of (and their behaviour towards) working-class young people (see also Fitzpatrick et al, 1998). The quality of youth provision might also be worth some scrutiny. However, in the government's view, addressing the 'incidence and perception of anti-social behaviour' is necessary if the 'most deprived communities' are to be 'revitalised' (Home Office, 2003a, para 4.53).

Young people congregate in groups, in part, *because of* concerns about safety[10]. They do so too because of established working-class cultural practices that exist in contrast to the privatism of households in middle-class suburbs and city-centre enclaves (Measor and Squires, 2000). To gather in this way was once regarded as normal in working-class communities. Indeed, it was widely regarded as beneficial for the healthy, social and psychological development of children whose need for sociability, peer support, autonomy from adults and practical education about dealing with conflict and so on was recognised (see also Warpole, 2003). Other factors help to explain young people's presence on the street, of course, such as quality of housing stock (overcrowding, for example), the relative cohesiveness of communities in the industrial city, the attractions of day-to-day sociability at little or no cost, and the way such gatherings reflect adult ways of being. But the spaces available for children to socialise (in the street, and the 'disused' spaces of the urban landscape [see also Hayward, 2004]) have been systematically reduced as a consequence of car ownership and land reclamation under renewal programmes. Already under threat from the dominant economic and cultural forces of neo-liberalism, which have ruptured traditional working-class communities and especially social relations between young people (Hall and Winlow, 2004, 2005), recent measures not only criminalise working-class young people, increase their chances of victimisation and create new antagonisms, they also represent a threat to the reproduction of *positive* working-class cultural practices where they remain. They reflect and sustain middle-class cultural values and the desire to create 'cornflake' family practices[11]. This is not to say that there are no problems with 'nuisance'; what is important, however, is that the strategies to deal with problems under current crime and disorder frameworks are counterproductive as far as securing 'community safety' for the most vulnerable groups *and* sustaining good neighbour relations are concerned (Stephen and Squires, 2003), which a commitment to communitarian values would imply.

Conclusion

Recent BCS data have shown that the most economically marginal and some affluent groups in urban areas face considerably greater risks of criminal victimisation in the contemporary period. It is clear, too, that the experience of the most disadvantaged is considerably underestimated by these data. The capacity to absorb the impact of some crimes is also borne disproportionately by the least advantaged. Moreover, this chapter has argued that 'social inclusion' policies have sustained and exacerbated relative deprivation under current frameworks and that they are founded on a number of classist assumptions that have perpetuated the cultural injustices visited on the urban poor. Together, New Labour's twin concerns to 'socially include' through the market, and to enhance public safety through crime and disorder reduction strategies, following the 1998 Crime and Disorder Act, not only reconfigure inequalities in cities, but have profound implications for victimisation, criminalisation *and* criminality. It has also been suggested that exclusionary dynamics are becoming more apparent on the one hand, yet on the other, paradoxically, are also increasingly obscured from view. Implicit in this analysis has been the suggestion that the 'criminalisation of social policy' debates need to be reconsidered in this context.

Notes

[1] House prices in Liverpool have increased dramatically (22% in 2004), taking average prices (£136,262) well beyond the means of many local families (www.liverpool.gov.uk/The_City/City_suburbs/index.asp).

[2] This is not necessarily the case, however; many asylum seekers, for example, are expected to subsist below minimum income levels.

[3] 'To be misrecognised … is to be denied the status of a full partner in social interaction, as a consequence of institutionalised patterns of cultural value that constitute one as comparatively unworthy of respect and esteem' (Frazer, 2000, cited in Morrison, 2003, p 140).

[4] These have the benefit of lessening the likelihood of stigma now associated with large-scale social housing provision.

[5] Joseph Rowntree Foundation consultation response to Office of the Deputy Prime Minister on *Planning Policy Guidance Note 3: Housing – Influencing the Size, Type and Affordability of Housing*, prepared by Julie Cowans in collaboration with Les Sparks, October 2003 (www.jrf.org.uk/knowledge/responses/docs/influencingthesizeofhousing.asp) (emphasis in original).

[6] www.number-10.gov.uk/output/Page6210.asp

[7] 'The deliberate choice not to interfere with conduct or beliefs, with which one disapproves' (Hancock and Matthews, 2001, p 99).

[8] Hancock (2001) discusses further the key influences on community mobilisation around crime and disorder, and the factors that can undermine and promote activity informed by Podolefski and Dubow's analysis.

[9] There are, it should be noted, examples of instances where communities characterised by increasing degrees of heterogeneity have remained relatively cohesive in their mobilisations around 'safety' in their neighbourhood. Space precludes further discussion, but Hancock (2001) and Donnelly and Majka (1998) explain the particular kinds of conditions that gave rise to these 'negative' cases.

[10] Rice, J., Bather, H., Slack, A., McHarron, S. and Slack, C. (2005) 'Section 30 scandal exposed', *Nerve*, no 6 (http://catalystmedia.org.uk/issues/nerve6/section30.htm).

[11] Term borrowed from Matthews (2003, p 7).

References

Carlen, P. (1996) *Jigsaw: A Political Criminology of Youth Homelessness*, Buckingham: Open University Press.

Coleman, R. (2004) *Reclaiming the Streets: Surveillance, Social Control and the City*, Cullompton: Willan Publishing.

Coleman, R. and Sim, J. (2005) 'Contemporary statecraft and the "punitive obsession": a critique of the new penology thesis', in J. Pratt, D. Brown, M. Brown, S. Hallsworth and W. Morrison (eds) *The New Punitiveness: Trends, Theories, Perspectives*, Cullompton: Willan Publishing, pp 101-18.

Coligan, N. (2005) 'New homes could ruin community', *Liverpool Echo* (9 May) (http://icliverpool.icnetwork.co.uk/).

Crawford, A. (1997) *The Local Governance of Crime: Appeals to Community and Partnerships*, Oxford: Clarendon.

Currie, E. (2003) 'Social crime prevention strategies in a market society', in E. McLaughlin, J. Muncie and G. Hughes (eds) *Criminological Perspectives: Essential Readings* (2nd edn), London: Sage Publications, pp 369-80.

Dodd, T. Nicholas, S., Povey, D. and Walker, A. (2004) *Crime in England and Wales 2003/04*, Home Office Statistical Bulletin, London: Home Office.

Donnelly, P.G. and Majka, T.J. (1998) 'Residents' efforts at neighborhood stabilisation: facing the challenge of inner-city neighborhoods', *Sociological Forum*, vol 13, no 2, pp 189-213.

Doward, J., Reilly, T. and Graham, M. (2003) 'Census exposes unequal Britain', *The Observer*, 23 November, p 7.

Etzioni, A. (1993) *The Spirit of Community*, New York, NY: Crown Publishing.

Etzioni, A. (1997) *The New Golden Rule*, London: Profile Books.

Fitzpatrick, S., Hastings, A. and Kintrea, K. (1998) *Including Young People in Urban Regeneration*, Findings, York: Joseph Rowntree Foundation.

Gilling, D. and Barton, A. (1997) 'Crime prevention and community safety: a new home for social policy?', *Critical Social Policy*, vol 17, no 3, pp 63-83.

Hall, S. and Winlow, S. (2004) 'Barbarians at the gate: crime and violence in the breakdown of the pseudo-pacification process', in J. Ferrell, K. Hayward, W. Morrison and M. Presdee (eds) *Cultural Criminology Unleashed*, London: Glasshouse Press, pp 275-86.

Hall, S. and Winlow, S. (2005) 'Anti-nirvana: crime, culture and instrumentalism in the age of insecurity', *Crime, Media, Culture*, vol 1, no 1, pp 31-48.

Hancock, L. (2001) *Community, Crime and Disorder: Safety and Regeneration in Urban Neighbourhoods*, Basingstoke: Palgrave.

Hancock, L. (2003) 'Urban regeneration and crime reduction: contradictions and dilemmas', in R. Matthews and J. Young (eds) *The New Politics of Crime and Punishment*, Cullompton: Willan Publishing, pp 129-53.

Hancock, L. (2004) 'Criminal justice, public opinion, fear and popular politics', in J. Muncie and D. Wilson (eds) *The Cavendish Student Handbook of Criminal Justice and Criminology*, London: Cavendish, pp 51-66.

Hancock, L. and Matthews, R. (2001) 'Crime, community safety and toleration', in R. Matthews and J. Pitts (eds) *Crime, Disorder and Community Safety*, London: Routledge, pp 98-119.

Hastings, A. (2003) 'Strategic, multi-level neighbourhood regeneration: an outward looking approach at last?', in R. Imrie and M. Raco (eds) *Urban Renaissance? New Labour, Community and Urban Policy*, Bristol: The Policy Press, pp 85-100.

Haylett, C. (2001) 'Illegitimate subjects? Abject whites, neoliberal modernisation and middle-class multi-culturalism', *Environment and Planning D: Society and Space*, vol 19, issue 3, pp 351-70.

Haylett, C. (2003) 'Culture, class and urban policy: re-considering equality', *Antipode*, vol 35, no 1, pp 55-73.

Hayward, K. (2002) 'The vilification and pleasures of youthful transgression', in J. Muncie, G. Hughes and E. McLaughlin (eds) *Youth Justice: Critical Readings*, London: Sage Publications, pp 80-93.

Hayward, K. (2004) 'Space – The final frontier: criminology, the city and the spatial dynamics of exclusion', in J. Ferrell, K. Hayward, W. Morrison and M. Presdee (eds) *Cultural Criminology Unleashed*, London: Glasshouse Press, pp 155-66.

Hirschfield, A. and Bowers, K.J. (1995) 'Crime patterning and the concentration of disadvantage on Merseyside', Paper presented to the British Criminology Conference, Loughborough, July.

Hirschfield, A. and Bowers, K.J. (1997) 'The development of a social, demographic and land use profiler for areas of high crime', *British Journal of Criminology*, vol 37, no 1, pp 103-20.

Hirschfield, A., Bowers, K.J. and Brown, P.J.B. (1995) 'Exploring relations between crime and disadvantage in Merseyside', *European Journal on Criminal Policy and Research*, vol 3, no 3, pp 93-112.

Home Office (2003a) *White Paper: Respect and Responsibility – Taking A Stand Against Anti-Social Behaviour*, Cm 5778, London: The Stationery Office.

Home Office (2003b) *Working Together: Tackling Not Tolerating Anti-Social Behaviour*, London: Home Office.

Hope, T. (1996) 'Communities, crime and inequality in England and Wales', in T. Bennett (ed) *Preventing Crime and Disorder: Targeting Strategies and Responsibilities*, Cambridge: Institute of Criminology, pp 165-94.

Hope, T. (1997) 'Inequality and the future of community crime prevention', in S.P. Lab (ed) *Crime Prevention at a Crossroads*, American Academy of Criminal Justice Sciences Monograph Series, Cincinnati, OH: Anderson Publishing.

Hope, T. (1998) 'Community safety, crime and disorder', in A. Marlow and J. Pitts (eds) *Planning Safer Communities*, Lyme Regis: Russell House Publishing, pp 168-80.

Hope, T. (1999) 'Privatopia on trial? Property guardianship in the suburbs', *Crime Prevention Studies*, vol 10, pp 15-45.

Hope, T. (2000) 'Inequality and the clubbing of private security', in T. Hope and R. Sparks (eds) *Crime, Risk and Insecurity*, London: Routledge, pp 83-106.

Hope, T. (2001a) 'Community, crime prevention in Britain: a strategic overview', *Criminal Justice*, vol 1, no 4, pp 421-39.

Hope, T. (2001b) 'Crime victimisation and inequality in risk society', in R. Matthews and J. Pitts (eds) *Crime, Disorder and Community Safety*, London: Routledge, pp 193-218.

Hughes, G. (2002) 'Crime and Disorder Reduction Partnerships: the future of community safety?', in G. Hughes, E. McLaughlin and J. Muncie (eds) *Crime Prevention and Community Safety: New Directions*, London: Sage Publications, pp 123-41.

Imrie, R. and Raco, M. (2003) 'Community and the changing nature of urban policy', in R. Imrie and M. Raco (eds) *Urban Renaissance? New Labour, Community and Urban Policy*, Bristol: The Policy Press, pp 3-36.

Jones, P. and Wilks-Heeg, S. (2004) 'Capitalising culture: Liverpool 2008', *Local Economy*, vol 19, no 4, pp 341-60.

Lea, J. and Young, J. (1993) *What is to be Done about Law and Order?* (2nd edn), London: Pluto Press.

Lees, L. (2003) 'Visions of "urban renaissance": the Urban Task Force report and the Urban White Paper', in R. Imrie and M. Raco (eds) *Urban Renaissance? New Labour, Community and Urban Policy*, Bristol: The Policy Press, pp 61-82.

Matthews, R. (1992) 'Replacing broken windows: crime, incivilities and urban change', in R. Matthews and J. Young (eds) *Issues in Realist Criminology*, London: Sage Publications, pp 19-50.

Matthews, R. (2003) 'Enforcing respect and reducing responsibility: a response to the White Paper on anti-social behaviour', *Community Safety Journal*, vol 2, no 4, pp 5-8.

Measor, L. and Squires, P. (2000) *Young People and Community Safety*, Aldershot, Ashgate.

Mersey Partnership (2004) 'Merseyside economic review 2004', Main Report (www.merseyside.org.uk).

Mooney, G. (2004) 'Cultural policy and urban transformation? Critical reflections on Glasgow, European City of Culture 1990', *Local Economy*, vol 19, no 4, pp 327-40.

Morrison, Z. (2003) 'Cultural justice and addressing "social exclusion": a case study of a Single Regeneration Budget project in Blackbird Leys, Oxford', in R. Imrie and M. Raco (eds) *Urban Renaissance? New Labour, Community and Urban Policy*, Bristol: The Policy Press, pp 139-61.

Podolefsky, A. and Dubow, F. (1981) *Strategies for Community Crime Prevention: Collective Responses to Crime in Urban America*, Springfield, IL: Charles C. Thomas.

Raco, M. (2003) 'Remaking place and securitising space: urban regeneration and the strategies, tactics and practices of policing in the UK', *Urban Studies*, vol 40, no 9, pp 1869-87.

Skogan, W.G. (1988) 'Community organizations and crime', in M. Tonry and N. Morris (eds) *Crime and Justice: A Review of Research Vol. 10*, Chicago, IL: University of Chicago Press, pp 39-78.

SEU (Social Exclusion Unit) (2001) 'A new commitment to neighbourhood renewal: A National Strategy Action Plan' (www.cabinet-office.gov.uk/seu/2001/Action%20Plan/contents.htm).

Squires, P. (1990) *Anti-Social Policy: Welfare, Ideology and the Disciplinary State*, Hemel Hempstead: Harvester/Wheatsheaf.

Squires, P. and Stephen D.E. (2005) *Rougher Justice: Anti-social Behaviour and Young People*, Cullompton: Willan Publishing.

Stephen, D.E. and Squires, P. (2003) *Community Safety, Enforcement and Anti-social Behaviour Contracts: An Evaluation of the Work of the Community Safety Team in the East Brighton 'New Deal for Communities' Area*, Brighton: Health and Social Policy Research Centre, University of Brighton.

Warpole, K. (2003) 'No particular place to go? Children, young people and public space' (www.groundwork.org.uk/what/publications/youth.htm).

Wilson, J.Q. and Kelling, G.L. (1982) 'Broken windows: the police and neighborhood safety', *Atlantic Monthly*, vol 249, no 3, pp 29-38.

Wood, M. (2004) *Perceptions and Experience of Anti-social Behaviour: Findings from the 2003/2004 British Crime Survey*, London: Home Office.

Young, J. (1999) *The Exclusive Society*, London: Sage Publications.

Young, J. (2001) 'Identity, community and social exclusion', in R. Matthews and J. Pitts (eds) *Crime, Disorder and Community Safety: A New Agenda*, London: Routledge, pp 26-53.

FOURTEEN

Community safety and young people: 21st-century *homo sacer* and the politics of injustice

Dawn E. Stephen

It is inherent in the especial character of law, as a body of rules and procedures, that it shall apply logical criteria with reference to standards of universality and equity. It is true that certain categories of person may be excluded from this logic ... that other categories may be debarred from access to parts of this logic ... and that the poor may often be excluded, through penury, from the law's costly procedures. All this, and more is true. But if too much of this is true, then the consequences are counterproductive.... If the law is evidently partial and unjust, then it will mask nothing, legitimate nothing.... The essential precondition for the effectiveness of law, its function as an ideology, is that it shall display an independence from gross manipulation and shall seem to be just. It cannot seem to be so without upholding its own logic and criteria of equity; indeed, on occasion, by actually *being* just. (Thompson, 1975, pp 262-3, emphasis in original)

The 'rights' and wrongs of 'community safety'

This chapter explores the impact of the now dominant aspect of community safety policy: the management of 'antisocial behaviour' through 'early interventions'. The opening necessarily lengthy quotation, therefore, firmly sets the tone for this critical exegesis of community safety and young people's place therein. The argument is that, instead of objective judgement, justice and inclusion, community safety has become a tool of partiality and exclusion through 'precautionary injustice' (Squires and Stephen, 2005a) techniques that increasingly demonise, and consequentially deny justice to, children and young people. As Goldson (2004, p 27) observes insightfully, 'the ideologies and domain assumptions that underpin 'risk' based early interventions are both intrinsically authoritarian and antithetical to long established principles of youth justice'. However, it is not merely that youth justice principles are being eroded through community safety discourses, but also that the very founding principles of British justice are themselves being dissolved. Accordingly, it is these 'ideologies and domain assumptions' to which Goldson refers that need to be considered first.

The first two weeks following the re-election of the Labour government in May 2005 produced a frenzy of derogatory representations of young people in 21st-century Britain. The Prime Minister's first press conference of his third term on 12 May 2005 raised the spectacle of 'yobbish' behaviour once more (see Office of the Prime Minister, 2005a). Likewise, in the same week, news that baseball hats and 'hoodies' were to be banned from the Bluewater shopping centre in Kent (see, for example, BBC, 2005a) and Chief Superintendent David Baines' comments about 'feral youths' rampaging through the streets (see, for example, BBC, 2005b) rekindled the spectre of 'out-of-control' young people. The Queen's Speech (see Office of the Prime Minister, 2005b) further underlined the government's strengthened commitment to addressing this visible manifestation of profound social malaise through the promotion of a 'culture of respect' (see Office of the Prime Minister, 2005c). Evidently still underpinned by the politically manipulative rhetoric of 'rights and responsibilities' (see, for example, Home Office, 2003), there was little sign that the government's responsibilities towards the rights of *all* citizens, especially those youngsters on the margins (see Goldson, 2004; Squires and Stephen, 2005a), would be addressed within this full legislative agenda. Nonetheless, through such symbolic rhetoric it is possible to appreciate the *realpolitik* of late modernity that ensures that contemporary politicians are faced with a harsh, and tacitly hopeless, reality. They are quite clearly, as Tombs and Hillyard (2004, p 54) contend, 'bereft of the means or inclination to devise social policy responses to social problems' and 'have turned increasingly towards the extension of the criminal justice system and the criminalisation of economically marginalised groups', none more so than children and young people, with profound consequences.

In focusing on this disquieting 'authoritarian drift' (Goldson, 2004, p 27), significant numbers of children and young people labelled as 'antisocial' are becoming recognisable as *homo sacer*, 'neither defined by any sense of positive laws nor a carrier of human rights' (Bauman, 2004, p 32). This shift, as Tombs and Hillyard imply above, is a pragmatic route to take, but it comes at great cost to those thus labelled, and indeed to the wider and deeper underpinnings of British justice traditions. In its acceptance of hearsay and subjective understandings of 'antisocial behaviour', the current direction of youth (in)justice, effected in and through seemingly benign community safety policies, is grossly manipulating the integrity of long-held reliance on objective 'evidence', 'equality before the law', 'due process' and 'justice' itself as children and young people – *ipso facto* miscreants – are increasingly sucked into contemporary net-widening (Cohen, 1985) processes 'with little concern either for their rights or for the principles of criminal law' (Bandalli, 2000, p 94). But, even saying that, given the wider 'policy harms' (Parker, 2004, p 240) endured by children and young people in the late modern neo-liberal state, it must be asked whether criminal law itself is a fitting arena in which to try to deal with their problems. It is, therefore, necessary to explore this question of rights within community safety discourses.

This erosion of rights was championed in the publication of the Five Year Plan *Confident Communities in a Secure Britain* (Home Office, 2004b). The Plan outlined the government's 'commitments to law abiding citizens' and set out to enable this supposed majority to feel safe through the fostering of 'strong and cohesive communities'. Tackling antisocial behaviour has been a key feature of this strategy (see Home Office, 2004b, section 2.4), which explicitly seeks to create a 'culture of intolerance' and a greater use of 'swift' measures to deal with antisocial behaviour, notably Acceptable Behaviour Contracts and Agreements (ABCs/ABAs), Parenting Contracts and Fixed Penalty Notices (Home Office, 2004b, p 49). Such measures embody the creeping populist authoritarian shift in youth justice in recent years by providing further insight into New Labour's symbolic politics (see Newburn and Jones, 2005) of 'respect' that offer headline-grabbing 'remedies' instead of profound or lasting understandings and solutions. These remedies find justification within idealised appeals to 'community', but the symbolic use of this elusive concept in the contemporary governance of disorder guarantees that 'community' is not designed to be inclusive to all because the tenuous bounds of inclusion rely, cynically, upon dichotomous constructions of 'law-abiding' and *Other*, as Flint explains:

> Technologies of governance in advanced liberal democracies involve the identification and classification of *autonomous citizens* capable of regulating their behaviour on the one hand, and on the other, identifying *targeted populations*, whose deviancy from norms of behaviour require government interventions. (Flint, 2002, p 249, emphasis in original)

Thus, although apparently benign in their common-sense appeal, community safety remedies suggest that the problems within, usually marginalised, communities can be addressed by focusing on the superficial symptoms of neighbourhood disorder (for example, the naive 'broken windows' theory advanced by Wilson and Kelling, 1982) rather than by addressing the much wider and deeper social, economic and political roots of social exclusion, and young people's disengagement (see, for example, Mizen, 2004; Parker, 2004; Tombs and Hillyard, 2004; Barry, 2005). Consequentially, acknowledging current trends towards 'swift justice' and the growing 'culture of intolerance', community safety is becoming a less than subtle stratagem rooted in an unjust and counterproductive 'institutionalised mistrust' (Kelly, 2003) of marginalised young people (see Stephen and Squires, 2004) in 'anti-nirvana' (Hall and Winlow, 2005).

Set firmly in the context of the neo-liberal-inspired diminution of welfare-based conceptions of and policy responses towards young people (see the excellent account in Mizen, 2004), this stratagem is founded on the belief that 'particular populations of young people pose a certain dangerousness' (Kelly, 2003, p 175).

Techniques of 'mistrust', notably 'antisocial behaviour' measures are employed to inflate the concept of 'dangerisation' (Lianos and Douglas, 2000) in order to mobilise late modern insecurities (see Squires and Stephen, 2005a). As such, and directly challenging suggestions that the government has not exaggerated the problems (House of Commons Home Affairs Committee, 2005, p 12), adults overestimate youth crime and the nature of their crime (Hough and Roberts, 2004) while variable conceptions of 'antisocial behaviour' (see Wood, 2004) enable politicians to inflate the extent of young people's antisocial agency (see Home Office, 2004d). With this in mind, the argument in this chapter will emphatically challenge the Home Affairs Committee's recent finding that:

> ... the definitions [of antisocial behaviour] should not be changed: they work well from a practical enforcement point of view, are helpful in focusing on the effect on victims and offer the flexibility that is essential to allow the problems of ASB [antisocial behaviour] to be highlighted and tackled where they are felt – at local level. (House of Commons Home Affairs Committee, 2005, p 3)

If anything, the very definition of antisocial behaviour assuredly encourages such excesses.

The 1998 Crime and Disorder Act (Home Office, 1998), in section 1(1)(a), defines 'antisocial behaviour' as behaviour that 'caused or is *likely to cause* harassment, alarm or distress to one or more persons not of the same household' (emphasis added). Alongside the use of civil rules of evidence, this ensures a further muddying of an already opaque legal, and indeed moral, quagmire. The suggestion that 'locally based definitions' of antisocial behaviour are required – consistent with appeals to 'community' within community safety discourse (House of Commons Home Affairs Committee, 2005, p 28) – could only serve to exacerbate matters.

These techniques have firm purposes (see Young, 1999), allowing society to justify exclusionary processes through the twin fallacies (see Squires and Stephen, 2005a) of late modernity: the 'epistemological' fallacy (Furlong and Cartmel, 1997) and the 'cosmetic' fallacy (Young, 1999), together consolidating 'the politicisation of youth and the criminalisation of young people' and masking the 'structural and age-related inequalities in society' (Barry, 2005, p 294).

In late modernity, these inequalities are compounded by a crisis of political legitimacy (see Flint, 2002), heightening fragmentation and 'the death of community' (Hall and Winlow, 2005, p 42), requiring governments to manipulate desires and responses (see Newburn and Jones, 2005) in the promotion of supposedly bottom-up community 'collective efficacy' (Sampson et al, 1999). For the individual, this 'death of community', as Hall and Winlow (2005) describe so effectively, 'marks the absence of collective means of coping with the constant threat of impoverishment, exploitation, cultural negation or expulsion', with the result that 'the prospect of being shoved rudely towards this terrifying precipice is now born by the individual' (Hall and Winslow, 2005, pp 42-3). Marginalised young people in late modern Britain are ill equipped for this new, harsh individualised reality. Undoubtedly, the unassailable victory of transatlantic neo-liberal ideology, especially in terms of youth justice (see Muncie, 2005), has ensured that society can absolve itself from responsibility for its citizens' welfare, not least that of the young miscreants in its midst. As a consequence, society deludes itself that it bears little obligation to offer support for their reintegration and inclusion. This view is reflected in the House of Commons Home Affairs Committee's analysis:

> It has been suggested that much anti-social behaviour by young people is really a matter of lack of tolerance, or inter-generational conflict. We conclude that, for the most part, this simply is not true. In particular, behaviour which invites a formal response (such as the use of enforcement powers) is almost always serious, persistent and non-contentiously anti-social. (House of Commons Home Affairs Committee, 2005, p 23)

If, then, so 'serious' and 'persistent', should not extant criminal law intervene? Clearly not. Instead, in community safety, we find 'burgeoning modes of repressive governance' (Goldson, 2004, p 27) whereupon the management of risk is devolved to responsibilised (see Garland, 2001, pp 124-7), watchful members of each community (see Flint, 2002) who collate the reams of questionable grey intelligence (Stephen and Squires, 2004) on which antisocial measures against young people can be enacted 'swiftly' and 'efficiently' without any need for the niceties of rights and principles long-enshrined in criminal law processes. Bauman captures this shift perfectly:

> The old Big Brother was preoccupied with *inclusion* – integration, getting people into line and keeping them there. The new Big Brother's concern is *exclusion* – spotting the people who 'do not fit' into the place they are in, banishing them from that place and deporting them 'where they belong', or better still never allowing them to come near in the first place. (Bauman, 2004, p 132, emphasis in original)

In this manner, the 'exclusionary potential' (Mizen, 2004, p 144) of community safety policies and practices is serving to consolidate young people's construction 'as an inherently problematic presence in the public realm' (Collins and Kearns, 2001, p 401). Thus, momentarily returning to the opening extract, the troubling result is somewhat reminiscent of the Black Act of 1723, which, as E.P. Thompson explained, was 'so loosely drafted that it became a spawning ground for ever-extending legal judgements' (Thompson, 1975, p 23). There is no other conclusion to be reached about the all-encompassing arbitrariness of today's 'antisocial behaviour' measures, thinly disguised as community safety. The next section, therefore, develops this argument by locating it within the wider policy arena for children and young people.

Every child matters?

A clear example of the maladroit handling of policy towards children and young people is found in the contrast between the national policy framework *Every Child Matters* (DfES, 2004a) and the associated 2004 Children Act, with the announcement by Charles Clarke, then Home Secretary, that local authorities will be able to 'name and shame' youngsters on Anti-Social Behaviour Orders (ASBOs):

> We know that too many communities are still blighted by the mindless behaviour of a few yobs, who can ruin the quality of life for everyone. Many offenders think that they are untouchable and above the law. If they thought that there would be a news blackout on their actions they must now think again. Publicising ASBOs has been tested in the courts and today we are making the position crystal clear – your photo could be all over the local media, your local community will know who you are, and breaching an ASBO could land you in prison. Publicity is part of proper enforcement, which is essential if we are to tackle anti-social behaviour and reassure communities that something is being done. (Home Office, 2005)

Now buttressed by the affirmation that "naming and shaming" is often essential to enforce ASBOs' (House of Commons Home Affairs Committee, 2005, p 73) and, as towns like Guildford construct 'Walls of Shame' (Quayle, 2005) or cities like Manchester produce leaflets carrying the names and photographs of children subject to ASBOs (Crook, 2005), it is clear to see that 'naming and shaming', as Smith (2005) states sharply, 'has become part of a national blood sport'. That other national blood sport, fox-hunting (supposedly banned in this same year) tended to be the exclusive preserve of conservative countryside folk. This new rather more inclusive, and quintessentially New Labour, urban blood sport can be enjoyed by all 'law-abiding citizens' and, in employing the ever-growing antisocial behaviour powers, children and young people are certainly proving easier quarry to ensnare in their natural habitats than foxes ever were.

Consequently, and clearly ignoring the long-standing caveats offered by sociology, not least the problems in defining 'deviance' and the risks associated with labelling (for example, Becker, 1963; Schur, 1971), this further erosion of children's and young people's rights breaches United Nations' principles, for example, the UN Convention on the Rights of the Child and the UN Standard Minimum Rules for the Administration of Youth Justice, both of which relate to respect for privacy and prevention of stigma (see Muncie, 2005; Smith, 2005). This is a heavy moral price to pay to 'reassure communities that something is being done'. It appears quite contrary to the government's purported desire 'that every child and young person is able to fulfil their full potential and those facing particular obstacles are supported to overcome them' (DfES, 2004a, p 2). What could be a greater 'obstacle' to a child or young person's successful development than having their mugshot and name displayed for all the world to see? Accordingly, in the contemporary rhetorical melange:

> Children and young people are caught up in a social and political context that persists in dividing the world into those perceived as 'vulnerable' and those seen as a threat. (Goldthorpe, 2004, p 115)

This is certainly not a new phenomenon (see Goldson, 2000; Parker, 2004), but the potency of the current problematic political emphasis on 'respect' and 'rights and responsibilities' (for example, Stephen and Squires, 2004; Such and Walker, 2004) lies in identifying and denouncing those young people deemed undeserving, or *homo sacer* (Bauman, 2004), in populist constructions. Politically symbolic rhetoric from both major parties essentialises marginalised young people as 'thugs' and 'yobs' (for example, Home Office, 2004a, 2004b, 2004c, 2005; Howard, 2005a, 2005b) to reinforce notions of dangerousness and thus justify increasingly repressive measures to contain these 'feral' and 'out-of-control' youngsters (Garland, 1996; Parker, 2004). 'Name and shame' and ongoing pejorative constructions will do nothing but serve to reinforce to those young people thus labelled that 'there are no obvious paths to a fully fledged membership' (Bauman, 2004, p 16) of *our community*; they are hitherto condemned to remain diaspora in the wastelands of utilitarian political opportunism mapped out in community safety discourses. And, given the dearth of meaningful commitment to troublesome children and young people, save in short-term-funded, headline-grabbing initiatives (for example, Parker, 2004) such as the worthy, but limited in scope, Youth Inclusion Project (www.crimereduction.gov.uk/youth15.htm), there appears to be no means of redemption or reintegration. Children and young people are merely to be vilified and employed purposefully for political ends.

Consequently, and in contrast to Michael Howard's electioneering assessment of Tony Blair's 'pussyfooting' (Howard, 2005b) performance, policy responses have been becoming increasingly conditional for children and young people (see Deacon, 2004 for a good discussion of conditionality in welfare). In place of formal law and welfare initiatives, stigmatising and condemnatory civil measures thinly couched in beneficent notions of community safety have progressively unfolded a raft of 'antisocial behaviour' measures (see, for example, House of Commons Home Affairs Committee, 2005, p 14) underpinned by a 'lack of respect for freedom and dignity of all, and lack of regard for established rights and systems of legality' (Hudson, 2003, p 73) for young people. Yet, undoubtedly, if politicians were to employ the same value-laden and harmful imagery for, and preside over the erosion of long-held legal principles with, any other 'minority' social group, there would seem to be ample grounds for legal redress on firm equal opportunities grounds. Perhaps then, this is why there seems to be an unwillingness by policy makers to address the rights of young people explicitly (for a good discussion of the tensions, see Freeman, 2005). It is therefore heartening to note, though, that some more enlightened media commentators are beginning to pick up on this point. A scornful report, and leader editorial, in *The Independent* offered a clear verdict: 'ASBOs are both illiberal and ineffective' (Verkaik, 2005). *The Independent* is not alone; merely two weeks earlier, Roger Smith's biting article in *The Law Gazette* concluded by calling for the abolition of ASBOs:

> ... stand-alone ASBOs are a jurisprudential Frankenstein, cobbled together in the satanic mills of the Home Office out of disparate parts of the justice system. Their effectiveness depends in large part on their ability to shock. They do. (Smith, 2005)

The greatest 'shock' has been to witness society's welcoming of increasingly punitive restrictions on children's and young people's agency. This is not to deny that important achievements have been made in the field of youth justice. *Every Child Matters: Change for Children in the Criminal Justice System* (DfES, 2004b, p 3) reports the 'visible and significant progress' made in how children and young people are dealt with and states that 'a key message of these reforms is the importance of services and agencies continuing to move towards prevention and early intervention' (DfES, 2004b, p 4). Laudable sentiments indeed, but this does not inspire much confidence in the light of the Five Year Plan (Home Office, 2004b), which is representative of a trend identified perspicuously two decades ago by Cohen (1985, p 53): '[i]ntervention comes earlier, it sweeps in more deviates, is extended to those not yet formally adjudicated and it becomes more intensive'. Lamentably, the continuation of this trend against 'youth nuisance' was given a clear green light:

> We have heard evidence that young people acting anti-socially should not be grouped together: there is a difference between a young person annoying residents by playing football and someone who is terrorising a local neighbourhood through a series of criminal and sub-criminal activities. We accept this: however, we emphasise that this does not mean that less serious ASB should be ignored. Activities such as playing football in the street are not necessarily harmless: persistent use of a garden gate, house wall or car or other inappropriate locations as goalposts – perhaps accompanied by abuse or threats when challenged – can amount to intolerable behaviour which should not be dismissed by the authorities. (House of Commons Home Affairs Committee, 2005, p 37)

Given that there are potentially no limits to that which can be construed as 'antisocial behaviour', nor the age at which children and young people can be sucked into the machinery of the 'antisocial behaviour' industry (Squires and Stephen, 2005a), New Labour's long-standing rhetoric of 'being tough on the causes of crime' appears to have become interpreted crudely as the minor incivilities that *may* (positivist certitude notwithstanding) eventually lead to crime, instead of tackling the circumstances within which antisocial behaviour develops and proceeds. Further, as Pitts (2005, p v) argues, 'the government's inordinate emphasis on stemming the criminality of young offenders has tended to eclipse the question of their social needs'. Apparently, the Select Committee regarded such conclusions as both inaccurate and premature:

> Overall, the clear message of the evidence is that there is more to do in terms of all means of tackling ASB – whether through diversion, support or sanction. It is not the case that the Government's ASB policies are overwhelmingly punitive towards children; nor is it true that its strategy is skewed towards enforcement. On the contrary, there is compelling evidence that in many parts of the country, legal powers are used only relatively rarely. We would emphasise therefore the need not to be led astray by the rhetoric but to focus on what is happening on the ground. (House of Commons Home Affairs Committee, 2005, p 44)

The voices of professionals, practitioners and individuals subject to ASBOs who were afforded the opportunity to be heard at the launch of ASBO Concern in April 2005 (see www.asboconcern.org.uk) merely two days after the publication of this report certainly offered a very different vista to these blandly misleading assurances. As Pitts (2005) has argued, with our exaggerated constructions of the dangerousness of young people, 21st-century Britain is developing a collective amnesia of the essential humanist truth that 'children and young people at risk of offending are no less children in need than any other child' (Goldthorpe, 2004, p 130). For politicians, every child may matter, but some appear to matter considerably less than others, notably those youngsters growing up in the marginalised housing estates throughout this country for whom community safety bears little relevance to the actuality of their daily lives (Stephen and Squires, 2004). If, then, community safety is not being realised for all citizens, it must, therefore, be asked what is being achieved? To facilitate a response to this question, it is germane to appreciate 'community', not in idealised terms, but as 'a means of government' (Rose, 1996, p 335).

The less-than-holy grail of 'community'

> Responsibility for crime control has moved from the centre and is increasingly exercised 'at a distance' by a combination of statutory, private and voluntary agencies. This change in formal responsibilities has been accompanied by a blurring of crime and disorder and the

collapsing of both into what is now called community safety. (Matthews, 2002, p 224)

This 'blurring' (see also Brown, 2004) is of profound concern, revealing an exponential effect of seemingly benign surveillance and intervention and subsequent chances of detection and sanction (Kempf-Leonard and Peterson, 2002) that has knock-on effects for the whole youth justice system (Goldson, 2004) and, as has been argued, for the wider principles of justice. Nonetheless, as stated earlier, the Five Year Plan (Home Office, 2004b) unfolded the government's 'commitment' to enable the 'law-abiding majority' (whomsoever they may be) to feel safe in their homes and local areas through the fostering of 'strong and cohesive communities'. However, the feel-good communitarian ideals implicit in such expressions of community safety mask the underlying shift from crime prevention to community safety (Gilling, 2001; Flint, 2002; Hughes et al, 2002; Matthews, 2002) in the governance of communities over recent years reflective of the changing control needs of the late modern, neo-liberal state (Foucault, 1991). Synchronous with this shift, the former, now deemed naive, notion that young people will eventually 'grow out of crime' (for example, Home Office, 1988, 1991) has been replaced by a pessimism (Audit Commission, 1996; Home Office, 1997) that focuses on risk and probabilities (Goldson, 2004) of offending rather than certainties. Supported by reams of superficial and value-laden, positivist-inspired 'indicators' from administrative criminology (Squires and Stephen, 2005a), instead of concerns about the welfare of children and young people, this pessimism ensures that, through the rhetoric and categories of community safety, those youngsters have become internalised as 'the universal symbol of disorder' (Burney, 2002, p 473). As this 'essentialised Other' (Young 1999), the apparently innocuous responses of 'civilianised' (Hope, 1998) crime prevention measures have become increasingly oppressive, focusing firmly on 'control by prevention' (Gilling, 2001, p 384) through the precautionary measures of ABCs, ASBOs and Dispersal Orders *inter alia* (see www.homeoffice.gov.uk/ crime/antisocialbehaviour/index.html).

Consequentially, the terrain of this 'era of governmentality' (Foucault, 1991, p 103) is mapped out by an understanding of 'community' as the paramount ideological 'means of governing crime and disorder' (Flint, 2002, p 249) primarily through young people, but extending to all whether 'antisocial' or not. Contemporary utilitarian political expediency accepts that nothing comes without cost and this is a maxim that 'law-abiding citizens' seem to have ignored. Yet when we pursue the ideal of 'community', it is necessary to reflect on another pertinent insight from Bauman:

> [T]here is a price to be paid for the privilege of 'being in a community' – and it is inoffensive or even invisible only as long as the community stays in the dream. The price is paid in the currency of freedom, variously called 'autonomy', 'right to self assertion', 'right to be

yourself'. Whatever you choose, you gain some and lose some. (Bauman, 2001, p 4)

The 'price to be paid' for chasing 'the [adult] dream' is becoming too high for many young people. In response to the Home Affairs Committee report, Frances Crook reminds us that 'children have a right to use public spaces, yet groups of children can be dispersed if their presence is thought to cause distress' (Crook, 2005). Thus the situation is such that contemporary community safety policies are denying young people the freedom to 'hang around' in public spaces when there is nowhere else to go, the freedom to 'be' and 'belong', and the freedom to take risks (see Squires and Stephen, 2005a, for a fuller discussion). In what has been described as a 'punitive spiral' (Flint, 2002, p 261), young people are being excluded, as Flint explains, 'from the civil rights of access to public space and commercial centres, further compromising their social rights of citizenship' (Flint, 2002, p 261). But, from an adult's point of view, this seems to be a fair price to pay in pursuit of the holy grail of 'community'.

One helpful illustration is found in the launch, in Brighton, of the Hollingdean Neighbourhood Agreement, which, mirroring the rhetoric of the Five Year Plan (Home Office, 2004b), aims to foster 'a safe and pleasant environment for residents to live in so that they can enjoy their homes and their local community' (Counsellor Gill Mitchell, cited in Sussex Police, 2005). Hailed by Counsellor Mitchell as 'a great example of residents, the city council, the police and other partner organisations working together to target anti-social behaviour', this agreement denotes acceptable and unacceptable behaviour for community residents. So far so good, but this is not a value-neutral terrain because the only group to be singled out for specific mention in the building of this nirvana is young people: 'It's all about encouraging young people to take more pride in their community', reports one local resident (see Sussex Police, 2005). The beguiling twin fallacies of late modernity provide such clarity of vision, such *probability*-based assurance that, in merely banning (potentially limitless) antisocial behaviours – tacitly young people's presence and agency within the public realm – the ills of marginalised estates can be cured and 'community' rekindled as the Home Affairs Committee avers:

> We welcome the introduction of a number of new powers to deal with ASB, including housing injunctions and demotions, anti-social behaviour orders (ASBOs) and dispersal powers. These can provide much-needed relief for communities suffering from the impact of nuisance behaviour. (House of Commons Home Affairs Committee, 2005, p 4)

Depicted as a 'triumph of behaviourism' (Brown, 2004, p 206), reliant on hearsay and bias, and framed within the insatiable ontological insecurities of late modernity (see Squires and Stephen, 2005a), empowered, responsibilised citizens, through

the 'enforcement of mutual obligations' (Deacon, 2004, p 924), are encouraged
to reaffirm hegemonic social and moral norms and values (see Flint, 2002) in the
reclamation of their communities from 'yobs', 'thugs' and 'neighbours from hell'.
Through current modes of 'contractual governance' (Crawford, 2003), the
miscreants are obliged to comply, or be banished, without being offered the
concrete tools to alter their behaviour, for example, leisure facilities or meaningful
employment, let alone fundamental educational provision and adequate welfare
safety nets. Consistently, the neo-liberal state is shown to be sorely lacking on all
such counts (for example, Lopez Blasco et al, 2003; Dolby and Dimitriadis, 2004;
Mizen, 2004; Webster et al, 2004; Barry, 2005), allowing the new youth justice
(Goldson, 2000; Pitts, 2001; Smith, 2003) to develop apace and further indulge
the twin fallacies as expressed clumsily here:

> Overall, the balance of the Government's strategy is about right. We
> welcome the resources put in by the Government into diversion and
> support, are satisfied that there are now enough powers in place to
> deal with ASB, and commend the Home Office Anti-social Behaviour
> Unit on its work to improve the response at local level. We welcome
> the suggestion from the British Crime Survey that there has been a
> fall in the number of people perceiving ASB to be a problem in their
> area, although we would need to see a consistent trend over time to
> draw any firmer conclusions.
>
> However, we conclude that the Government's strategy is being
> undermined by different philosophies, methods and tactics amongst
> key players. In particular, we were disappointed to hear that some
> social services departments, local educational authorities, Children
> and Adult Mental Health Services, Youth Services and children's non-
> governmental organisations (NGOs) are often not fully committed
> to local ASB strategies. The failure to attend meetings of Crime and
> Disorder Reduction Partnerships is just one symptom of this. Yet
> many perpetrators of ASB, both young and adult, are the very people
> with complex needs and therefore with whom these organisations
> are already, or should be, working. (House of Commons Home Affairs
> Committee, 2005, pp 3-4)

'Complex needs' and punishment cannot be conflated in this fashion. The
fundamental issue here, therefore, seems to be that the committee failed to
comprehend that the philosophies of welfare and justice models of dealing with
problem children and young people (see Muncie, 2005) can be quite antithetical.
Certainly the kinds of ASBO cases highlighted by Harry Fletcher from the
National Association of Probation Officers reveal starkly the asinine inhumanity
of the growing shift away from welfare (see Fletcher, 2005). Accordingly, within
this ideological lacuna, the failure of leading welfare personnel to participate as
the committee suggests could be interpreted as those practitioners offering a

direct challenge to current hegemonic discourses and practices (Squires and Stephen, 2005b). The welfare and human rights-based organisations represented by ASBO Concern would appear to offer such practitioners a more expressive, and concerted, means of resistance to the values inherent in the current climate; a climate captured by Garland so effectively:

> There has been a marked shift of emphasis from the welfare to the penal modality.... The penal mode, as well as becoming more prominent, has become more punitive, more expressive, more security-minded. The welfare mode, as well as becoming more muted, has become more conditional, more offence-centred, more risk conscious.... The offenders ... are now less likely to be represented in official discourse as socially deprived citizens in need of support. They are depicted instead as culpable, undeserving and somewhat dangerous individuals. (Garland, 2001, p 175)

The condemnatory, and morally questionable, antisocial behaviour measures inherent in contemporary community safety discourses offer no greater support for Garland's thesis. In accepting the populist representations of, and responses to, children and young people's 'antisocial' agency within community safety discourses, the 'law-abiding citizens' of Great Britain have opened up a Pandora's box of increasing penetration into, and regulation of, their own lives. More significantly, the good citizens also risk losing the capacity for compassion and liberality on which British democratic principles of justice were founded.

Time to rethink 'community safety' for young people

This chapter has been written with clear subjectivity, and no apologies are made for taking this line. Having initially become concerned with community safety discourses and practices while working with families whose children were subject to the callous arbitrariness of inappropriate antisocial behaviour measures (Stephen and Squires, 2003), there did not seem to be much scope for objectivity – ironically, rather like the measures themselves. With consolidating 'antisocial behaviour' developments (for example, Home Office, 2004b) and powers, through the 2002 Police Reform Act and the 2003 Anti-Social Behaviour Act, alongside continuing, and indeed magnifying, demonising rhetoric from politicians (for example, Home Office, 2005b), concerns about the injurious potentialities of community safety continue to grow, not least in the abject breaches of rights and principles of justice, as this chapter has demonstrated.

One mother's desperate pronouncement highlights graphically the central humanist truth in this troubling new reality: 'They're still children and entitled to be children. Community safety needs to be about keeping all children safe' (Stephen and Squires, 2004, p 364). Yet, the Honourable Members of the House of Commons Home Affairs Committee (2005) and the government's new agenda (as set out in the 2005 Queen's Speech [Office of the Prime Minister, 2005b]) missed a vital opportunity to reframe the direction of current policy as this mother implored. There is no denying the fact that many communities are 'blighted' by the behaviour of *some* children and young people, but laws already exist to tackle any acts of criminality without the need for recourse to legally and morally spurious 'antisocial behaviour' measures.

Notwithstanding, through the new politics of injustice, *all* children and young people growing up on marginalised estates are being constructed as *homo sacer* (Bauman, 2004), as 'culpable, undeserving and somewhat dangerous individuals' (Garland, 2001, p 175), and, in not challenging these representations, we are denying them, and ourselves as a wider community, safety, if not also humanity. Law must be just and based on 'logical criteria with reference to standards of universality and equity' (Thompson, 1975, p 262), but these standards simply do not exist as far as 'antisocial behaviour' measures are concerned. Consequentially, the current climate is denying a whole generation security, as Mizen poignantly notes in comments about New Labour's youth policy as a whole: '[it] may thus ostensibly lay claim to safeguarding tomorrow's future, but the reality is that it is much more likely to continue to misspend our youth' (Mizen, 2003, p 473). Politicians, the media and the public continue to fail to appreciate that, unless we guarantee structural, and thus ontological, safety for marginalised and disaffected children and young people through inclusive welfare-based initiatives that safeguard the rights enshrined within the 1998 Human Rights Act and other international treaties (see Muncie, 2005), community safety will remain a 'dream' (Bauman, 2001), and a very disturbed dream at that.

References

Audit Commission (1996) *Misspent Youth*, London: Audit Commission.

Bandalli, S. (2000) 'Children, responsibility and the new youth justice', in B. Goldson (ed) *The New Youth Justice*, Lyme Regis: Russell House Publishing, pp 81-95.

Barry, M. (ed) (2005) *Youth Policy and Social Inclusion: Critical Debates with Young People*, London: Routledge.

Bauman, Z. (2001) *Community: Seeking Safety in an Insecure World*, Cambridge: Polity Press.

Bauman, Z. (2004) *Wasted Lives: Modernity and its Outcasts*, Cambridge: Polity Press.

BBC (2005a) 'Mall bans shopper hooded tops' (http://news.bbc.co.uk/1/hi/england/kent/4534903.stm, accessed 11 May 2005).

BBC (2005b) 'Feral youths on "rampage of fear"' (http://news.bbc.co.uk/1/hi/england/manchester/4554611.stm, accessed 17 May).

Becker, H. (1963) *The Outsiders*, New York, NY: Free Press.

Brown, A. (2004) 'Anti-social behaviour, crime control and social control', *The Howard Journal of Criminal Justice*, vol 43, no 2, pp 203-11.

Burney, E. (2002) 'Talking tough, acting coy: what happened to the Anti-Social Behaviour Order?', *The Howard Journal*, vol 41, no 5, pp 469-84.

Cohen, S. (1985) *Visions of Social Control*, Cambridge: Polity Press.

Collins, C.A. and Kearns, R.A. (2001) 'Under curfew and under seige? Legal geographies of young people', *Geoforum*, vol 32, no 3, pp 389-403.

Crawford, A. (2003) '"Contractual governance" of deviant behaviour', *Journal of Law and Society*, vol 30, no 4, pp 479-505.

Crook, F. (2005) 'Abolish ASBOs for children', Press release, The Howard League for Penal Reform, 5 April.

Deacon, A. (2004) 'Justifying conditionality: the case of anti-social tenants', *Housing Studies*, vol 19, no 6, pp 911-26.

DfES (Department for Education and Skills) (2004a) *Every Child Matters: Change for Children*, DfES/1081/2004, Nottingham: DfES Publications.

DfES (2004b) *Every Child Matters: Change for Children in the Criminal Justice System*, DfES/1092/2004, Nottingham: DfES Publications.

Dolby, N. and Dimitriadis, G. with Willis, P. (2004) *Learning to Labour in New Times*, London: Routledge Falmer.

Fletcher, H. (2005) *Anti Social Behaviour Orders: Analysis of the First Six Years*, Briefing for the launch of ASBO Concern, 7 April, London: NAPO.

Flint, J. (2002) 'Return of the governors: citizenship and the new governance of neighbourhood disorder in the UK', *Citizenship Studies*, vol 6, no 3, pp 245-64.

Foucault, M. (1991) 'Governmentality', in G. Burchell, C. Gordon and P. Miller (eds) *The Foucault Effect: Studies in Governmentality*, Chicago, IL: University of Chicago Press, pp 87-104.

Freeman, M. (2005) 'Beyond rhetoric: extending rights to young people', in M. Barry (ed) *Youth Policy and Social Inclusion: Critical Debates with Young People*, London: Routledge, pp 55-68.

Furlong, A. and Cartmel, F. (1997) *Young People and Social Change: Individualisation and Risk in Late Modernity*, Buckingham: Open University Press.

Garland, D. (1996) 'The limits of the sovereign state: strategies of crime control in contemporary society', *British Journal of Criminology*, vol 36, no 4, pp 445-71.

Garland, D. (2001) *The Culture of Control: Crime and Social Order in Contemporary Society*, Oxford: Oxford University Press.

Gilling, D. (2001) 'Community safety and social policy', *European Journal on Criminal Policy and Research*, vol 9, no 4, pp 381-400.

Goldson, B. (ed) (2000) *The New Youth Justice*, Lyme Regis: Russell House Publishing.

Goldson, B. (2004) 'Authoritarian drift', *Safer Society*, no 23, pp 27-8, Winter.

Goldthorpe, L. (2004) 'Every child matters: a legal perspective', *Child Abuse Review*, vol 13, no 2, pp 114-36.

Hall, S. and Winlow, S. (2005) 'Anti-nirvana: crime, culture and instrumentalism in the age of insecurity', *Crime, Media, Culture*, vol 1, no 1, pp 31-48.

Home Office (1988) *Punishment, Custody and the Community*, Cmnd 424, London: HMSO.

Home Office (1991) *Safer Communities: The Local Delivery of Crime Prevention through the Partnership Approach*, Report of the Standing Conference on Crime Prevention ('the Morgan Report'), London: HMSO.

Home Office (1997) *No More Excuses*, Cm 3809, London: HMSO.

Home Office (1998) *The Crime and Disorder Act*, London: HMSO.

Home Office (2003) *Respect and Responsibility – Taking a Stand Against Anti-Social Behaviour*, London: Home Office.

Home Office (2004a) 'Call For local heroes', Press release 216/2004, 29 June.

Home Office (2004b) *Confident Communities in a Secure Britain: The Home Office Strategic Plan 2004-08*, London: Home Office.

Home Office (2004c) 'Confident Communities in a Secure Britain: Home Office publishes Strategic Plan', Press release 237/2004, 19 July.

Home Office (2004d) *Perceptions and Experiences of Anti-Social Behaviour*, Findings 252, London: Home Office.

Home Office (2005) 'Yobs will face the consequences of their actions', Charles Clarke, Press release 042/2005.

Hope, T. (1998) 'Are we letting social policy off the hook?', *Criminal Justice Matters*, vol 33, pp 5-6, Autumn.

Hough, M. and Roberts, J.V. (2004) *Youth Crime and Youth Justice: Public Opinion in England and Wales*, Bristol: The Policy Press.

House of Commons Home Affairs Committee (2005) *Anti-Social Behaviour*, Fifth Report of Session 2004-05, Volume 1, London: The Stationery Office.

Howard, M. (2005a) 'Taking a stand against the yob culture', Speech, 31 March (www.conservatives.com/tile.do?def=news.story.page&obj_id=121091, accessed 31 March 2005).

Howard, M. (2005b) 'Taking a stand against yob families', Speech, 6 April (www.conservatives.com/tile.do?def=news.story.page&obj_id=121442, accessed 6 April 2005).

Hudson, B. (2003) *Justice in the Risk Society*, London: Sage Publications.

Hughes, G., McLaughlin, E. and Muncie, J. (2002) *Crime Prevention and Community Safety: New Directions,* London: Sage Publications.

Kelly, P. (2003) 'Growing up as risky business? Risks, surveillance and the institutionalized mistrust of youth', *Journal of Youth Studies*, vol 6, no 2, pp 165-80.

Kempf-Leonard, K. and Peterson, E. (2002) 'Expanding realms of the new penology: the advent of actuarial justice for juveniles', in J. Muncie, G. Hughes and E. McLaughlin (eds) *Youth Justice: Critical Readings*, London: Sage Publications.

Lianos, M. and Douglas, M. (2000) 'Dangerization and the end of deviance: the institutional environment', *British Journal of Criminology*, vol 40, no 2, pp 261-78.

Lopez Blasco, A., McNeish, W. and Walther, A. (2003) *Young People and the Contradictions of Exclusion: Towards Integrated Transition Policies in Europe*, Bristol: The Policy Press.

Matthews, R. (2002) 'Crime and control in late modernity', *Theoretical Criminology*, vol 6, no 2, pp 217-26.

Mizen, P. (2003) 'The best days of your life? Youth, policy and Blair's New Labour', *Critical Social Policy*, vol 23, no 4, pp 453-76.

Mizen, P. (2004) *The Changing State of Youth*, Basingstoke: Palgrave Macmillan.

Muncie, J. (2005) 'The globalization of crime control – the case of youth and juvenile justice', *Theoretical Criminology*, vol 9, no 1, pp 35-64.

Newburn, T. and Jones, T. (2005) 'Symbolic politics and penal populism: the long shadow of Willie Horton', *Crime, Media, Culture*, vol 1, no 1, pp 78-87.

Office of the Prime Minister (2005a) Transcript of Prime Minister's Press Conference, 12 May (www.number-10.gov.uk/output/Page7481.asp, accessed 12 May 2005).

Office of the Prime Minister (2005b) 'The Queen's Speech', 17 May (www.number-10.gov.uk/output/Page7488.asp, accessed 17 May 2005).

Office of the Prime Minister (2005c) 'Government aims to foster a culture of respect', Press release, 17 May (www.number-10.gov.uk/output/Page7488.asp, accessed 17 May 2005).

Parker, R. (2004) 'Children and the concept of harm', in P. Hillyard, C. Pantazis, S. Tombs and D. Gordon (eds) *Beyond Criminology: Taking Harm Seriously*, London: Pluto Press, pp 236-50.

Pitts, J. (2001) *The New Politics of Youth Crime: Discipline or Solidarity?*, Lyme Regis: Russell House Publishing.

Pitts, J. (2005) 'Youth crime. Election campaign report', *Community Care*, 3-9 March, pp i-xii.

Quayle, C. (2005) 'Institutionalised spite', *Red Pepper*, April, pp 29-31.

Rose, N. (1996) 'The death of the social? Re-figuring the territory of government', *Economy and Society*, vol 25, no 3, pp 327-56.

Sampson, R.J., Morenoff, J.D. and Earls, F. (1999) 'Beyond social capital: spatial dynamics of collective efficacy for children', *American Sociological Review*, vol 64, no 5, pp 633-60.

Schur, E.M. (1971) *Labeling Deviant Behaviour: Its Sociological Implications*, London: Harper and Row.

Smith, R. (2003) *Youth Justice. Ideas, Policies, Practice*, Cullompton: Willan Publishing.

Smith, R. (2005) 'Shocking behaviour', *The Law Gazette*, 17 March (www.lawgazette.co.uk/features/view=feature.law?FEATUREID=226678, accessed 11 April 2005).

Squires, P. and Stephen, D.E. (2005a) *Rougher Justice: Young People and Anti-Social Behaviour*, Cullompton: Willan Publishing.

Squires, P. and Stephen, D.E. (2005b) 'Rethinking ASBOs', *Critical Social Policy*, vol 25, no 4, pp 517-28.

Stephen, D.E. and Squires, P. (2003) *Community Safety, Enforcement and Acceptable Behaviour Contracts*, Brighton: Health and Social Policy Research Centre, University of Brighton.

Stephen, D.E. and Squires, P. (2004) '"They're still children and entitled to be children". Problematising the institutionalised mistrust of marginalised youth in Britain', *Journal of Youth Studies*, vol 7, no 3, pp 351-69.

Such, E. and Walker, R. (2004) 'Being responsible and responsible beings: children's understanding of responsibility', *Children and Society*, vol 18, no 3, pp 231-42.

Sussex Police (2005) 'Neighbourhood Policing News', 5 April (http://sussex.police.co.uk/npt/brighton_east/district_news.asp, accessed 7 April 2005).

Thompson, E.P. (1975) *Whigs and Hunters: The Origin of the Black Act*, London: Allen Lane.

Tombs, S. and Hillyard, P. (2004) 'Towards a political economy of harm: states, corporations and the production of inequality', in P. Hillyard, C. Pantazis, S. Tombs and D. Gordon (eds) *Beyond Criminology. Taking Harm Seriously*, London: Pluto Press, pp 30-54.

Verkaik, R. (2005) 'Out of control ASBOs a "menace to society"', *The Independent*, 2 April, p 9.

Webster, C., Simpson, D., MacDonald, R., Abbas, A., Cieslik, M., Shildrick, T. and Simpson, M. (2004) *Poor Transitions: Social Exclusion and Young Adults*, Bristol: The Policy Press.

Wilson, J. and Kelling, G. (1982) 'Broken windows', *Atlantic Review*, March, pp 29-36.

Wood, M. (2004) *Perceptions and Experience of Anti-Social Behaviour: Findings from the British Crime Survey 2003/04*, London: Home Office.

Young, J. (1999) *The Exclusive Society*, London: Sage Publications.

FIFTEEN

Conclusion: contradictions and dilemmas: the rise and fall of community safety?

Peter Squires

We began this excursion into the field of community safety policy making with a series of questions about what may have been achieved in its name. We conclude, having reviewed many dimensions of this area of policy development, with a fairly substantial charge sheet against it. The 'official' history of community safety tells a story locating the origins of community safety policy development in a revitalisation of local democracy as municipal authorities sought to resist an increasingly centralised and increasingly punitive and largely situational response to problems of crime and disorder. At the same time, the renewed priority afforded to victims (the community of victims) and the broader academic legitimation provided by 'left realism' appeared to suggest that the prevention of crime and the maintenance of law and order could form part of a wider project of progressive and inclusive social reconstruction.

We have only fleetingly glimpsed such holistic ambitions on two previous occasions in the UK, each, perhaps not surprisingly, related to the coming to power of a seemingly left-inclined government. Thus, in 1946 Hermann Mannheim outlined a programme for criminal justice and social reconstruction (Mannheim, 1946) linking the ambitious post-war reforms that culminated in the welfare state with the central goals of a criminal justice system. Less than two decades later, the Labour Party Study Group convened by Lord Longford, produced its report, *Crime: A Challenge to Us All* (Labour Party, 1964), advocating a wholesale reform of juvenile justice based on viewing the welfare and support needs of young offenders as uppermost and their punishment as secondary. Two decades on, it is arguable that the emergence of the 'community safety' perspective can be understood in the context of a similar political sequence. However, it might be equally debateable just how 'left-inclined' the new Blair government really intended to be, but the scale of the government's ambition for a wholesale reorientation of criminal justice around crime prevention and community safety seems fairly clear (though always with a wary eye on what the *Daily Mail* might be saying, after all 'tough on crime' but also 'tough on the causes of crime': Muncie, 1999, 2000).

The full impact of New Labour's criminal justice reforms may have taken some time to emerge, but the policy agendas emerging from the Morgan Report (Home Office, 1991) and the Commission on Social Justice (1994), with its 'social inclusion' agenda and what it termed the 'justice gap' (Commission on Social Justice, 1993), certainly played their part. However, not dissimilar to the ways in which the equally ambitious reforms of 1946 and 1964 were watered down, resisted or otherwise thwarted in practice, no sooner had the community safety perspective emerged on the political scene than it began to change. Telling illustrations of this might be detected across the field. A first concerns the marked U-turn in conceptions of youth offending.

Youth offending is an important area on which to focus, given the prominence that youth problems and, especially, perceptions of youth indiscipline have assumed on governmental agendas. As early as 1988, a Home Office Green Paper, *Punishment, Custody and the Community* (Home Office, 1988) had articulated a view of youth offending consistent with a wide-ranging research base and with which even the most ardent labelling theorist would have found favour:

> Most young offenders grow out of crime as they become more mature and responsible. They need encouragement and help to become law-abiding. Even a short period in custody is quite likely to confirm them as criminals.... They find themselves labelled as offenders and behave accordingly. (Home Office, 1988, p 6, para 2.15)

Three years later, the influential Morgan Report, regarded by many as the political mainspring of the community safety perspective, concluded its analysis of the troubling behaviour of young people: 'the vast majority of criminal activity by this age group involves less serious offences and a considerable amount constitutes behaviour which is rowdy or anti-social rather than strictly criminal' (Home Office, 1991). Furthermore, the report concluded, 'most young people grow out of delinquency as they move through adolescence' (Home Office, 1991, p 24). Given the significance that antisocial behaviour has now assumed in government priorities (Squires and Stephen, 2005), it is particularly instructive to note that, for Morgan, antisocial behaviour was here clearly distinguished from criminal acts.

Only five years after the publication of the Morgan Report, the focus had changed entirely. The James Bulger murder case had been a crucial turning point, and the 1996 Audit Commission, paving the way for New Labour's youth justice reforms, reflected the new, less tolerant, attitude. Young people no longer 'grew out' of crime. Thus: 'young males are not growing out of offending as they used to' (Audit Commission, 1996, p 12). In 1997, the new Home Secretary introduced his tough-sounding youth justice White Paper, *No More Excuses*, with the following words:

> For too long we have assumed that young offenders will grow out of their offending if left to themselves. The research evidence shows that

this does not happen. Today's young offenders can easily become tomorrow's hardened criminals. As a society we do ourselves no favours by failing to break the link between juvenile crime and disorder and the serial burglar of the future. (Home Office, 1997, p 1)

Nipping crime 'in the bud' was to become the order of the day, 'to intervene early and effectively before crime becomes a habit [in order to prevent] today's young offenders becoming tomorrow's career criminals' (Home Office, 1997, p 2). Yet as a number of commentators have argued, this new 'early intervention' orthodoxy was 'at odds with established theory, research findings and practical experience' (Goldson, 2000, p 257). For a wider critique, see Squires and Stephen (2005, ch 4). Yet if this sudden U-turn on prevailing conceptions of youth offending – in the absence of substantial new research findings and largely in the face of established theory, research evidence and practical experience – can be seen as one of the wheels falling off the community safety 'bandwagon', it was certainly not to be the only one.

A second area whereby the broader, perhaps more ideological, ambitions of community safety rather lost out in the translation to policy and legislation concerns the passage of the 1998 Crime and Disorder Act (CDA) itself and the responsibilities it conferred upon Crime and Disorder Reduction Partnerships (CDRPs). As we have seen already, the concept of community safety was initially defined in terms of a very purposeful and significant step beyond the more conventional discourse of crime prevention. Increasingly, in local government circles, the phrase 'crime prevention' was reinterpreted to mean the promotion of a sense of community safety and the securing of improvements in the quality of life of residents by reference to a wide range of social issues, the tackling of certain risks and sources of vulnerability and the development of policies on a broad range of fronts (ADC, 1990; Coopers and Lybrand, 1994). The idea became well established over a relatively short period of time, defining, in turn, a distinctly local government approach to social crime prevention.

Thus, according to the Local Government Management Board in 1996, community safety entailed the idea of 'community-based action to tackle the causes and consequences of criminal, intimidatory and other related anti-social behaviour. Its purpose is to secure sustainable reductions in crime and fear of crime in local communities. Its approach is based on the formation of multi-agency partnerships between the public, private and voluntary sectors to formulate and introduce community-based measures against crime' (LGMB, 1996, p 1).

And, as the London Strategic Policy Unit (1986) put it, 'using the concept of community safety rather than crime prevention was deliberate, in order to set the agenda in a positive way, emphasising people rather than property, and the roles of local authorities, community and tenants' groups rather than the police' (p 2). Moreover, the report continued, shifting focus away from the 'situational' approach to crime prevention, which had prevailed in the UK for many years, and towards a renewed conception of social crime prevention, using the concept of community safety recognised that 'improving the physical security of individual houses and estates, while useful, will not on its own necessarily improve people's safety or sense of security in their own homes and neighbourhoods. A sense of safety is related to the relations among the people who live in the neighbourhood, and to their fears about crime as well as to their personal experience of crime' (London Strategic Policy Unit, 1986, p 5). Furthermore, according to this approach, safety also needed to be addressed by local people becoming involved and responsible for taking coordinated action in their own residential neighbourhoods in conjunction with statutory agencies.

It was then but a short step to the full Morgan Report partnership agenda. Morgan spelled out the important differences of emphasis in the ideas of crime prevention and community safety:

> The term crime prevention is often narrowly interpreted and this reinforces the view that it is solely the responsibility of the police. The term community safety is open to wider interpretation and could encourage greater participation from all sections of the community.... We see community safety as having both social and situational aspects, as being concerned with people, communities and organisations including families, victims and at risk groups, as well as with attempting to reduce particular types of crime and the fear of crime. (Home Office, 1991)

Despite such an 'ideological' endorsement of the community safety paradigm, and the fact that the Morgan Report has been, quite rightly, credited with planting community safety on the national political agenda, where it was eagerly picked up by the renewed Labour party, a number of other agendas were developing that also impacted on the government's landmark crime and disorder legislation. Prominent among these was the 'disorder management' agenda, which later coalesced into the campaign against 'antisocial behaviour' (see Chapter Fourteen in this volume). Other contributors to this volume (Matt Follett and Barry Loveday, in Chapters Six and Seven, respectively) have discussed the issues concerning the relationships between local authorities and the police arising from the CDA, but here it is enough to note the change of emphasis reflected in the new legislation.

Whereas before 1998 actively promoting 'community safety' had been at the heart of the new policy, the new legislation was concerned with the more familiar goals of 'preventing crime' and 'tackling crime and disorder' and established Crime and Disorder *Reduction* Partnerships to put this into effect. In the guidance issued to the newly established CDRPs (Home Office, 1998) on conducting their crime audits and drafting their crime and disorder strategies, the notion of 'community safety' was almost entirely absent. By contrast, the concept 'community' was employed in conjunction with ideas of 'consultation' and 'accountability' in order to underline the democratic legitimacy of the policy processes in question. CDRPs were cautioned against generating unachievable aspirations around vague 'quality of life' criteria or unspecific perceptions of problems (indeed, addressing the fear of crime itself posed a significant dilemma in just this sense) and advised to concentrate on 'realistic' crime reduction targets. Undoubtedly, in this shift from 'community safety' to crime and disorder reduction, something was being lost.

A third area of retrenchment in the conception of community safety concerns another similar redefinition of purpose to that just described. As we have seen, a key foundation for much of New Labour's policy development in the 1990s had its origins in the Commission on Social Justice (1994). The Commission's report was the source of the 'social inclusion' agenda that, in particular, identified the complex overlaying of social problems (including crime, disorder and antisocial behaviour) in the nation's most deprived and marginalised areas. The report confirmed a social policy version of the 'inverse care law', which stipulated that in those areas where social needs were greatest, the public and social care agencies were the least equipped to tackle them, resources were least readily available, exacerbating social problems (especially crime, disorder and antisocial behaviour) were at their most acute and the resident populations were least able to cope. Areas with long-term social and economic problems were receiving fragmentary, short-term and event-driven crime and disorder management responses, and, in turn, whole communities were being over-controlled yet simultaneously under-protected (Campbell, 1993).

In 1993, the Commission on Social Justice published a short report, *The Justice Gap*, giving a label to this collective set of circumstances and defining the failure to ensure principles of equal citizenship (Commission on Social Justice, 1993). From the perspective of the discourse of community safety, this encapsulated the impossibility of ensuring criminal justice in the absence of broader social justice, as evidence began to mount regarding the devastating impact of crime and disorder and concentrations of victimisation in the most deprived areas. In practice, as Crawford has commented, a higher priority was nevertheless still given to 'crime prevention – as opposed to poverty prevention' (Crawford, 1998, p 121) but over time, in the hands of the Home Office, the social justice gap has become a question of criminal justice procedures and system performance, or justice through effective enforcement (Home Office, 2002). Notwithstanding broader questions of inequalities and disadvantage, social justice is to be achieved by ensuring that offenders are efficiently and appropriately apprehended, charged, prosecuted and punished. Relatively little is said here of addressing the reasons for young people becoming offenders in the first place or of assisting them in moving on to less harmful or problematic lifestyles. Perhaps it goes without saying, but, once again, this represents a rather more restricted ambition for a policy discourse premised on 'community safety' and 'social justice'.

A final difficulty for the community safety policy agenda, closely related to the above, concerns the themes raised especially in Dawn Stephen's chapter in this volume. Here we are concerned with the ways in which community safety policy has become, contrary to the ambitions of some of its original enthusiasts (Gilling and Barton, 1997), something of a 'trojan horse' for the further criminalisation of social policy that has now become largely overrun by antisocial behaviour enforcement. An explanation for this outcome can clearly be found in what we have referred to as the 'enforcement deficit' conception of antisocial behaviour (Squires and Stephen, 2005).

We have already noted the ways in which the social inclusion and community safety policy agendas were always closely associated with questions of 'quality of life' and 'peace of mind' – especially in some of the more deprived areas. Community safety was always intimately connected with broader questions of safety and security, with how people felt about where they lived, their perceptions of various risks and their levels of fear. In this respect, drawing on the Wilson and Kelling (1982) 'broken windows' tradition, Hansen et al (2003) have described the underlying rationale for taking antisocial behaviour more seriously. The problem resides, they argue, in the way that the criminal justice system has tended not to take terribly seriously minor or isolated acts of nuisance committed by individuals, yet in so doing it has tended to overlook the accumulating impact of incivilities, harassment and antisocial behaviour for the *victims*. In other words, there is a mismatch between the 'accumulating distress for victims and [the] non-accumulating impact for offenders' (Hansen et al, 2003, pp 81-2). Antisocial behaviour enforcement action helps address the cumulative impact of disorderly and offending behaviour. 'Refocusing attention from crime to antisocial behaviour occurs because of a failure of criminal justice to punish persistence in crime in ways commensurate with community impact' (Hansen et al, 2003, p 87). Taken overall, this is said to constitute an 'enforcement deficit' or a 'justice gap'. The politicisation of antisocial behaviour, therefore, appears as an attempt to close the 'justice gap' through more effectively targeted and streamlined enforcement.

A particularly telling example of this purportedly 'enforcement-driven' solution to community safety problems posed by young people (as Stephen has argued, often represented as virtual outsiders in their own communities) arose in Campbell's review of Anti-Social Behaviour Orders for the Home Office in 2002. The supposed 'enforcement deficit' was said to contribute to a sense of relative impunity enjoyed by juvenile offenders. Campbell drew upon the familiar populist constructions of juvenile impunity (and the supposed licence it gave to youthful troublemakers) and noted that juveniles 'were able to commit their anti-social behaviour in the full knowledge that there were few criminal sanctions that could touch them' (Campbell, 2002, p 2). Swifter and more effectively targeted enforcement was the key. With this in mind, the rapid escalation in concern about antisocial behaviour might be seen as the writing on the wall for an older conception of community safety. Alternatively, it could be seen as the most predictable outcome of it, a new localised and specific enforcement priority emerging from its erstwhile community safety shell. None of this need be inevitable; on the contrary, it will reflect (for example, as Follett has argued in this volume) the forces and relations, interests and contexts set in motion within the field of community safety politics.

From this volume

Judging from the contributions to this volume, the politics of community safety is now more of a contested terrain than at any previous time. A number of themes have emerged: community safety as an 'incomplete' project, as a 'contested' project, as a 'flawed' project and, now, as a project being transformed – or overrun, if you prefer – by other priorities, especially, perhaps, enforcement and a new punitiveness. Perhaps it goes without saying, but although the different contributions referred to below are discussed in relation to these different themes for purposes of illustration, many of the chapters could be used to illustrate more than one of the themes.

An incomplete project?

We have seen a range of contributions pointing to community safety as still an incomplete project. Judged from the 'social division of welfare' perspective with which we began, we have had arguments that there are indeed winners and losers within community safety. We have seen that some sections of the community, if they have not actually lost out in the community safety stakes, may not yet have derived the benefits attained by other sections of the population.

Thus Carlie Goldsmith has described the ways in which young people's needs, especially the needs of some of the young people in the most acute and deprived circumstances, are overlooked in a criminal justice system that seeks primarily to discipline and punish and may be exacerbating their problems. As we have noted above, the chapter might also be used to illustrate the profound limitations of an enforcement- and punishment-centred approach to youth justice. Likewise, Paula Wilcox has drawn attention to the potential limitations of a gendered conception of community safety that may prioritise public crime, disorder and antisocial behaviours while lacking a purchase on more privatised and hidden forms of victimisation and abuse. Domestic violence has undoubtedly been a national stated priority for CDRPs, but its relative invisibility still militates against the development of effective and sustainable responses.

Similarly, Derek McGhee, while noting the considerable progress achieved in breaking down the barriers to more constructive relationships between the police and lesbian, gay, bisexual and transgender communities, thereby enabling the more effective prioritising of homophobic hate crimes, raises important issues of community representation and agency (especially police) accountability that might still frustrate the development of effective policies. On the other hand, for Marian FitzGerald and Chris Hale discussing minority ethnic experiences of community safety, an important issue concerns the seemingly contrary implications of national policies relating to crime reduction and security and more localised community safety and quality of life outcomes. Their conclusion that 'the government does not appear to have produced any race equality impact assessment of its community safety policies' (p 86) is particularly telling. Enforcement-led or security-driven priorities may well exacerbate community tensions and diminish trust and confidence in the police. We have been here before.

A contested project?

There are also those who have argued that community safety is and will remain an essentially contested project – perhaps this may explain something of why it is (and may remain) incomplete. In their different ways, both Matt Follett and Barry Loveday discuss a range of 'provider' issues relating to community safety policy development. Follett's concern began with his recognition of the extent to which the 'community safety agenda' emerged as a primarily practitioner-oriented discourse, developing at a national level and only subsequently becoming a field in which local politicians (councillors) came to engage. Of course, as soon as community safety is opened up as a political field in this way, it becomes a field of political contestation like any other in which competing local political interests and priorities may rise or fall. In the process, they may even submerge some of the priorities ('minority group interests') that, at its inception, the community safety agenda might have been presumed to promote.

In a similar manner, Barry Loveday's discussion of police contributions to community safety policy development reinforces this sense of the field as a contested terrain, not just locally but in relation to Home Office national priorities too. While there is a clear suggestion that local police managers are supportive of CDRP arrangements, and gain a good deal from them, partnership working brings many difficulties and further institutional changes may still be necessary to get the best from, and render more accountable, the new structures and arrangements. A not dissimilar set of issues arises in respect of Mark Button's discussion of the contribution of private sector policing and security agencies. As Button acknowledges, the contribution of the private sector to community safety is often somewhat overlooked. Two related issues apply here. On the one hand, the commercial, business and retail sectors, the most frequent employers of private security, are looked on as if they are not really parts of the community, even though CCTV scheme development, to which many similar observations apply, was once a major plank of community safety policy development (LGMB, 1996). On the other hand, private security is sometimes regarded as a particularly sectional interest with aims and objectives, narrowly commodified conceptions of security and safety, sometimes quite contrary to our more familiar and traditional conceptions of community. This may well be true, although as Button notes, the private security sector is undoubtedly here to stay. Therefore, the challenge for local democracy must be to 'ensure appropriate accountability and governance' (p 136) in order to prevent its pursuit of narrow sectional interests.

Finally, in this review of 'contested' community safety practice, we have had

Adrian Barton's analysis of the limitations imposed on potentially effective outreach work in drug treatment programmes by 'audit-driven, one-size-fits-all approach[es] to social provision', a perverse consequence of which might be that 'the criminal justice system's apparent audit and control needs will overrule real community safety benefits' (p 149). While Barton's work illustrates well the potentially contradictory nature of relationships established between substance misuse projects and priorities and broader community safety policy objectives, it might equally well be taken to illustrate the dangers of primarily enforcement-led strategies.

A flawed project?

For a number of contributors, however, it was not so much that community safety had become (or, indeed, that it may always have been) a politically contested project, but rather that there may have been something almost inherently flawed about this approach to the governance of crime and disorder. Thus, from the outset, Dave Whyte and Steve Tombs register their concern that community safety strategies have generally ignored, and therefore failed to develop adequate responses for, corporate crime. The field of crime prevention, they argue, 'within which community safety has assumed a central place – is one that is narrowly focused ... on the crimes and incivilities of the relatively powerless' (p 163). Although they draw attention to what they call the 'regressive tendencies' of community safety, they argue that there need be no necessary reason for failing to include corporate and business criminality issues in the community safety brief. But, in order to achieve this, they add, the forms of interest representation that currently comprise community safety partnerships need to be developed – indeed, politicised further – to allow access to a wider range of safety issues and concerns rather than simply those defined by dominant corporate interests (Coleman, 2004).

In a similar sense, Sandra Walklate's concern about victims and the community safety policy processes also addresses a question about how 'interests' are represented within this sphere of policy making. Her central argument, emerging from a perspective on the politics of victimisation and the need to take victims seriously, here deploys a more 'critical victimology' to ask whether the concepts of victimhood embedded within community safety policy development essentially distort conceptions of victimhood (or draw only rather selectively on conceptions of victims) in order to reinforce the state's existing security, safety and risk management agendas. Community safety policy, in this sense, might be seen as flawed insofar as it serves primarily as an exercise in the legitimation of political authority and established priorities. Lynda Measor's chapter has also illustrated aspects of this wider issue. Although the work began as a study of teenage pregnancy in selected areas, the fieldwork soon revealed patterns and relationships of power and authority within relatively 'marginalised' communities that lay substantially beyond the state and exercised a far stronger grip on behaviours and alliances than any artificial constructions of 'community safety'. In 'fractured and divided communities', she argues, simplistic appeals to the 'community as a whole' may be worse than useless and will, anyway, probably fall on deaf ears. What community development writers refer to as 'social capital' may exist in a variety of forms, not all of it taking a form consistent with equal rights and justice, but when people are confronted by problems they cannot otherwise resolve, their resort to their own resources ought not to surprise us. Thus, the chapter also makes a case for a more engaged cultural criminology, if only to resist the kinds of emerging bureaucratic agendas described by Walklate.

Overrun by enforcement?

The final theme emerging in the chapters by Hancock and Stephen concerns the extent to which the relatively progressive 'community safety agenda' may, in more recent times, have become overrun by the 'antisocial behaviour bandwagon' (Squires and Stephen, 2005; Squires, 2006), by the increasing 'recriminalisation of delinquency' (Singer, 1996), and a broadly based 'new punitiveness' informing criminal justice policy (Pratt et al, 2005). As Lynn Hancock argues, recent enforcement initiatives, especially regarding antisocial behaviour, 'not only criminalise working-class young people [and] increase their chances of victimisation ... they also represent a threat to the reproduction of *positive* working-class cultural practices' (p 212), while reflecting and sustaining broadly middle-class cultural values. There are important parallels here with the chapters by Measor and Goldsmith. Rather similar to Dawn Stephen's chapter, Hancock adds that the strategies employed to tackle current crime, disorder and antisocial behaviour problems are also potentially counterproductive insofar as providing 'community safety' for the most vulnerable groups *and* promoting community cohesion are concerned. Inasmuch as the social inclusion agenda is infused by a highly disciplinary subtext, Hancock might equally agree that the community safety agenda is deeply flawed.

In like mind, Dawn Stephen begins her contribution by reference to the 'rights and wrongs' of community safety, developing an argument that 'youth justice principles are being eroded through community safety discourses' (p 219). Her analysis draws on Cohen's 'dispersal of discipline' thesis to question the balances between welfare, support and punishment made available to disadvantaged and 'at-risk' young people. The national policy framework may insist that 'every child matters' (DfES, 2003), but some children and young people seem to matter rather less than others – until, that is, they commit offences or indulge in allegedly 'antisocial' acts and behaviours, at which point they appear to begin to matter more than others in a climate of hostility and demonisation surrounding 'troublesome youth'.

References

ADC (Association of District Councils) (1990) *Promoting Safer Communities: A District Council Perspective*, London: ADC.

Audit Commission (1996) *Misspent Youth*, London: Audit Commission.

Campbell, B. (1993) *Goliath: Britain's Dangerous Places*, London: Methuen.

Campbell, S. (2002) *A Review of Anti-Social Behaviour Orders*, Home Office Research Study 236, London: Home Office Research and Statistics Directorate.

Coleman, R. (2004) *Reclaiming the Streets: Surveillance, Social Control and the City*, Cullompton: Willan Publishing.

Commission on Social Justice (1993) *The Justice Gap*, London: Institute for Public Policy Research.

Commission on Social Justice (1994) *Social Justice: Strategies for National Renewal*, London: Vintage Books.

Coopers and Lybrand (1994) *Preventative Strategy for Young People in Trouble*, September, ITV Telethon/Prince's Trust.

Crawford, A. (1998) *Crime Prevention and Community Safety*, Harlow: Longman.

DfES (Department for Education and Skills) (2003) *Every Child Matters*, Cm 5860, London: The Stationery Office.

Gilling, D. and Barton, A. (1997) 'Crime prevention and community safety: a new home for social policy?', *Critical Social Policy*, vol 17, no 1, pp 63–83.

Goldson, B. (2000) 'Children in need or young offenders? Hardening ideology, organisational change and new challenges for social work with children in trouble', *Child and Family Social Work*, vol 5, no 3, pp 255-65.

Hansen, R., Bill, L. and Pease, K. (2003) 'Nuisance offenders: scoping the public policy problems', in M. Tonry (ed) *Confronting Crime: Crime Control Policy under New Labour*, Cullompton: Willan Publishing, pp 80-94.

Home Office (1988) *Punishment, Custody and the Community*, Green Paper, Cmnd 424, London: HMSO.

Home Office (1991) *Safer Communities: The Local Delivery of Crime Prevention through the Partnership Approach*, Report of the Standing Conference on Crime Prevention ('the Morgan Report'), London: Home Office.

Home Office (1997) *No More Excuses*, Cmnd 3809, London: HMSO.

Home Office (1998) *Guidance to Statutory Crime and Disorder Partnerships*, London: Home Office.

Home Office (2002) *Narrowing the Justice Gap*, Justice Gap Taskforce Report, London: Home Office.

Labour Party (1964) *Crime: A Challenge to Us All*, Report of the Home Affairs Study Group (chaired by Lord Longford), London: The Labour Party.

LGMB (Local Government Management Board) (with Association of District Councils, Association of Metropolitan Authorities and Association of County Councils) (1996) *Survey of Community Safety Activities in Local Government in England and Wales*, London: LGMB.

London Strategic Policy Unit (1986) *Community Safety*, London: London Strategic Policy Unit.

Mannheim, H. (1946) *Criminal Justice and Reconstruction*, London: Routledge and Kegan Paul.

Muncie, J. (1999) 'Institutionalised intolerance: youth crime and the 1998 Crime and Disorder Act', *Critical Social Policy*, vol 19, no 2, pp 147-75.

Muncie, J. (2000) 'Pragmatic realism: searching for criminology in the new youth justice', in B. Goldson (ed) *The New Youth Justice*, Lyme Regis: Russell House Publishing, pp 14-34.

Pratt, J., Brown, D., Brown, M., Hallsworth, S. and Morrison, W. (2005) *The New Punitiveness: Trends, Theories, Perspectives*, Cullompton: Willan Publishing.

Singer, S.I. (1996) *Recriminalising Delinquency: Violent Juvenile Crime and Juvenile Justice Reform*, Cambridge: Cambridge University Press.

Squires, P. and Stephen D.E. (2005) *Rougher Justice: Anti-Social Behaviour and Young People*, Cullompton: Willan Publishing.

Squires, P. (2006) 'New Labour and anti-social behaviour', *Critical Social Policy*, vol 26, no 1, pp 144-68.

Wilson, J.Q. and Kelling, G.L. (1982) 'Broken windows', *Atlantic Review*, March, pp 29-38.

Index

Page references for notes are followed by n